To: Michael

Family Affairs

With warm compliments.

J. Sorie Conteh

J. Sorie Conteh.

Other novels by the author
The Diamonds
In Search of Sons (SLWS CR-8)

Family Affairs

14619 Good Hope Rd. Silver Spring.MD.20905.USA

ISBN: 978-9988-1-3984-1

This is a work of fiction. Except in a few obvious instances, names, places, organizations and incidents are either products of the author's imagination or have been used fictitiously. Any resemblance to actual events, places, or persons alive or dead is purely coincidental

First published 2011
Sierra Leonean Writers Series /Africa Future Publishers
c/o Mallam O. & J. Enterprises
120 Kissy Road, Freetown, Sierra Leone
publisher@sl-writers-series.org

Printed in India by : Jaipal Printing Press
1011, Bhawani Peth,
Pune 411 002.

Cover design by Isata N. Conteh

Dedicated to my senior brother:
P.C. Maxwell (paddy) Abu Robert Ngaquee 11.
Fakunya Chiefdom, Moyamba District, Sierra Leone

CHAPTER ONE

It was another rainy season in Talia, sometime after Giita died in childbirth, trying to produce more grandsons for her mother-in-law. Since the death of his daughter, Kinie Ndomawaa had tried hard to regain his emotional equilibrium, but he was still floating in a sea of bafflement about the world he inhabited. He kept asking himself why his beloved daughter, Gitta, died. Why had that happened, he wondered. Why? Why should someone die in the process of bringing precious lives into this world? Oh God, he would lament in anguish, why should parents ever have to bury their children? Even the ancestors would be troubled to see that once again, things had not happened in the right order.

As he walked towards his in-laws' house, he was again thinking about God's mysteries and the many ways in which they manifested themselves. Ah, yes, that is how God maintains a certain balance in this universe, he said to himself. He makes some things simple and straightforward and others complicated. So we experience situations that are difficult to explain; how the wicked among us prosper and the holy barely manage to make ends meet; how some people spend most of their days enduring life rather than enjoying it. We experience both abundant wealth and enormous poverty and wretchedness. Some people live healthy lives while others languish in illness. In some places, it rains and rivers overflow their banks and cause disasters. In other places, there is lack of rain and drought is the result; no crops grow and people die of famine. We witness pain and joy. The same God does all these things. Yes, how else can one explain some of the human anomalies we experience every day? It also explains why Hindowaa and his mother are such opposite poles of God's creation.

Hindowaa, according to Kinie Ndomawaa's thinking, represented God's straightforward, simple creations whereas his mother represented the opposite. She had chosen to maintain an iron grip on her son's household instead of remarrying after her husband's death. And it was she who had pressured Hindowaa into trying to have more sons with Giita by threatening to look for another wife for him. Ndomawaa was convinced that this was what had triggered Giita's desperate search for more sons and eventually led to her death. He promised himself that one day he would confront Hindowaa and his mother on the matter.

"Kinie Ndomawaa, biwah, biseh", a woman greeted him.

"Eeem, biwah, biseh, kahun yeihnaa? (How do you do, and how is your health?)" he replied.

"When did you arrive?" the woman asked.

They were now face to face and Kinie Ndomawaa was trying hard to avoid making eye contact with her. So long after his daughter's death, people continued to express sympathy and condolences whenever they saw him and as a result, he continued to experience the agony of bereavement. He knew from experience that the woman would soon begin to cry. Another person saw him talking to her and greeted him from a distance. Ndomawaa returned the greeting.

"Ah,dunyafuu. Dunyafuu," the woman exclaimed, bemoaning the emptiness of the world without a beloved daughter. "You and your daughter look so much alike; so good looking! Who would not know that you are her father? Look at your neck, your forehead. You look so much alike! My brother, it is the will of God and our ancestors. But at least you have your grandchildren, especially the twins. They are so lovely. God is great. We are also proud of your granddaughter, Kunaafoh. She is doing a wonderful job in this chiefdom and beyond. We are so proud of her. The child has made a name for herself since she started working. Look at the number of people she has cured of all types of diseases! Everybody says that her injections are so powerful that just one is enough to make you well, no matter what was wrong with you."

Jatu, the woman speaking, had had a taste of being ostracized by the community until Kunaafoh came to her rescue. She, like a number of men and women who had had old sores, had been accused of being a witch. Everyone, even children, had tried to avoid them. Kunaafoh was able to determine that these people were suffering from diabetes. She had treated them successfully and the news had spread all over Talia that she could perform miracles. She was now revered in the community.

"What that child did for me I shall never forget until the day I die," Jatu went on. "Look at me; I am well, and people who never used to talk to me now talk to me and even visit me. People eat the food I cook. Before that, it was not possible. Look what happened, Kinie Ndomawaa, look what happened! God sent your daughter to come and cure us. Now we are human beings again. She gave us back our dignity. Before she came, we lived in this community but were not part of it. I know that many people will not understand what I am telling you Kinie Ndomawaa. You have to have experienced it to appreciate what I am telling you. Oh, your daughter is a good doctor! When last did you see her?"

"Every time I come here, I visit her," Ndomawaa

replied. "But you know the missionaries; they are very cautious and don't allow you to walk into the mission if you don't have a specific reason for the visit. You cannot just go there, then sit and talk as you like, even as a grandfather. However, lately, they have become a little more tolerant of me and they give me latitude to come in and see my granddaughter. My sister, Kunaafoh is God's gift to the family and me. Now everyone in the chiefdom is proud to have the first female doctor. I am sure that Giita, too, is happy where she is… I am going to visit my son-in-law, and hope I find him at home," Ndomawaa informed her as they went their separate ways.

Alone again, his thoughts returned to Hindowaa and his mother.

I don't understand. I really don't understand how a man can stand being bullied by a woman. Yes, my mother had lots of influence on me, but we discussed matters and she often agreed with me if she thought my opinion on an issue was reasonable. She was a reasonable woman and always tried to please me. Hindowa's case baffles me. What is more worrisome is that he is a Wunde man like me. He is even an Ngombuwaa. How could he have taken such a big title in the Wunde Society and yet behave contrary to the values of the fraternity. I am sure that his father will not be happy in his grave about this. I am equally certain that even his grandfather will not be happy about this situation. They will consider him a man who has betrayed his manhood and position in the Wunde fraternity. I know he is a good man when he is not under the influence of that mother of his.

He noticed that people were looking at him curiously. Some of them had probably guessed that he was heading towards his in-laws' house. As he approached

Nyake's house he changed direction to avoid it, knowing that Nyake would engage him in a long conversation. However, he then bumped into Nyamakoro, the woman who was famous in the town for becoming rich by baking cakes. She was a great admirer of his and also liked to engage him in long conversations. Ndomawaa sighed, feeling as if he had run from the frying pan to the fire. He knew that his plan to see his son-in-law as soon as possible would now have to be postponed for as long as Nyamakoro wished, because he would find it difficult to tear himself away once they started talking. Many people believed that Nyamakoro had the tongue of a 'Jalibaah,' or griot - a sugarcoated tongue. Ndomawaa prayed that the woman would be considerate enough not to keep him talking for too long.

"When did you come?" Nyamakoro asked him.

"I have been here for only three days."

"Three days! and nobody told me you were here? I am going to cook for you; I shall tell my husband. I shall cook for you tomorrow morning, so don't eat anything before I send food for you. You cannot come to this town and leave without me cooking for you. I even feel guilty that you have been here for three whole days and I did not prepare food for you."

"You know that when I come here, I run around a lot. I wanted to see the chief to discuss a number of things, but decided that I should see my son-in-law first. So far, I have not even seen him. I am on my way to his house and pray that I shall find him at home this time."

"My brother, that in-law of yours, is his mother's captive," Nyamakoro remarked. "They say that he has been like that ever since his father died. It is sad for a man to be that way. As for me, I would not like to have a husband or son like that. I would not feel secure. In my day, we respected our men. They took firm decisions on family issues. Now things are different. When you look at Hindowaa, he looks so strong and yet he is under his mother's thumb. It is a shame, because he is a good man. I am afraid for them, because if you allow your house to be run by your mother, you risk the wrath of the ancestors. The ancestors will be angry with Hindowaa one day and teach him and the entire household a sad lesson. I pray that he changes for the better and does not allow this state of affairs to continue."

Ndomawaa was glad to hear Nyamakoro say out loud what many people in the town and outside thought regarding Kigba's domination of her son. Many of them had come to the conclusion that Hindowaa had compromised his manhood. Some had even begun to doubt whether he deserved the coveted Wunde title of Ngombuwaa.

He could not refuse an invitation to visit Nyamakoro. Once in her house, she said,"You know, Kinie Ndomawaa, I have known you for a very long time. I came to know you even more when you daughter married Hindowaa here in our town. I need to bring something to your attention, provided you promise to keep it a secret. You need to take an oath as a Wunde man. It is a very serious issue."

Resigning himself to being in Nyamakoro's company for even longer than he had anticipated, Ndomawaa pulled his stool closer to her and his eyes widened inquiringly as he waited to hear what she had to say.

"Ah, nyapui (woman) Nyamakoro, let me tell you one thing," he assured her, "I am among the very few people in this our chiefdom that is a member of both the

Wunde and Poro secret societies. Our secret societies survive because we maintain a very high degree of secrecy; it is the hallmark of these societies. So I promise you that I will not tell anyone, dead or alive that you said this or that to me. If I have reason to mention it anywhere, I promise you that I shall never, never mention your name as the source of the information. I swear to my Wunde and Poro fraternities."

"My first husband was also a member of both the Wunde and Poro fraternities. He was not supposed to belong to them but wanted to show your people that he had accepted their culture, tradition and customs. It also helped his business. The only problem was that when he passed away, there was a lot of confusion because the Poro fraternity wanted to monopolize the funeral ceremonies and the Wunde fraternity objected. It took many consultations and the intervention of the elders before the matter could be resolved. Anyway, the funeral ceremonies were grand. I think both fraternities should find a way to avoid such conflicts in the future."

"Yes, and that was not the first time we had such a problem here and elsewhere," Ndomawaa agreed. "In our own town, we have succeeded in coming to an agreement over what to do when such a situation arises, but I won't tell you about it now because I am very anxious about what you have to tell me. As you can see, I am not young anymore, and my heart is not as strong as it used to be. When I am anxious, I feel very uncomfortable."

"Heh, look who is talking about not being young anymore," Nyamakoro scoffed, though in a friendly way. "You are still a young man." Then, she became serious and lowered her voice. "Anyway, my brother, while there is no one here to listen to us, tell me, and be honest about it, do you really know Kigba, Hindowaa's mother, very well? All my life, I have lived in this town and I love it. This is where I married and had my family. This is where my husband died and received a wonderful funeral. This is where I shall die and be buried. The people here can be kind, sympathetic and generous; but the few who are not are dangerous, very, very dangerous. That is why they say that our witchcraft here is more potent than in other places in the chiefdom. You yourself, don't you believe this? Don't you see it? Ndomawaa tell me. Answer my questions. You don't belong to this town, but you know it as well as I do."

"You see, my sister, since my daughter married Hindowaa, we became one family. However, to tell you the truth, I never been close to Kigba. She is a very slippery woman. I also discovered that she is very secretive, maybe because she has a big title in the women's secret society. I learned very early that she has great influence over her son and two daughters. In fact, I think she exerts too much authority over them. I made these observations over a long period. I am sure you know her better than me since all of you live here in Talia."

"Kinie Ndomawaa, I knew your late mother very well. She was a good woman. We met several times during the many initiation sessions in your town and here. That was how we became friends until her death. That was a long time ago but I still recall how we used to sit, just the two of us, and talk about your town and Talia. We used to talk about the good old days when this chiefdom prospered in the ginger trade. Those were good times. Oh yes, very good times. As a business woman, I know what I'm talking about. Your mother and I would talk about the initiation festivities - how they were grand and no initiates died during the period. But things have changed. Now, you cannot trust people, and witchcraft has become a threat to all of us."

Ndomawaa was beginning to feel impatient. He cleared his throat as if he was about to say something, but remained silent and kept staring hard at Nyamakoro as she continued her rambling introduction to whatever it was that she wanted to tell him.

"My brother, I know how much you have endured in life. You lost your wife and now your daughter, Giita. I feel your pain because I also lost my husband at a time when I needed him very much. I went through a lot of pain because some people believed I was responsible for his death. Oh, there was nasty gossip in this town. You also know how people used to say they knew why I was prosperous. This town is very dangerous and full of malicious gossip. Now, I keep to myself and my current husband most of the time and I am happy."

As she continued speaking, Ndomawaa began to rub his nose frequently. Nyamakoro noticed his impatience at last and hurriedly came to the point.

"Let me tell you about Kigba. There is a common belief here in Talia and I think even beyond this town, that she possesses a djinn. My brother, I don't think that this rumor has no substance. Wherever you have smoke, there must be fire; that is what our people say. We the women with titles in the women's society also believe that Kigba has a djinn. It is a male djinn which is why she never remarried after her husband died. Her possession of the djinn also makes her a suspect in her husband's death. Do you know he died?" Ndomawaa shook his head. "He drowned," Nyamakoro told him with a significant look. "He drowned in a shallow river, where even babies swam safely. Just imagine. The man used to go fishing even when our river here was overflowing its banks, yet he died in shallow water; and what is even more surprising, it happened during the day. Kigba's husband's death is still the biggest mystery in this town. How can you explain it? Do you know that even our chief knows about this matter of Kibga's djinn? He knows. I wanted to pass this information on to you so that you become aware of the kind of people you are dealing with. Be very careful, my brother, now that I have brought this to your attention."

"Thank you, my sister. Thank you very much," Ndomawaa said. "You are a very dependable sister. Thank you. You know, when I was coming to Talia three days ago, I had this feeling that I would find out something useful. My sixth sense never fails me. Let me also tell you that for a very long time, I have had the feeling that there is something mysterious and hidden about Kigba. Have you noticed how she only makes the briefest eye contact with you and then withdraws her gaze? I am convinced that she has four eyes. I told my late daughter about it and told her to take necessary steps to protect herself from her mother-in-law, but she never took me seriously. Oh, how I wish she were alive today!"

For several moments there was an atmosphere of pain in the room and Ndomawaa and Nyamakoro maintained a solemn silence before either of them spoke again.

"My sister, I have benefited a lot from this visit to Talia," Ndomawaa said finally. "Do you know that sometime ago, some of us, I mean the men here and in my own town, started asking why Kigba had not remarried like you did when your husband passed away. We said, 'She is relatively young and good-looking, but has no husband.' What is even stranger, and this supports the belief that she possesses a male djinn, is that no one has ever associated her with a male friend. So the question is, how does she manage as a woman? It is suspicious, because as you know, it is not a normal thing for a woman to stay unmarried. This baffles us, the men. Now I am beginning to understand why she is not married. It is the djinn that is responsible. I tell you, there are women and even some men who are like that. From now on I shall be very careful in my dealings with her...Tell me, do you know if Hindowaa knows about this aspect of his mother's life? I am just curious. Parents don't usually reveal such secrets to their children unless they want to pass the spirit over to the children when they know that they are going to die. In this case, if Kigba decides to pass the djinn, she will pass it on to her elder daughter and not to her son. That is how it works. I would like to find out if Hindowaa is aware of what is happening under his nose."

"Hmm, my brother, I don't think the son is aware. How can you even ask such a question? My guess is that if anyone is aware in the family, it will be the elder daughter who should be the next beneficiary of the spirit. Don't behave as if you are totally ignorant of our customs. Like you said a moment ago, the woman has no man, so it makes sense that she has a male and not a female djinn. What would both of them, female and female do with each other?"

They both laughed heartily at the idea, the first time they had laughed during the visit. Though it was growing dark, the town had become lively for there was no prospect of rain.

"I shall keep to my promise and send you food tomorrow morning," Nyamakoro called out to Ndomawaa when he finally strolled away in the direction of his son-in-law's house. "And don't forget what I said earlier. Don't eat anything until you receive what I am going to cook and send for you tomorrow."

From a distance, Ndomawaa could see Hindowaa in the hammock, but he could also see other people on the veranda. He had hoped that he would find his son-in-law alone so they could carry on a one-to-one conversation. He had also hoped that he would not meet Hindowaa's mother in the house because he wanted maximum privacy with his son-in-law. On reflection, he decided that it would be a waste of time to proceed to Hindowaa's house with visitors there, so Nyake became the choice for his next visit. He changed direction and headed that way, thinking deeply about what he and Nyamakoro had discussed. The more he thought about Kigba, the more human behavior puzzled him. How could a woman become so powerful in a male-dominated society and nobody seemed to be concerned about it? Was the chief not aware of Kigba's masculine characteristics, or was he turning a blind eye to them because she was championing his wish to marry Kunaafoh? Why had it taken so long for Nyamakoro to tell him about Kigba? Was it that she assumed he knew about it because of his relationship with the family? Why was it that Nyake, whom he liked and respected, had also not mentioned it to him even by way of man-to-man gossip? Was it possible that Nyake was not aware of this aspect of Kigba's life? He remembered that he and Nyake had had several discussions, and had joked about Hindowaa and his mother, but not once did he recall Nyake saying anything relating to Kigba's spiritual connections. Strange, he thought as he walked along. He wanted to bring the subject up with Nyake but wondered how to raise it. He was also baffled by the fact that

Nyamakoro had chosen to bring up the subject. Was there a motive behind it? He could not answer the question. Yes, he certainly believed Nyamakoro was right. Why had Kigba not remarried and why was she always on the backs of her son and daughters who were adults with their own families? Why could she not leave them alone? As he went along, he was searching the recesses of his mind for examples of women of Kigba's age who had been widowed and remained unmarried. As far as he could recall, there was only one such woman in the entire chiefdom; but she had been married for a long time and was no longer young when her husband died. Also, she was very fat which had intimidated even the most adventurous men.

From a distance, Ndomawaa could see Nyake lying in his hammock and was glad because he could not face the prospect of going to Hindowaa's house only to find his visitors still there. Someone greeted him just outside Nyake's house.

"Ah, Kinie Ndomawaa, how are you?"

The man was short and heavily built, with a long, bushy beard and a belly which protruded as if he were eight months pregnant. He looked perfectly content, however, and not aware of his unattractive and untidy appearance.

"Ndakei, how are you?" Ndomawaa responded warmly when they came face to face. Nyake had observed them and decided to eavesdrop on their conversation.

"When did you come?" the man asked.

"Three days ago."

"What! ndakei, when you come here if I don't meet you by chance you don't visit your old friend. Why? What have I done to you? You could at least come and let us drink palm wine together, enjoy kola nuts, and talk about the good old days."

Ndomawaa felt embarrassed at being caught out by the short man and was silent for a moment as he tried to think of a good enough excuse for not paying him a visit. In the end he said only, "Ndakei, I apologize. You are right. Forgive me. The next time I come I shall pass by your house and we shall drink palm wine and eat kola nuts together. Everybody tells me that your palm wine is one of the most potent in Talia. I look forward to seeing you the next time I come. You see, I am still trying to sort things out after the death of my daughter."

Mention of his late daughter drew a sympathetic response.

"Ndakei, one thing we shall always remember your daughter for is the granddaughter she left with you," the man said. "Thanks to her, we now have a doctor we are all proud of in this town and the whole chiefdom. People's ailments are now cured. Every day people go to the clinic and when they come out they say what a good doctor your granddaughter is. They talk highly of the potent injections she gives. Before she came, we had one white doctor who hardly gave injections. All she gave were tablets, some powdered medicines, or sometimes some sweet liquid medicine that took a long time to cure you. Now that we have our own daughter, who knows about medicine and our diseases, we get powerful injections. They are so powerful that when you walk out of the clinic, even your head feels it, and you have to drag your foot. That is good. May God bless her and may her mother rest in peace."

Ndomawaa was moved almost to tears by the short man's words as they went their separate ways. When he entered Nyake's veranda, he found him lying in his hammock with his clay pipe firmly sandwiched by his lips. The atmosphere was peaceful with the skies outside still free from any threat of rain, and people were going about their normal nocturnal activities. He announced himself by saying,

"My granddaughter has told me that as we get older, we should avoid the hammock. She says it is not good for our posture and will affect our backs."

"Ndakei Ndomawaa, good evening," Nyake said, ignoring the remark.

"Ndakei Nyake, good evening. How are you?" Ndomawaa had sat down close to him. "How is the family?"

"Thanks to God, they are all well," Nyake responded, puffing away at his pipe. "When are you returning?"

"Ndakei, the way things are now, I cannot say exactly when I will be returning. I came here to discuss very important matters with my son-in-law, but we have not been able to find time to talk because he always has visitors. At this very moment his house is full of people. That is my problem. I had hoped to talk with him today, but it has not been possible. I am coming from Nyamakoro's house and by the time I leave here, he will probably be sleeping." He sighed, adding inconsequently, "I like the smell of your tobacco."

"Ah, ah, you have not smoked since your granddaughter arrived. You said she told you that smoking is not good for your health. Now you are telling me that I should not lie in my hammock, because your granddaughter said it is not good for my back. Well, if she continues like that she will one day say that we should not eat because it is not good for our stomachs. That is what happens when they know too much of the white man's book. I hope she did not say you should not drink palm wine anymore and eat kola nuts. Ndakei, let me tell you something. These days, anything that you really enjoy, the doctors will tell you it is not good for your health. My father and my grandfather lived to a ripe old age. They used their hammocks, smoked their tobacco and drank their palm wine and bamboo wine to the very end. When my father died, he was over eighty years old and he walked as straight as a ghost. He never stopped smoking, drinking and eating kola nuts. Now, I am beginning to fear that one day your granddaughter will say that at our age, we should stop woman business. Can you imagine that?" Both men laughed and laughed and laughed.

"Ah, before I forget, let us share a gourd of palm wine; it is fresh. My brother brought me some this evening when he came from the farm. He taps good wine."

"Do you know that since I arrived, that is three days ago, I have not had a single drop of palm wine? My granddaughter has not told me not to drink palm wine, but then she has not actually seen me drinking, so I'll wait and see."

"Boi-Komah," Nyake called out to one of his daughters.

"Naah," the girl answered.

"Waah." (Come).

"Nyagbeh keh keh. (Here I am, father)."

"You know where your uncle put the palm wine. Bring it for us with two cups, and then, go and ask your mother to send us some kola nuts."

The girl assembled the gourd of palm wine and the cups and ran back into the house to deliver her father's message.

"Yes, your in-law must be busy, running up and down," Nyake remarked as they started to drink. "It is a long time since we met even though we don't live far from each other. Anyway, I do understand his situation. He is living under the same roof as his mother. It is not easy for a grown man to be in that position."

"It is interesting that you are making such a comment. Nyamakoro and I were discussing the same issue of Hindowaa still clinging to his mother's wrapper. We concluded that it is a strange thing in our culture. The way I see it, ndakei, to your parents, you are always a child. Perhaps that is the way Hindowaa sees it too. How else can you explain it?"

"Listen to me, ndakei," Nyake replied, "listen carefully. Where in Talia, or your town or anywhere in our chiefdom have you known or witnessed this type of closeness between a mother and her adult son? We have been discussing this among ourselves. Unfortunately, no one has brought this to Hindowaa's attention. People say that it is not our business to interfere in their domestic affairs, and indeed, they are right. Why should we get involved in their household affairs? It does not affect us, so why get involved? We really do not have a case to make against Hindowaa and his mother, do we?"

"I agree with you," Ndomawaa admitted.

"But, ndakei, let me tell you something in confidence. This town of ours is well informed about things that you and I think are big secrets. People know things that would surprise you. I tell you, people are well informed even though they pretend to be ignorant." They were now emptying their second cups of palm wine. "Don't you ever underestimate the intelligence of people in this town. Sometimes they know more about what is going on in your household than you do. People get rudely shocked when they find out how much others know about their domestic affairs."

"Ndakei, you are correct. That was the impression I got from Nyamakoro when I visited her. We had a long conversation and she said almost the same things you are now telling me."

"Ndakei Ndomawaa, let me share a secret with you. This time I really mean a secret. You understand what I am saying, eh. You and I are Wunde men and Lawaas for that matter. Tell me, why has Kigba not remarried since the death of her husband? Look at Nyamakoro. Her husband died, and she remarried. Look at Sande'nya. Her husband died, and she remarried. Look at Magundia. Her husband died, she remarried. I can go on like this; you know what I mean. So what happened to Kigba? After all she is not that old, she is beautiful and she looks healthy. How does she manage her life without a man, you understand what I mean? To be honest with you - and this is between us - there was a time I thought of having a relationship with her. You think she was interested? She never even looked at me. No. She certainly did not encourage me. And I am not that old. Look at my wives, they are young. Anyway I gave up. So how does she survive without a husband? Strange," Nyake mused.

"Ndakei, I agree with you. My own feeling is that maybe she has no appetite for a man. Perhaps she lost it after her husband died." Ndomawaa suggested, and both men laughed until Nyake began to cough.

"Ndakei, you will kill me," he wheezed, still chuckling. "How can you say that she has lost appetite for a man? No one loses appetite for that thing. Don't deceive yourself. Even if you are as old as creation, it is the one thing you don't lose appetite for. It is true and you know it."

"That is the point I am making, Nyake. That is the point. Now we are talking. So how do we explain this? I do not have an answer. Your town is unique in that you are the only people that have this type of situation. So it is you who should explain it to me. Why in your town, and only your town?"

"Tell me. Did Nyamakoro tell you anything or did she answer that question during your conversation with her this evening?" Nyake asked. He was trying to prod his friend into divulging information. However, though slightly tipsy by now, Ndomawaa remembered his solemn promise to Nyamakoro.

"No, she never told me anything; you know how secretive women can be sometimes. Perhaps she has no information on Kigba. Or, if she knows anything, maybe she does not trust me. After all, I come from another town."

"Ah, but that is just why she should trust you - because you are an outsider. Let me tell you another secret about Talia. We love people from outside more than we love each other. That is one of our problems and that is why we are where we are today. We can do anything to please other people, but when it comes to each other, we only pay lip service. When our own people make efforts to move ahead in life, to prosper, we become jealous of them and do everything to bring them down to our level if we can. That is common and we know it. It will take us a long time to get out of that habit in this town. How long? I don't know. You see Nyamakoro herself, her people came from outside many, years ago. She is prosperous because of our generosity to outsiders. She is now the richest woman in this town. There are other people like that here. They came as strangers and we gave them shelter; later they became more native than we were. They even challenged our nobility and wanted to contest the chieftaincy. One day, I mean it my brother, if we continue like this, outsiders will become chiefs in our chiefdom, and our people will support them. They support anyone or anything from outside this chiefdom. As I told you earlier, I shall share this big secret with you and I trust that as Wunde men it shall be a secret between us until eternity."

Ndomawaa moved his stool closer to his friend as if he wanted to capture every single word emerging from Nyake's mouth.

"They say that it is a family thing, but what I don't know is whether it is from the father's side or the mother's. But it is a family thing which she has inherited."

"What family thing? I don't understand what you mean by family thing."

The two men were almost whispering now, and Nyake let out the secret.

"Hinii loh nge'yaah, keh djini mia." (She has a husband, but it is a djinn).

For a moment, Ndomawaa clamped a hand over his mouth, which was half open, then the two men returned to doing justice to the palm wine in silence.

"Kooh, ndakei!" Ndomawaa exclaimed inwardly, looking over his shoulder. To Nyake, he seemed overwhelmed by the news.

"Ndakei Nyake," he said, "if this is the case, then it explains many things. Yes, all my bafflement will now be put into perspective. Yes, ndakei, there must be an element of truth in this idea, because, for us Mende people, it is not a normal thing what is happening in

Hindowaa's household. It is not normal at all. You know what I mean. I am so happy. This trip of mine has been rewarding. I was completely in the dark, but now I have seen the light. Thank you, my brother. This will be a secret I shall keep till eternity. Thank you very much. But tell me, ndakei, is her son aware of this?"

"That is the big question," Nyake replied. "We here in Talia have been asking the same question. Is Hindowaa aware of this? It is a big question and we need to find the correct answer to it. If we can get to the bottom of it, then it will explain and put into the right perspective many of our concerns about the situation in their household."

"Ah, ndakei, human beings are too hard to understand," Ndomawaa remarked. "When you see Kigba from the outside, you will not think that she is part of this kind of thing. You say she did not pay any attention to your advances? Well, she must be satisfied and faithful to what she has. It must be a very strong djinn." They laughed again. Nyake said,

"Ndakei, you will give me a headache this evening. You make me laugh so much. But you are right. She must be very content with what she has. Wonders shall never cease. But what is bad about this is that she never gave me an opportunity to prove myself. She has no basis for excluding me. It is very unfair; don't you think so?"

"Maybe, you should protest to the chief," Ndomawaa replied in the same jocular way. "Present your case as forcefully as you have just spoken and maybe the chief will give you a hearing. But face it. You are now an old man and she has a strong djinn."

"To tell you the truth, there are many people in this town - and this is also a big secret. Many people who believe that Kigba's husband's death had an element of mystery to it," said Nyake, becoming serious again. "Tell me, if it was not because of the djinn, how could the husband have died so easily? Drowned in shallow water. The matter was discussed during the Wunde ceremonies for his funeral, but it was only gossip and still is."

"Have you ever recalled in living memory, here in this your town or the chiefdom, any woman whom you can compare to Kigba?"

After a moment's thought, Nyake shook his head.

"I know that Mamie Yoko was very powerful, but not in this respect. You know what I mean. We still talk very fondly of her today. No, she was not like Kigba. What also baffles me is why she put no pressure on her daughter, Boi-Komah, who has two daughters and a son, but she was ready to exert pressure on Hindowaa to have more sons with my daughter. It was constant pressure. My daughter told me all about it."

"If you want me to be honest with you this evening, only Kigba can answer that question or perhaps her son, Hindowaa... Ndake Ndomawaa, the way I see all this is that something good came out of your daughter and Hindowaa - I mean, your granddaughter, Kunaafoh. Look how much good she has brought to this town and the chiefdom. People who had sores that did not heal have now been cured. This is something we should be grateful for. Sampa had her goiter treated and now her beautiful neck can be seen. It used to be so distorted by the goiter, not to mention the discomfort she had to endure. People said that she could not be cured, and we all accused her of being a witch. She was ridiculed and scorned by the entire community, an outcast among her own people. Now she is a happy woman. Ndakei, this is good for our town and its people."

"Thank you, ndakei. Thank you for these kind words. I am consoled by them. It is because of comforting thoughts like these that I have been able to retain my sanity. It has not been easy for me at all, to be honest with you. I know that my daughter, Giita, will come back one day; and when she comes back, I shall give her the same name. She was special, and I am not saying this because she was my daughter. I know that you and many others in this town had a very high regard for her," Ndomawaa told his host.

Nyake was still lying in the hammock, not caring about the effect it would have on his back as he got older. "One day when I was coming from our town, I met a woman by the river," Ndomawaa went on. "She had finished washing her clothes. I did not recognize her but she called my name without hesitating. She greeted me nicely and started thanking me. I was confused and felt that she had mistaken me for someone else. Then she said to me, 'Kinie Ndomawaa, you don't know me, do you?' I told her that her face looked familiar, but I was unable to put a name to it. She said, 'I know you. You are the father of Giita and your granddaughter is Sister Kunaafoh. I almost went blind but now I can do many things by myself. Everybody here in Talia said that I was a witch and that was why no medicine could cure me. Now I can see. Do you know who cured me?' She started crying as she said. 'It was your granddaughter. God will bless you. God will bless her and I know her mother is peaceful where she is.'

On hearing about this incident Nyake asked kindly, "Tell me, how did you feel when the woman said that to you? There is no doubt that your granddaughter has brought fame to this town and the chiefdom. But, let me also warn you before you get a nasty surprise one of these days. Do you know that there are many others in this town who say that your granddaughter is doing things that they don't understand? Yes, many people come to me and gossip. They are worried. Why? Because they say some people are now rejecting the idea of witchcraft saying that Sister Kunaafoh has powers that witches do not have, otherwise, how else could she cure all those ailments that afflicted people in this town? They are worried. Look at the way she treated our well known Kinie Mbaqui who had the most chronic sore here in this town. The man can now put on shorts and move around with pride. He is not ashamed anymore, thanks to your granddaughter. My fear is that one day people are going to ask the chief some very hard questions about your granddaughter's powers. Anyway, let us wait and see. For now, we look at your granddaughter and consider what she is doing as good. We see it as the work of God and our ancestors. Let me promise you that I shall stand up to anyone that comes up with any concerns about Kunaafoh's ability to treat people whose diseases seemed incurable in the past."

Ndomawaa was again comforted by Nyake's comments. He knew that Nyake was expressing the feelings of many in Talia and the chiefdom. He was equally pleased that so much information had been divulged about Kigba's possession of a djinn. He now had enough ammunition to confront Hindowaa and his mother about the circumstances surrounding his daughter's death.

When he took leave of Nyake, Ndomawaa still had a glimmer of hope that he would find his son-in-law alone on the veranda. It was still fairly early and people were continuing to go about their business; so he tried to avoid being stopped by anyone who wanted to exchange greetings. From a distance, he saw a flickering light at Hindowaa's house and there were still people on the veranda. He knew who they were - the same ones who would always wait until the last drop of palm wine had been squeezed out of all the gourds. He knew each of them by face and by name. He slowed his pace as he approached his in-laws' house and decided against trying to engage Hindowaa in any discussion that evening. From his conversations with Nyamakoro and Nyake, he felt satisfied with the progress he had made towards finding the reason for Giita's premature death. Armed with what he had heard, he intended to confront mother and son at a time and place of his own choosing. It was only a matter of time, so he waited in patience as the night progressed to the following day.

■

CHAPTER TWO

Giita's bereaved husband and father were sitting side by side on Hindowaa's veranda the next afternoon, united in silent grief as they remembered the tragic day of her death. Threatening clouds intensified their sadness as they painfully recalled the downpour that had dispersed the crowd waiting at the house for news of the birth of her twins. Clouds massed over the town; people walked faster to their destinations. Animals, too, rushed for shelter.

"Daemia (In-law)."

Giita's father always addressed Hindowaa as 'in-law', and Hindowaa addressed him in the same way. Still in a contemplative mood, Hindowaa jerked in his hammock as if he had not expected the silence to be broken. Instead of answering his father-in-law, he just turned towards him so that they were now facing each other at a comfortable distance. The clouds continued to threaten rain and it became evident that it was going to come down heavily before the day was over. Giita's father went on,

"My daughter, my eldest child, your former wife, died not all that long ago. Since then, I have been trying to find out why she died. She was not an old woman; and she certainly was not a witch. Just look at the number of children she left behind! My daughter was a peaceful and loving person. She never hurt anybody."

At this, Hindowaa sat up, his mouth slightly agape. He realised that his father-in-law had much more to say.

"My daughter did not die a natural death," the older man continued. "Yes, she did not die a natural death. Everywhere I have gone to find out why she died, the story is the same. She did not die a natural death. And I also have to tell you that everywhere I have gone, they have told me that the future is not promising for this household."

This information gave Hindowaa such a jolt that he rose from the hammock at once.

"What are you saying, daemia? I don't understand. What are you saying?"

"Daemia, I have told you what I discovered when I sought the wisdom of diviners on the matter. They have been unanimous in their opinions. Not one of them has told me anything different. I did not tell any of them that I had visited other diviners, so you can see why I believe what they all told me. For the sake of my five grandchildren I am telling you this so that you can take necessary steps to prevent further calamity befalling your house. You have to cleanse your house because now that my daughter has gone forever, my grandchildren are all that I have left. In my own way, I intend to find out those responsible for her death and fight them directly or indirectly. I shall fight them, daemia, I tell you, I shall fight them during the day, at night, during the rainy season and during the dry season. I shall fight them. Daemia, I shall fight them here on earth and after I depart from this world. I shall fight them. You know as well as I do that my daughter left me with five grandchildren - your children. We should protect them at any cost. And, daemia, there is something else which I shall tell you about when I am ready. It concerns your mother. "

Ndomawaa's voice was bitter and distressed as he spoke that afternoon. Hindowaa, too, felt anguished as he listened. It seemed to him that it was in sympathy with his father-in-law's mood that the clouds were threatening a downpour. As they continued to gather, the atmosphere darkened within and without.

"Why did Giita die?" his father-in-law lamented. "What did she do? What did I do that was responsible for this tragedy? Why me? Why you? Why? Why?"

His voice was shaking and he turned his face away from Hindowaa. His eyes reddened but he shed no tears. The rain came down then and the deluge soon engulfed the town though some people defied it and continued to go about their business.

"Daemia, please tell me more", Hindowaa urged his father-in-law. "Did they say someone else is going to die in this house? Did they?"

Hindowa was now pacing up and down the veranda with both hands clasped behind his back. Rain pounded the zinc roof, making a deafening sound, but they continued to talk.

"Daemia, death is just one aspect of tragedy," Ndomawaa told his son-in-law. "A house can fall apart without someone dying. Misery comes in many forms. To tell you the truth, the diviners were not precise about the nature of the calamity. What they said was that this house will experience problems, very serious problems. You know that there are malicious people all over the place. This is why I decided to come and warn you so that you and your mother can do something together to prevent your house from falling apart. We went through a very turbulent time when my daughter was trying to have more sons, and look how she ended. We have suffered a lot, daemia."

As he continued to ponder the circumstances leading to his daughter's death Hindowaa's father-in-law became even more distressed and soon afterwards took his leave. As the rain kept up its relentless assault, Hindowaa began to mull over what the old man had told him.

It was just yesterday that I was taking stock of my situation in this world. Just yesterday, that I remembered how tormented I was when Kortu died. Perhaps our father has cursed me for not attending my brother's funeral even though I performed all the rituals connected with his death. Deep, deep down in my heart, I knew that I should have been at his funeral. It was not very long after that that Giita died in labour... Otherwise, I cannot say or understand why that happened to me. And now, my father in-law is telling me that my house is threatened with another calamity. What does this mean? I need to confer with my mother about this prediction. We need to alert the ancestors. Are they aware of it and are again failing to warn us?

The rain continued to pour down, though with less intensity. Darkness had taken over the town, but human activity was not yet at a standstill. Hindowa called out to Boi-Kimbo, his second wife. She was busy preparing his favorite sauce for the evening meal and came running from the kitchen, one hand pressed against her chest as if she was alarmed. She was surprised to find Hindowaa on his feet, and staring into space, but said only, "I am here."

"Where is my mother?" he asked without looking at her. She noticed that his voice was unusually subdued.

"She told me that she was going to the chief's compound, but that was a long time ago, even before the rain started. She also told me that from the chief's compound she would pass by Kinie Nyake's house before coming home."

There was a brief silence during which Hindowaa decided that since the rain had now lessened considerably, he would go and look for his mother at the chief's compound. If he did not find her there, he would go on to Nyake's house. He planned to avoid the main road and take another less frequented route, then when he got close to the compound, he would look for some errand boy to go and call his mother. He told Boi-Kimbo that he was going out without mentioning his destination or how long he would be away.

The rain had cleansed the air and as he strolled through the back ways leading to the chief's compound, Hindowaa could smell the freshness rising from the vegetation, coupled with the strong fragrance of the mangoes that had dropped during the heavy rain. The trees along the way swayed in rhythmic response to the calm evening breeze. He continued to saunter towards the chief's compound with his left hand firmly anchored in his pocket as if to secure some precious item there. The nearer he came to the compound, the slower his pace became because he was wondering why his mother had not told him where she was going. Why the chief's compound and Nyake's house? And how could his mother decide to visit the chief and Nyake without telling him? Feeling weighed down with a sense of despondency and confusion, he paused for a moment and stared into space, then he heard a noise and saw a little boy coming towards him.

Hindowaa beckoned to the boy who approached him gingerly. He was of average height for an eight-year-old, with big bulging eyes. Hindowa also noticed that his nose was smeared with snot which was almost dripping into his mouth.

"Good evening, maada (old man)," the boy greeted him as they studied each other. There was a moment's silence before Hindowa said,

"My mother went to the chief's compound. Please go and see if she is still there and tell her that I sent you to call her. Her name is Yeea Kigba."

"Yes, maada," the boy answered. He walked briskly towards the chief's compound, but felt a little apprehensive because it was not an ordinary house where people could just walk in casually. He approached the compound from the back, and slowed his pace. He was wondering how he would enter it without attracting too much attention when he saw a messenger coming out of the gate. He went towards the man and greeted him politely.

"Please, sir, I am looking for Yeea Kigba. Her son says she came to see the chief and asked me to come and call her. Is she in the compound?"

"She left some time ago and I believe she is now at home," the messenger answered. He looked in the direction from which the boy had come and added kindly,

"Be careful as you go that way, there are snakes and other creatures of the night that can hurt children."

Quite unafraid, the boy ran off towards Hindowaa, who was still standing where he left him, looking anxious.

"Was she there?" he asked, even before the boy opened his mouth.

"No, maada, they said she left some time ago."

"Thank you. I shall tell your father that you are a good boy, and give you three pence to buy some lunch when you go to school - that is a promise. Now go straight home and be careful for snakes. You hear me?"

The boy sped home, thinking about the money and wondering whether the man would keep his promise.

Hindowaa trekked home again along the same narrow pathway. He wished he had brought his torch, for the town was now charcoal dark and he was aware that creatures of the night might be on active duty, waiting for anyone careless enough to come their way without taking necessary precautions. One question continued to trouble his mind. What did his mother want to discuss with the chief and Nyake? He hoped she had not engaged them in any discussions about his daughter, Kunaafoh, marrying the chief. As far as Hindowaa was concerned, that matter was not negotiable and he hoped his mother understood that. He was glad he had his father-in-law's full support that Kunaafoh should remain a nun and a doctor because she was a great asset to the community. But then, if his mother did not talk about Kunaafoh's marriage, what else could she have discussed with the chief, he wondered, his forehead creased with anxiety.

Since my father-in-law told me that my household is threatened, I cannot relax. Losing my wife was bad enough. Now he also tells me that there is something else concerning my mother that he wants to discuss with me another time. What is it? When will he tell me about it? I am so confused. And my mother is not helping matters. What business does she have with the chief? How many other people has she visited without my knowledge? Anyway, I am absolutely determined that Kunaafoh will not marry our chief. And I am equally certain that even our ancestors will support my position. I will make it clear to my mother once more that my daughter will never marry our Chief. Not while I am alive, well and breathing. I shall also ask the missionaries to explain to her that nuns do not marry or bear children. I only hope that mother has not taken any money from the chief to influence her on this matter. That would be a grave mistake because if the marriage does not take place, she or the family will have to refund it and I already owe money to many people in this town.

Approaching his house, he saw no light. Was his mother back, he wondered, or was she still out doing her rounds? He hoped she had already returned because he was eager to talk to her; his night would be even more disturbed if he failed to discuss this burning subject with her. He knew that despite her age, she did not sleep early. Many a time he and the rest of the household would fall asleep before her even though she retired early. If he found his mother in bed, he would ask Boi-Kimbo to go and see if she was asleep. And if she had not returned from her mission, he would send Boi-Kimbo to go and search for her in town. He knew all the likely places. If she was not at Nyake's house, he knew she would be visiting the woman who made snuff and sold tobacco. If the latter were the case, then he knew that his mother would not be coming home anytime soon. However, he made up his mind that whatever happened, he would wait up for her. He was determined to find out if she knew of anything threatening the Hindowaa household and likely to bring on the calamity Ndomawaa had spoken of.

"Good evening," Boi-Kimbo greeted her husband as he entered the house. An Aladdin lamp glowed so feebly in the parlor that it was almost dark. Boi-Kimbo's twins had gone to bed and there was a sense of peace though crickets, frogs and other creatures of the night were busy making sounds that interrupted the stillness.

"Has my mother returned yet?" Hindowaa asked. His anxiety made him sound aggressive.

"She came in a long time ago and after eating, went into her room," Boi-Kimbo replied in a submissive tone, tightening her wrapper which had slipped off her youthful and delicate waist.

"Is she asleep?" Hindowaa asked, as they moved towards their own bedroom. Boi-Kimbo did not answer the question, saying instead, "Food is ready; shall I bring it?"

"I shall tell you when I am ready to eat. Is mother sleeping?" Hindowaa asked again.

"I don't know if she is awake or asleep. As you know, it is hard to tell. I think that sometimes she stays awake for most of the night."

"How would you know that? Are you a witch or a ghost?" Hindowaa joked.

"If I were a witch or a ghost you would have known it by now. Sometimes your mother tells us stories about things that happen late at night when everyone in the town is supposed to be asleep - stories about dogs barking at odd hours. She sometimes hears strange noises and asks us if we heard them at such and such time. I wonder why she can't sleep."

Hindowaa tapped on the door when they reached his mother's bedroom, then waited and listened, his heart beating fast. He heard no movement and could not see any light. Was she awake or asleep? he wondered. He was relieved when she answered in a sharp voice, "Yaemia (Who is it)?" He imagined her hurriedly tying her wrapper since she had not expected anyone to come to her room at that time of day.

"Nyamia, Hindo (I am Hindo)."

As he entered the room, Hindowaa smelled fresh and potent palm wine and looked around quickly to see if there was a gourd visible. Sometimes generous people brought his mother palm wine which she preferred to enjoy alone since such presents did not often come her way.

"How was your day, mother?" They were now seated but had not yet made eye contact. As he waited for her to answer, he continued to survey the room hopefully because he could still smell palm wine.

"The rain has been too much," his mother grumbled. "It caught me at the chief's compound, so I stayed there until it ceased. Then I went to see Nyake and I spent a long time with him. As you know, he always has something to say and will not let a person leave early. After I left his house, I came home, ate some food and decided to come to bed; but I wish I had gone to see Yaetoma. My snuff is finished and all the children are now asleep. It is a good thing I have some palm wine; otherwise I would not have been able to sleep tonight. I was not asleep when you came in. I heard you asking your wife if I had come back."

Hindowaa was not at all pleased to hear that his mother had indeed visited the chief and Nyake. Familiar places, he said to himself as he looked at her prematurely aging face. So what was discussed?

"Mother, I have been thinking about something Giita's father told me this afternoon. It worried me very much. Soon after he told me that, he went away.

Hindolo's mother sat up straight and for the first time since he entered her room, looked directly at her son, her large, beautiful eyes bulging even more.

"What was it about, my son, tell me?"

She sounded troubled and continued to stare into Hindowaa's eyes. She then took a very deep breath as if she were about to fall into a trance, and moved her stool nearer to him. There was a short silence as she waited for him to continue.

"Since Giita's death, I have had many sleepless

nights, thinking about the circumstances that led to her death. The children, the older twins, still don't understand the meaning of death and they keep asking me when their mother will come back, and why she has stayed so long? Oh! How it makes my heart ache. It is just too painful. I have had several dreams about Giita that suggest that she is angry with me and with some other people, including you, my mother. Now her father came to tell me something very disturbing. That is why I am here to talk to you tonight. I cannot keep these thoughts to myself any longer. My mind is as heavy as a stone."

Hindowaa's mother leaned forward, looking even more nervous.

"Yes, my son, I am with you and prepared to listen. Tell me. What is it all about? You say Giita is angry? She is angry with me? What did I do to her? She gave us five children, three sons and two daughters. I am pleased with her. I am sure if she had lived longer, she would have given me more grandsons. I thank God, she gave us three healthy sons and I shall always pray for her and ask our ancestors to guide her in the other world where I know she has arrived safely. Why should she be angry with me?"

"Mother, when Giita's father came here today, he looked worried, and indeed he was worried. I could feel it. I could feel it. He was sweating..."

"Hindo, I am listening," his mother said, trying to hide the nervous impatience she was feeling. "What was he worried about? What did he say he was worried about? There are just the two of us in this room and I believe everyone else is asleep. Tell me why you have come to see me."

"Daemia told me that since the premature death of his daughter, he had had no rest over the matter and therefore went to see several diviners."

"And what did they tell him?"

"Well, he said all the diviners informed him that Giita's death was not due to natural causes. Mother, if I were much older, I would have collapsed when he told me that. He also said that unless we cleanse this house, another calamity will befall my household. I tried to find out from him whether other members of the family would die, but at that point he became philosophical, saying death is just one element in the realm of human tragedies. This means that something terrible could happen to this house without anyone dying. What this could be I don't know, mother, I just don't know. Also, he said he had other issues of concern to discuss at a later date. With what he told me, and the unpleasant dreams I have had about Giita, I have been seriously worried, mother. This is why I am here."

Looking uncomfortable and visibly shaken, Kigba moved her stool further away from Hindowaa.

"My son, this is very troubling news. Here we are, still reeling under the pain of Giita's death, and now we are told about some other bad thing coming to this house?"

Contemplating the new threat to her family made her angry, and she continued more forcefully, "Hindo, all I can do is to promise to fight this to the bitter end. I shall tie my wrapper as tight as I can make it and fight any evil elements in this town that want to destroy our household. Where are our ancestors in this situation facing us? Where are they? I agree with Giita's father. This town will destroy us if we don't put our heads together and fight back. As for me, I am ready. I shall challenge them and let them know that I am not an ordinary woman. I am also a Sowie, head of the women's secret society. I shall challenge them. That is all I can say for now. I am sick and tired of the evil in this town. This time, the devil will not succeed. No, he will not succeed while I am alive and well."

Kigba paused for breath then went on in a slightly calmer tone.

"Have you informed anyone else, I mean your two sisters and their husbands? They should be informed immediately. All the immediate family members should be told so they can be on the alert. They should know that there are forces out there - very ugly forces that want to bring this house down. We should also inform the ancestors immediately. I shall not rest until we have fortified ourselves. Do you hear what I am saying, Hindo?"

"Mother, you are the first person I have told about this. I came earlier and Boi-Kimbo told me that you had gone to the chief's compound. I then went to look for you, but learned you had already left for home."

His mother was obviously still considering what to do about what he had just told her, and he waited, staring at her. Kigba rose from the stool and fidgeted with an old basket under her bed while her son watched her movements closely. She took out a small bundle wrapped in leaves and untied it. She took out some fresh kola nuts which she divided into two and started eating one piece. Hindowaa stretched out his hand for the other piece.

"Mother, if I may ask, what was the purpose of your visit to the chief's compound?"

Kigba continued chewing the kola nut for a minute or two before answering him.

"Heeh heeh, Hindo, so I am now a child. I am your child who should say where I am going, when I shall be back and what the purpose of the visit is. When did you start this interrogation business on your mother, hm? Anyway, you know that the chief is our future in-law. Whenever I have time, I visit his compound and we talk in-law talk. He has also been very generous to me. He gives me money and gifts. He is a very good person and as you know, I like him. I shall do everything in my power for him to marry Kunaafoh."

It was in a grave voice that Hindowaa said,

"Mother, did I hear you correctly? Did you say that you discussed the prospects of Kunaafoh marrying the chief and that he has been giving you money and gifts?"

"You are correct," she replied. She now sounded quite relaxed and continued chewing the kola nut. Her jaws moved slowly, like a pregnant she-goat chewing on the cud.

"Oh, I forgot. Would you like some palm wine? It is very good. It was Kinie Kolugbonda who thought of me today and dropped this gourd. He is such a kind man. Tomorrow when Boi-Kimbo cooks, I shall tell her to prepare one dish for him. He is so kind to me."

Hindowaa silently accepted his mother's offer and started pouring the wine into his cup before speaking again.

"Mother, I thought we had come to the understanding and conclusion that Kunaafoh could not marry the chief or anyone else because she is a nun. We also agreed that we should find another female member of the family to give to him. Giita's father also supported our position and I have been thinking of approaching the chief about it. Now you have put me in an embarrassing position. How do I now proceed on this delicate matter?"

"Hindo, you and I agreed about my granddaughter's marriage to our chief." His mother's tone became stubborn, her expression sour. "I made my position known to you many, many times. My only choice is our chief and I don't understand what the problem is. Kunaafoh is now an adult. Her breasts are full. Men look at her with lust. Do you want her to stay without a husband? She goes around this town dressed in white like a ghost, with something like a snake around her neck. If she does not marry, how will she ever have children? Tell me that. What is the matter with you? I brought you into this world because I am a woman and was married to your father, a man. That is how children are born. Where did you hear about a girl not getting married? The ancestors must be turning in their graves."

As if to distance himself from his mother's animosity, Hindowaa moved his stool further away.

"Mother, nuns do not marry. They do not bear children. All the Catholic nuns and priests are not married and have no children. They are devoted to God and Christ. That is how this religion has been from time immemorial. I have told you this whenever the subject has come up. This is why Kunaafoh cannot marry the Chief or anyone else."

"Who is this Christ you are referring to," his mother demanded angrily. "Is he a man, a ghost or a mermaid? I don't know. I don't know book and you don't know book, yet you know so much about the white man's religion. So God said that women should not marry and have children if they belong to the white man's religion? Tell me, I don't know. How can my granddaughter be married to someone nobody can see? I think you have lost your mind, or perhaps you have been bewitched. Is it because Kunaafoh went to the white man's land and learned the white man's book that she should not marry and have children? My son, I am sorry for you. I pity you. You see, that is why it is not good to send girls to the white man's land. Look at the rubbish we are now hearing - that women should not marry and have children. Hindo, you make me sick, sick and sick. One thing I will tell you is this. If I don't die, I will live to see Kunaafoh, my grandchild, married to our chief. Don't involve me in your madness. Even Giita, in her grave will not forgive you if her daughter remains unmarried and childless. That is all I have to say, Kinie Nuuyaabaah (Mr. ingrate)."

The night was now advanced, but mother and son continued their bitter argument on the subject of Kunaafoh's marriage. Hindowaa was not convinced by anything his mother had to say. In the end, he said to her, "Mother, I think the best thing for us to do is to wait until the whole family meets again on this matter, but as for me, I am determined that Kunaafoh will not marry anyone. She is my daughter. I also told you that her grandfather supports my position. The community supports my position. And I know that God and our ancestors support my position. I am not defying you, but this is the will of God. So let us leave this matter for now. God knows as well as you that I am not an ingrate."

At that, visibly enraged, Kigba stood up and started pacing from one end of the room to the other, breathing hard.

"Heeh, heeh. Hindo. Hindo. You are challenging me? You are challenging your mother, your mother who brought you into this world? I who carried you in my belly for nine months. I who had one of the most difficult struggles to bring you into this world? It is I that you are challenging? I who saw you naked, washed you and put trousers on your behind, and cleaned you up when you went to the toilet? It is I that you are now challenging?"

In her agitation she started sweating even though the room was comfortably cool. “Oh, my ancestors, listen to this. I hope you are listening. I shall curse you, Hindo. I shall curse you if my granddaughter does not marry our chief. In fact, I shall move out of this house just to show my disgust if you refuse for my granddaughter to marry our chief. You are now a mad child. I mean a mad man. You should be walking the streets in rags.”

Confused and disturbed by his mother’s ranting, Hindowaa could only stare at her in silence. Her threat to curse him was upsetting. The palm wine now tasted sour and stale.

“Let me take this opportunity to tell you something,” she went on. “My late grandmother once told me that it was not safe to have only one son. She also said that in many families, there is always a fool or mad person. She said it was better if one had only one daughter and several sons because an only son could prove either a blessing or a terrible disappointment. According to her, only sons could go either way in life. They could be successful or become burdens on the family. That is, they could prove useless, mad, sick, or become criminals. I don’t know where she got that idea from, but the way you are behaving makes me believe what she told me. You must be getting sick in the head, sitting here telling me that my granddaughter will never marry or have children. I have to look for a medicine man to cure you of your madness. Chai! You make me sick! My grandmother was right.”

“But, mother, let me ask you a question,” Hindowaa said after that outburst. Kigba was waiting for the question while Hindowaa was waiting for her to tell him to proceed. For a moment silence reigned. Finally he summoned enough courage to ask his mother the question he had always wanted to ask.

"Why is it that you have never asked my sister, Boi-Komah, when she will give you more grandsons? She has two girls and a boy. I had two boys and a girl with Giita before she had the twins whom she never lived to see, love and raise. What is the difference?" That question offended his mother even more and she continued to berate him.

"I knew that one day you would ask me such a question. I knew it, so I am not at all surprised that you are bold enough to ask it tonight. My son, I am more concerned about you, you my only son. Boi-Komah is married and her husband will take care of her, protect her and provide for her and the family. You are a man. That is the difference. If you don't know it, let me tell you tonight so that you can keep it in your head. I shall teach you a lesson if you defy me over this matter. I am warning you, Hindo. I shall not allow you to have your way. You are my child no matter how old you are. Do you hear me? You are my son, and only son; you understand? I shall talk to your sisters about this. I want them to understand that you have grown too big - that you now feel you can challenge me. Oh! My mother will be turning in her grave as she listens to us. Your father too will be turning in his grave and your grandfather also. You can be sure that they are listening to this conversation, and all of them will be wondering whether you are the same Hindo they used to know. They will not believe that in this world today, children dare to argue with their parents. Yes, things have changed indeed. How dreadful the world has become. Chai! Chai!"

Hindowaa had not expected his mother to react so

vehemently and point a threatening finger at him. Until this incident, he could not recall any time she had become so angry with him. She seemed absolutely furious. The night was advanced and he wanted to go to bed but could not leave the room without her permission, knowing that if he were to take leave of her she would be further offended. He waited for the right moment, feeling stifled.

"Let me make this known to you and I want you to understand it very well. I shall visit the grave sites of your father and grandfather tomorrow. I will tell them about this situation and appeal to them to let you know that it is necessary for Kunaafoh to marry our chief. I shall tell them that you are the first member of the family to advocate the non-marriage of women. I know how they will feel and react. They will think that something has gone terribly wrong with your mind."

Hindowaa knew that his mother was serious, but he too had made up his mind not to give in to her. He decided to visit his father and grandfather's graves and communicate with them regarding Kunaafoh's future and the family crisis it was causing.

"I shall also talk to Ndomawaa about this matter. He has never told me that both of you had agreed that my granddaughter should stay unmarried and childless. I have never ever heard that a woman should not marry. Ah, Hindo, if someone had told me this in the form of a story, I might have believed it. Yes, I would have believed that there are women, created by God but who refuse to marry and have children because they belong to the white man's religion." She laughed contemptuously.

Hindowaa's tone remained conciliatory but firm as he responded.

"Mother, I want you to understand that I have not

challenged you on this matter. All I want to say to you is that we discussed it once and I thought we had come to the understanding that we would find another woman for the chief. I have never challenged you. I know that you are my mother and you brought me into this world; but I think I should be allowed to decide on matters concerning my own daughter. Yes, I am your son, but an adult son, not a child, not a dependent child. I shall continue to appeal to you so that we resolve the matter as a family."

"Oh, Ngewo. Ngewo, (Oh God, God)," Kigba answered. "You are no longer a child. I know that. Yes, I know that. Kinie Berewa (Mr. Big Trousers). You now put on big trousers; very big trousers, so you are no longer a child. You are telling me to my face, me, your mother. Ah, I don't know what this world is coming to. You children of today, you are cursed - burdens to your parents who brought you into this world. I shall talk to your sisters and Kinie Ndomawaa so that all of us can meet as a family to discuss this matter. However, I want you to understand that my position will not change because I have on several occasions assured our chief that my granddaughter will be his next wife. I shall not approach him to say I have changed my position. What will he think of me?"

Hindowaa said nothing more and mother and son agreed to retire. They were both mentally exhausted and needed sleep. Nature was completely silent. The creatures of the night had ceased their activities. Hindowaa took leave of his mother and walked wearily to his room where he found his wife, Boi-Kimbo, fast asleep. She was snoring in blissful abandon, completely in harmony with the silence of the night.

■

CHAPTER THREE

The fierce and continuous barking of dogs shattered the early morning silence. It was the time just before dawn when people derived the most pleasure from their sleep and did not want to be woken up. Kigba, however, was already up and had left the house. She vividly recalled the last time she visited the grave sites of her husband and Hindowaa's grandfather. It was not long ago that she had made the visit. The barking of dogs always reminded her that it was the right time to make the visit to the grave sites. People believed that that was the time the spirits of the dead returned to their graves at the end of their nocturnal wanderings. Dogs were believed to be psychic and able to see the spirits of the dead as they returned to their abode. This was why they barked in the early hours of the morning.

This particular visit was of immense importance to Kigba for she was deeply worried over developments in the family. Her heart was heavy as she walked towards the grave sites located at the south side of the house. They had been covered by overgrown shrubs despite frequent visits by family members.

I hope they don't think that I am visiting them too often, Kigba thought as she approached the grave sites. I hope they will not be angry with me; but it is their duty to protect us, guide us and resolve our problems. Yes, I know that the last time I was with them, they were reluctant to grant my request. It was the time when I came to plead with them to give me more grandsons because Giita was pregnant. They told me that they had consulted with the older ancestors who told them that Giita had already been allotted her quota of children, two boys and a girl. When I insisted, they said they would oblige but at a cost. I now know the cost; Giita delivered her twins but died in labor. So sad. This time, however, the issue is not very complicated; and I see no reason why anyone should die as a consequence. Yes, there is no reason for anyone to die. All they need to do is to prevail on Hindowaa to behave himself. I know that they will support my position. It is simple. A woman cannot be a woman in our community if she is not married; and a woman cannot be a woman if she cannot to bear children, many children. I shall inform them of this strange idea which Hindowaa is trying to introduce in the family, the town and the chiefdom. I know that they will be angry with him and take measures to knock sense into his big head."

The barking of the dogs did not distract her as she went. She made a detour from the main footpath and went through the bush road that led to the grave sites. Her skin became wet as she navigated her way through the dew-soaked bush. She was dressed in white, and part of her bare feet and face were smeared with white clay as was the custom on such occasions. When the dogs stopped their barking she told herself that all the spirits of the dead had returned to their respective graves. It would have been terrible if she came and found that they had not yet returned. That would have meant that she would be speaking to them in their absence. It was always better to speak to them while they were in their graves.

It was still dark and the morning was now silent, providing the appropriate environment for the departed to listen to her. She had prepared food for her husband and her son's grandfather. She also had some rice flour and kola nuts. Before she left, she would pour libation for the departed and had brought along a small gourd of palm wine for that purpose. She also had two goat horns.

The graves of Hindowaa's father and grandfather lay parallel to each other and Kigba sat between them with both legs outstretched. She was alone with her husband and Hindowaa's grandfather. She felt the cold morning wind piercing her body even as she tried to make herself more comfortable. When she heard the croaking of frogs not far from the big river, she knew that time was against her and began her communication with the departed.

"My husband and maada Kaapu greetings. Greetings also from the entire family. How are you all? How are those who went before you and those before them and those after them? How are they all doing? We on this side of the divide know that things are not bad with you over there. We know because we have not dreamed any bad dreams. We know because all the food we have been offering to you all has been eaten. We know because all the libations we have been offering, have been well received. We thank God and all of you."

"We are happy that you came to check on us."

When Kigba heard the voice, she felt as if she was in trance. The voice was remote but clear, but in her state of anxiety she could not determine whether it belonged to her husband or Hindowaa's grandfather. She would listen more carefully when the next response came.

"I am pleased to hear your voice," she said. "I am pleased to be with you this morning. I want to tell you that there is nothing wrong with the family. Our health is good. Hindowaa is well. His wife, Boi-Kimbo, and her children are well. The twins have grown big. I love them. Teneh, Boi-Komah and their husbands and children are all well. My husband, it is a long time since I saw Fanday, but

I learned from relatives that she is doing well. She will be coming to visit me soon. The harvest last season was good and we are looking forward to making a bigger farm this year when the rains stop."

She heard the voice again. "It is the wish of the ancestors that all will materialize."

"I am sure you are wondering why I am here this morning. I am not here to disturb you. I am here to tell you about a development in the family that needs your timely intervention. All of you! As you know, I am not getting any younger. I live with Hindowaa, your son and grandson; so you see there is nothing that is seriously wrong with the entire family. We thank you for guiding all of us. We know that you will not forget your family on this side of creation."

"We are doing what we should do and will continue to do so," the voice told Kigba. This time, she knew it was Hindowaa's grandfather.

"I am here because I need you. Hindowaa is behaving strangely, stupidly and irresponsibly these days, and I am worried. I have come to the conclusion that he is not well in the head. Imagine; just imagine. He is saying that Kunaafoh should not marry our chief. He says that Kunaafoh belongs to a religion that does not allow women to marry and have children. I never heard this before. Nobody in the family ever heard such strange things. The people in Talia and the chiefdom have never heard this before. This type of thinking is coming from a member of our family. A man. You will not believe that Hindowaa is now challenging me on this issue. I told him that as long as I am alive, I will make sure that my granddaughter marries our chief. One night, we argued for a long time over this matter and we separated without agreeing on the issue. He said we should hold a family meeting even though his strange mind is already made up against Kunaafoh marrying our chief. I know how you will feel when you hear this strange news. Things are now happening that you will never have dreamed of in your lifetime. I am here to appeal to you to come to my assistance in order to resolve this matter, which is threatening the Hindowaa household. If not addressed the family will break up. I am pleading with all of you on the other side of the big divide to help me resolve this matter."

Kigba felt exhausted after passing on all this information and the short interval before a response came seemed like an eternity. She even thought she had lost contact with the ancestors and was relieved when she again heard a voice saying,

"We shall investigate and come back to you on this matter. It is serious, so we need to hang heads."

"I have heard you and thank you many times," Kigba said. "I shall wait to hear from you and promise not to come to any final decision before that."

She poured libation, placed some food, kola nuts and the two goat horns by the grave sites before continuing. "I shall come again to find out the result of your deliberation on the matter, then I shall tell Hindowaa, Teneh, Boi-Komah, Nyake, Nyamakoro, Fanday, Kinie Bokai, nyahapui Miatta and her husband your final decision. I thank you for listening to me and I say goodbye. Please continue to rest in peace."

"Go in peace," the voice said as Kigba was leaving. This voice was also clear and she knew that it was her husband who had said goodbye. The frogs were still croaking as she walked away with a sense of relief that she had addressed her concerns to her husband, Hindowaa's grandfather and the rest of the ancestors. She heard familiar voices from a distance and slowed down her pace for she was not prepared to talk to people going very early in the morning to fetch water from the river. They were mostly women and girls with buckets and other containers delicately balanced on their heads.

"Good morning Kigba." The voice startled her.

"Good morning," she responded reluctantly.

"Where are you coming from so early in the morning?" The woman was surprised because Kigba would not be fetching water when there were young people in her house to do so every morning and evening.

"Can't you see my face and feet? Can't you see the way I am dressed? What do you make of all this? Don't you pay respects to your departed ones?" Kigba's voice was unfriendly; at least that was how the woman interpreted her tone. Other women heading towards the river avoided them and walked away.

"I am sorry if my question offended you, I should have known better. You know that I am getting old. How are they all? I hope they are fine and there is peace there."

As she walked away, the woman said to herself,I was just trying to be nice and look at the way she reacted. Next time, I will shut my big mouth so that I don't get into trouble. She thinks I am her son whom she bullies. I don't blame her. it is Hindowaa that I blame for his docility. No wonder his contemporaries make fun of him. Sheeeuuur.

That was why I dreaded coming on the main path, Kigba grumbled inwardly. People will ask you questions just to provoke you. How come she did not notice my face, feet and my dress? How could she possibly misinterpret my situation? As if she has never visited grave sites. She has lost her husband, father, and grandfather. Does she want to tell me that she does not visit them, prepare food for them and pour libation for them? Of course, she does. So why is she asking me questions? Hypocrites. They always want to poke their noses into people's business

"Good morning, yaae Kigba."

One of the children belonging to the house greeted her as she was going indoors. The household was now alive and the morning's domestic activities were already under way.

"Yeea Kigba, good morning," Boi-Kimbo greeted her mother in-law. She had not seen her yet that morning but did not ask why she was dressed in that manner and where she was coming from.

"Your son asked about you before he left the house."

"Your children are still in bed?" Kigba asked without responding to Boi-Kimbo's information.

"Yes, they are still in bed," Boi-Kimbo replied. She sensed her mother-in-law's foul mood and steeled herself for any eventuality.

"That is how you spoil children. They should be up and ready to fetch water from the river and clean the house. They are now big and they are girls. Don't you know that girls are supposed to be up early? You want to spoil these children. I have been noticing this for some time but decided to ignore it. Don't spoil my grandchildren. They are girls. When they grow up and get married, how will they take care of their husbands?"

"It is only because today is Saturday and there is no school that they are sleeping late, Yeea."

Boi-Kimbo was angry about her mother-in-law's interrogation and interference with the way she was bringing up her daughters, but refused to react in a way that would provoke a confrontation between them. She suffered in silence knowing that whatever happened, her mother-in-law would have the upper hand.

"I have been waiting for the right moment to ask you a serious question." Kigba told Boi-Kimbo who looked confused.

"Do you know how old your daughters are? They will soon be old enough to be initiated into the Sande Society. When are you going to have the next grandchild, the son? What are you waiting for?"

Boi-Kimbo had known that one day Kigba would ask her that question and replied crossly,

"Yeea Kigba, I shall become pregnant when God decides. I am not responsible for my own pregnancy; at least that is what I know. It is God that gives children."

"You twist you face when I ask you a question? Are you trying to talk back to me? I know it is God that gives children. Well, why has He not given you another one since you gave birth a long time ago? That is the question I am asking you. Are you sure you are clean with my son. These days, one cannot be sure with children like you. Your eyes are open even before you are born. I shall watch you closely from now on to see what you are up to."

Boi-Kimbo's eyes reddened and she began to cry.

"It is only because of my father, otherwise, I would have packed my belongings and taken my children and gone home, she said to herself as she collected a container and headed toward the river. Her children were still sleeping. It was Saturday and she refused to wake them up. How long can I put up with such treatment from this woman? She controls her children, especially my husband; she controls my children and me. Hindowaa cannot do anything about it because he has decided to submit himself totally to his mother. The only time in his life he has said no to his mother is about Kunaafoh. Apart from that, he allows his mother to rule this house as if she were the head of the house. I now believe what people say about her. She is a witch and she also possesses the djinn. Why does she hardly sleep at night? What does she do all night staying awake? Giita, my mate, you were an angel and I know that you are now in heaven. All the things you told me about Hindowaa and his mother are true. I see it daily. I experience it weekly and live it monthly; it has become an eternal nightmare for my children and me. Please pray for me so that I can get out of it before I go crazy. If I had not met you and you had not treated me like your daughter and enlightened me, I would have lost my sanity by now. I was lucky to have had a wonderful mate like you. As you said, this is the House of Fear and not the House of Love. It is indeed a House of Fear, thanks to Hindowaa's mother and to Hindowaa's submission to her. This is my life and the life of my children."

The day had started pleasantly enough but it soon became clear that the weather would change and rain would take over the sky. Many people had disappeared to their farms or traveled to other places that day. Now that she had visited her husband, Hindowaa's grandfather, and other ancestors and informed them of developments in the household, Kigba was determined to confront her son again on the subject of Kunaafoh's marriage. Her strategy was to consult as many people in Talia as possible and find out their views on the matter before the family met. So far she had not briefed her daughters, Teneh and Boi-Komah, about the differences between herself and Hindowaa over Kunaafoh because they had praised

Kunaafoh and her profession. She had been told many times how proud they were of their niece. They had never expressed any concern that Kunaafoh had not married and still had no children. For them, what was important was that their niece had become famous. They were proud to be associated with a relative who was so admired in the town and beyond. Kigba therefore felt a little apprehensive at the thought of summoning her two daughters for consultations on the matter.

Teneh, the elder, had adopted an independent attitude when dealing with her mother, especially when Kigba tried to interfere in her domestic affairs. They had had several mild but hostile exchanges. Boi-Komah, on the other hand, was still her mother's baby and consulted Kigba on matters concerning her own household. However, like her elder sister, Teneh, she was also independent-minded and principled and had already made up her mind about how she would respond if her mother ever tried to question her about not having more sons. Fortunately, that hadn't happened yet.

Kigba summoned her two daughters to a meeting on a very pleasant day. She had planned it such that she would have minimum interruptions while they were together. They met at Teneh's house while her husband was away, fishing, the children had gone to school, and Boi-Komah's husband had traveled to another village. The atmosphere was therefore ideal. Boi-Komah had prepared a delicious meal, which the three women had eaten prior to any discussions. The daughters had no idea why their mother had summoned them. Boi-Komah thought the meeting might be to discuss her inability to have more sons, but Teneh refused to speculate. She and her husband were satisfied with the number of children they had.

Kunaafoh had appreciated their decision and gave her support. If Kigba was unhappy about it, she would not try to impose her views because she knew Teneh's character. That was a closed matter as far as Teneh was concerned and Kigba knew it. She began by saying,

"One thing I am happy about, my children is that both of you know how to cook. I am happy I taught you how to cook properly. You see, you can sustain a marriage if you know how to cook and take care of your husband. Mende men generally like their stomachs and love women who can take care of them. Believe me, if you don't know how to cook, they will look for other women even if you are as beautiful as a mermaid. Also, when you were in the Sande Society, you did a lot of cooking. I am very happy with you, my children. As for you Boi-Komah, it took you a long time to know how to cook potato leaves sauce. That was your greatest challenge but in the end, you prevailed. Teneh had no problems with preparing most of the main dishes."

By this time, they were all in the big parlor of the house. The daughters did not comment on Kigba's observations, knowing that her comments in praise of their culinary skills were irrelevant to the purpose of the meeting.

"You know your late father," Kigba went on, "he loved me because I knew how to cook. He had a good appetite. After eating well he would do anything I wanted him to do for me, especially when he had drunk his palm wine. That was why some people believed I controlled him. He simply liked his stomach and I knew how to take care of him in that way. I am grateful to my mother who taught me how to cook and take care of my husband. So I am happy for you."

Kigba had been watching her daughters carefully as she spoke. When they began to show signs of impatience, she hurriedly said,

"My children, we are meeting here today at my request. I don't know whether you have noticed that there is a rift in the house between your brother and me. It was in the making even before Kunaafoh disappeared and it continued after she came back. It is not an easy matter and I have in fact consulted my late husband and your grandfather about it. It concerns Hindowaa's refusal for Kunaafoh to marry our chief and have children."

The two women listened to their mother. Boi-Komah coughed twice and cleared her throat to interrupt, then decided not to. She thought it would be better for Teneh to be the first to speak. However, Teneh did not intervene and their mother continued to address them.

"One night, Hindo and myself spent almost the entire time discussing the question of Kunaafoh's marriage to our Chief. We did not agree about it. He told me that Kunaafoh belongs to a religion that does not allow women to marry or have children. That is such an outrageous idea. Just imagine - Hindowaa does not know book, but he has accepted such a terrible idea. I have put the case to our people who have left us behind. I spoke to them a week ago and they promised to look into the matter. I shall revisit them and find out their opinion. I told them that Hindowaa is now challenging his mother who brought him into this world. Oh, how I suffered with his pregnancy! I told him that of the three of you, it was his pregnancy that gave me the roughest time. I could have died in labor trying to give birth to Hindowaa yet he is the only one now challenging me. This is the world we are living in today."

Tears started falling from Kigba's eyes and her children did not speak for a while; then Teneh said, "Mother, to tell you the truth, we were wondering why you wanted to see us together but could not come up with any good reason. Now we know why and we thank you very much for wanting to involve us in our family matters."

Boi-Komah chimed in, "Mother, you started by commenting on our ability to cook well and said that has helped to make our marriages successful. Well, that may be true, but there are other reasons for the success of our marriages. I personally don't think that our ability to cook well is one of them..."

Kigba was fidgeting with her head tie as she listened to her daughter. Teneh was delighted by what her sister had said and picked up the thread of the comments.

"Mother, even though we are not educated, I want to tell you that from what we learn from other women, these days cooking is not just for women. Men also cook, whether they are married or not. In fact our niece has been very kind to us in telling us that in the white man's country, where she went to study, both men and women cook."

Kigba scowled in disapproval as she listened to this, and she interjected angrily, "Teneh, I hope that you and your sister do not listen to all that your niece tells you. If women don't cook what will be their role in the house? You see, this is the problem; this is what I have observed about people who go to the white man's land. When they come back they tell us that women should not marry and women should not have children. This is the problem I now have with your brother in respect of Kunaafoh. I don't want to think that you too support his position. God forbid! So men should cook for you to eat? Ah, ah. Are you saying then that men should now tie wrappers and you should wear the trousers? My children, your generation wants to turn the world upside down. Your grandparents and ancestors will turn in their graves if they hear this." Wagging a finger at them, she went on, "Now, let me warn both of you. Do not allow yourselves to be influenced by Kunaafoh. Some people are getting worried about the things she has been doing since she came here. They say she is now making people not believe in our traditions and customs because she has cured many of the diseases that were associated with witchcraft. Can you believe what she is doing to this town and chiefdom? Please, don't allow her to influence you."

"We understand how you feel," Teneh said to pacify her mother; but Kigba's lips curled in displeasure.

"Do you really?"

"Yes, mother; we understand how you feel," Boi-Komah hastened to assure her. Teneh, however, added, "But, mother, even though we are not educated, we know what is good when we hear it. We agree with our niece about many things she tells us. She really understands our culture and is not opposed to women marrying and having children. We have had several conversations with her.

"What did you say, Teneh? Did I hear you say you support Kunaafoh's position? Did I hear you say that, my child?"

Kigba stood up, adjusted her wrapper and sat down again. A brief silence ensued; then pointing an accusing finger at Boi-Komah, she said.

"And you, my little child, did you hear what your

sister said?" Her tone was threatening, but Boi-Komah refused to be intimidated. She answered politely but firmly, "We are your children. This is a fact and we shall never contest it. But there is also another fact which is that Teneh and I are now adults, married with children. We make decisions and take responsibility for our decisions. Your days and ours are different. Kunaafoh, belongs to a religion. She has gone through all the training required and she has also studied to become a doctor. The religion does not allow people like her to be married and to have children. My sister and I see nothing wrong with this. Please try to understand and spare yourself all the trouble caused by not accepting this situation. In any case, Kunaafoh, is not really your problem, mother. She is not your daughter, only your granddaughter. It is our brother who has the main responsibility for Kunaafoh. If Giita were alive she, too, would have been be responsible for her, not you the grandmother. I am sorry, mother but this is the truth."

Teneh nodded in support of her sister.

Without saying a word, Kigba left the room briefly. On her return, her daughters watched her movements as if she were getting ready to perform in a play - a comedy perhaps. The clouds outside seemed about to release a downpour. Without sitting down, Kigba resumed the conversation.

"Yes, Boi-Komah,' she said in a caustic tone. "You are my last child and my breast milk is still in your mouth. Your mouth has my milk and yet you dare open it to tell me all this nonsense this afternoon. I am happy that your elder sister heard all this rubbish."

Convinced that she had also spoken for her elder sister, Boi-Komah sat as still as a well-preserved statue in a museum. Her calmness only increased Kigba's agitation.

"Teneh, have you heard what your sister has told me this afternoon?" she almost screamed. "You are my witness. I shall inform our ancestors. Boi-Komah has now grown very big. I suckled her for almost one and a half years before I weaned her. I weaned her only yesterday, and now listen to what she is telling me - that women have the right to decide not to marry and have children. Oh! My mother is turning in her grave. My father, too, is turning in his grave to hear this baby saying such things."

"Mother, please sit down and don't get angry. It is not good for your heart," Teneh said, also adopting a calm attitude. "It will affect your health. Please sit down before I talk."

The parlor was now growing dark as the clouds outside continued to threaten rain. Kigba sat down and gathered her wrapper between her legs. She moved her stool further away from Boi-Komah which only made her daughter smile. Teneh, too, was smiling as she went on "Mother, we have been here for a long time now. Let us not prolong this meeting. What I want to tell you is that I support everything Boi-Komah has said, and she said it very well. Our brother is the main guardian when it comes to our niece. You are a grandmother. We are your children. When we were to marry, you had a say in the matter. When it comes to grandchildren, you have very little say. Please leave it to our brother and respect his views. Kunaafoh is his daughter. I am begging you. Please."

"Ah, ah. A long time ago, before any of you were born, I mean a very, very long time ago, there used to be waves of disaster in this chiefdom from time to time. They said it was due to the anger of the ancestors, caused by the community's failure to comply with sacred ethical values. Once, the ancestors became so angry that they unleashed madness on the community and many people were afflicted. I heard that at that time, you would come across people laughing non-stop for many hours, or people running, running until they fell down and died. I remember this story when I see mad people passing around in this town and hope and pray that nothing like that ever happens again because I think that if it comes, it will start in the Hindowaa household. To tell you the truth, I think that both of you are either becoming mad, or are mad already. I shall just have to tie my wrapper very tightly and fight all of you now that you have joined your brother in fighting me. I accept the challenge."

Kigba got to her feet and was already standing by the door about to leave the house when Teneh started pleading with her to be cautious.

"Mother, we are not challenging you. It is not a battle. Wait a little and do not leave. This is a family matter and you have expressed your views. Don't we also have the right to express our views? If you were not prepared to discuss the issue, why then did you call us for a meeting? It is as if you had already taken a position and only wanted to inform us about it. You are our mother; we know that. But please allow us as adults to express our views on matters that concern the family."

Far from being appeased, Kigba retorted, "Of my three children, you are the only one whose pregnancy was not complete. It lasted for less than nine months and our people believe that babies born too soon mature very slowly and even at old age, behave like children. I can now confirm that. You are older than Boi-Komah yet you don't show it. Instead, you sit here this afternoon and are not ashamed to agree with your junior sister. If she is not mature, it is because she is the younger child, with my breast milk still in her mouth; but look at you, the elder one, displaying the same madness. I shall fight all of you as I have promised. Let me get out of here before the rain starts pouring."

She stalked away, wrestling with her wrapper, which seemed to be falling off her waist, so angry that she continued muttering as she went. Her daughters looked on without feeling any remorse.

"Boi-Komah, mother has to learn the hard way that things are changing," Teneh remarked as they were about to part. "Why should she think that she has any say over her granddaughter's marriage? It is not her business. Why she thinks that the family cannot offer the chief another woman, I don't know. I suspect that there is a deal between herself and the chief and if she is not careful, she may live to regret it. Just imagine! the chief already has many wives yet she wants to surrender our young and educated niece to him. I am happy that our brother has taken a very firm decision on the matter. He has our solid support even though he has not yet consulted us."

Meanwhile, feeling bitterly disappointed, Kigba continued to reflect on her meeting with her daughters. All my children want to fight me. It is Hindowaa who has poisoned their minds. I have told him that I will curse him if he defies me on this issue. Look at the way Boi-Komah spoke to me - a child of yesterday who still has milk in her mouth. Then that big fool, Teneh, supporting what her younger sister says. I just don't know what has gone wrong with her too. How could she support her younger sister?"

She was already on Nyamakoro's veranda when the

rain came down heavily on Talia. Some of the school children had already arrived while those who were late returning home were running, already drenched.

"You are lucky. You made it just in time before the rain started," Nyamakoro greeted her. "Welcome, and how are you today?"

"The last time we met was a week ago. How have you been, mba?" Kigba responded. "Is your husband in today?"

"Let us get into the house, otherwise we shall get wet. The wind is blowing the rain into the veranda... My husband traveled to Moyamba and will be coming back after two days."

"Ah, this is a good sign for me, mba - that your husband has traveled. You see, I am here for a private talk with you about a sensitive matter. Do I look like a mad woman to you? No? You see, I am coming from a place where I was made to feel like a mad woman. That is why I am asking you, mba."

"Mba, don't say such things. It is not good to have such a feeling about yourself. What led you into such thinking this late afternoon? You don't look like a mad woman and you have never shown mad tendencies."

"I was just telling my daughters a story we were told when we were much younger. I don't know whether you, too, were told the same story. Apparently, once, a long time ago, when you and I, and even our own parents were not yet born, a wave of madness visited this chiefdom. They said it was like a natural disaster and lots of people were afflicted by it. Previously sane people began to act strangely - bursting out laughing and continuing until they choked, or running until they collapsed and died. It seems, the ancestors were angry and were taking revenge on the community."

Nyamakoro laughed and laughed until she thought she herself had caught the madness that attacked the chiefdom all those years ago.

"Mba, you will kill people with such stories," she gasped. "I have never heard such a thing, but it sounds believable. I do know for a fact, that the ancestors can take revenge on an entire community, or on individual family members, especially when they feel neglected. That is why we have to be very careful about the way we conduct ourselves. But, what led to this story, if I may ask?"

The two women were now seated in the parlor even as the rain continued to wash the town.

"You know, mba, our family has never given the chief a wife, so I want him to marry Kunaafoh, my granddaughter. This idea was on even before Kunaafoh disappeared and went to the white man's land. Now that she has come back, I told my son that we should proceed with the matter. Would you believe that he is opposed to the idea? I visited his father and grandfather's graves last week and informed them about this development. Now I have just found out that my daughters support his position. I felt as if I was going mad. That was why I asked you whether I look like a mad woman."

"Mba, before we continue, I have a little food and some nice cakes which I made this morning. Otherwise, I have some kola nuts which we can share."

"Mba, to be honest with you, my stomach is full," Kigba answered. "I ate at my daughter's place. Let us share a kola nut instead."

"Mba, you said that you want Kunaafoh, the daughter of Giita, Sister Kunaafoh, the Catholic Sister and medical doctor, to marry whom - our chief?" Nyamakoro asked as she divided the kola nut.

"You are correct, mba."

"Mba, don't say that aloud. Don't you know that the people who belong to that religion don't marry? They serve God and mankind. The men don't marry. The women don't marry. The men don't have children. The women don't have children. That is how the religion is, mba. Don't you see the way they all dress? They serve God. They serve Christ. They serve mankind. Don't talk about Kunaafoh marrying anybody."

Kigba's mouth fell open and her big eyes stared at Nyamakoro.

"Ah, mba, I am beginning to believe that the madnessI told you about just now is returning to Talia. That can be the only reason people are saying that women should not marry and have children. So, mba, if you were told not to marry and have children, you would agree? Tell me; would you agree? It is simply madness and I will curse my son."

Kigba had finished half of the piece of kola nut Nyamakoro had given her and bit hard on the other half. Nyamakoro said, "Mba, you see me, I don't know book, but there are certain things that I know because I have seen them with my own eyes. The missionaries have been here for a very long time. We have seen the Catholic priests and nuns. I have never seen one that was married with children. I don't know where you got your idea from that a Catholic nun could marry and have children. Kunaafoh is a Catholic nun and a doctor. She has been doing good work in this town and beyond. That is her own calling, as the white people would say. We should all be proud of this daughter of our town and chiefdom who has brought us so much fame. This is a blessing to you and your family. You should be proud and grateful to God. This is all I have to say to you as a friend of long standing. You know our people have a saying: 'God does not descend from heaven to come and talk to you. It is people whom He sends to talk to you,' so please listen to me."

'Oh, my ancestors! I don't believe this," Kigba lamented, but in a sarcastic tone. "I don't believe my ears today. Mba, mba. You, too, have been infected by this madness. We need our own doctors, our own native doctors to drive it from your head. We need a diviner to deliver all of you."

Nyamakoro continued eating her kola nut for a moment before responding to this ourburst. When she spoke, it was in a firm and serious manner.

"Mba, to be honest with you, I really don't know why you came to see me. From what you said, I thought you came to seek my opinion. What I have told you is from the bottom of my heart and I did not mean any harm. However, I now detect an angry tone in your voice, so I don't think we should continue this discussion. I have never been mad in my life."

Kigba was shaken and confused by Nyamakoro's response. She had known her friend for a long time and they had never had serious misunderstandings on any issues. She had come, convinced that Nyamakoro, being a woman of high social standing in the community, would support her position, or at least be sympathetic to her. Instead she had supported the position of all her children. Now, Kigba was not sure who was mad. Nyamakoro was the most senior woman she had contacted.

"Mba, tell me, how would you have had children, you as a woman, if you were not married? When did you ever hear in our community that just because you belong to the white man's religion you should not marry and have children? Now, you are talking like the people who know book. You have children. They are all married with children. Why was it that you did not advocate for their non-marriage so that they could serve Christ, God and mankind? All of you confuse me on this matter. And another thing; we still don't know if Kunaafoh has been initiated into the Sande secret society. We don't know if she was initiated when she was in the white man's land. All these concerns continue to worry me as a grandmother. Why won't you sympathize with me instead of taking this hard attitude on a matter as simple as this?"

Quite unmoved by this rebuke, Nyamakoro said to Kigba, "If I were a nun, a Catholic nun and a trained doctor, I would neither marry nor have children. I have given you my opinion on this subject and I have done so very sincerely. At this moment, I have nothing more to say except to wish you well. Perhaps, I should go and see the chief and tell him to summon the town crier to tell people to be on the alert for this madness that you say is attacking the town."

Kigba felt that Nyamakoro was mocking her and left the house without saying good-bye.

The rain had ceased and it was just starting to get dark when she ventured outside. As she trudged through the cool refreshing darkness, she thought about Nyake. It dawned on her that she should have consulted him before her own daughters and Nyamakoro. She also knew that he was fearless and would not hesitate to say what he thought about any issue. Even the chief had mentioned how much he valued Nyake's counsel though he thought there were times when Nyake was too brutal with the truth. She knew that Nyake was her son's confidant, and wondered whether Hindowaa had already contacted him on this family matter. Since it was not too late, she thought it would be a good idea to visit Nyake and conclude her consultations. She was sure Nyake would be awake, lying in his hammock, either smoking his pipe or drinking his evening palm wine. She was silently cursing Nyamakoro as she walked towards Nyake's house. The woman was behaving as if she knew the white man's book, and that was only because she was the richest woman in Talia. Why had she not answered the question about whether she would have allowed her daughters to remain unmarried and childless?

From a little distance she could see Nyake lying in his hammock. However, she was disappointed to observe two other men with him. She could not turn back because Nyake had already spotted her and would be expecting her. She cursed the night and the men sitting on the veranda. She knew them both, Laaga and Simbo - Talia's predators and parasites who moved around drinking and eating outside their own homes

"Ah, my wife, welcome. How are you tonight?" Nyake called out cordially the minute she stepped on to the veranda. Laaga and Simbo also greeted her as she looked around for a seat.

"I am not going to ask you what I have done to deserve this long overdue visit," Nyake joked as Kigba sat down.

"I have not seen Hindowaa for some time now," one of the other two men remarked.

"He is around," Kigba said. "You know that moving around this town in the rainy season is not easy. He is around."

Nyake noticed that she looked uncomfortable in the presence of the two men, and tried to tease her out of it, saying, "My wife, it is good that you have come because the night is cold and an old man will need a hot cover to keep him warm."

Everybody laughed, including Kigba. She said, "Actually, I came to see you about something confidential, but since you have visitors, I shall come another time."

"No. No problem. In fact, my visitors were just about to leave when you arrived."

At this pointed remark, Nyake's visitors started taking leave of him and soon disappeared into the darkness which gave Kigba an intense feeling of relief. She really wanted to to conclude her consultations on this issue of Kunaafoh's marriage to the chief.

"They are everywhere in this town," Kigba remarked sourly. "If you go down town; you will find them there. They move from place to place, but not always in search of food and drinks. No, it is mostly to gossip. That is their trademark. There are many of them in this town. My son has never told me that Laaga, who taps palm wine, gave him a drop, or that Simbo, who hunts, gave him a pound of meat. Since he runs an open house, they are both constant visitors. My husband, let me tell you and you should know this, perhaps, better than me, those men are gluttons."

"Don't talk too loudly, they have not gone far yet. Some people have long ears, like horns; they can hear from a long distance," Nyake said, to their mutual amusement. "There are Largas and Simbos in every community. That is life."

"But, don't they know that people in this town are tired of entertaining them? They are almost like brothers and are always together even though they are married. I wonder how their wives feel about it? They must be ashamed," Kigba said.

"My wife, maybe their wives are not even aware of what they are doing. Do wives know what their husbands are up to when they leave their homes? They don't tell them where they are going and for what reason. I am a man; so I know what I am talking about."

"You are right. My late husband never told me where he was going and when I should expect him back. He would walk away casually and come back hours later both during the day and in the evenings. I never questioned him… You know, my husband, you are a very wise man. I wish we all looked at things the way you do. But again, we all can't look at life the same way and that is why God made us physically the same, but the way we think differs from person to person, even among family members."

"Ah. From the way you are talking, I recognise the influence of my brother, I mean your late husband. He was one of the wise men in this town. I wish many more of us were like him; he was wise and courageous. He stood for principles and personal credibility until he died. He never compromised on them."

"My husband, thank you very much. Principles and credibility were very important in our lives. I wish my son were here, I really wish he were present so that he could learn from you. Right now we have a very big problem in the house. We are fighting about it and I do not intend to lose. It will be a fight to the finish. I have already paid your friend, I mean my late husband, and Hindowaa's grandfather, a visit to tell them what is going on. My husband, my credibility is at stake. It is at stake with our chief."

His curiosity aroused, Nyake asked, "What are you talking about, my wife? I don't understand."

"Has Hindowaa not told you about our fight? I was sure he must have mentioned it long ago - my proposal that Kunaafoh, my granddaughter should be given to our chief as a wife. I proposed it even before Kunaafoh disappeared from this town. Now that she has come back, I told Hindowaa that we should proceed with the arrangements. Think about it, my husband. We informed our chief about the marriage a long time ago. He is waiting for us to start the proceedings but now Hindowaa is against it, telling me that Kunaafoh belongs to a white man's religion that does not allow women to marry and have children. It is a shame. How do I now go before our chief and say, 'I am sorry, the Hindowaa family cannot fulfill its obligation'. My husband, this is where we stand. I told Hindowaa that as his mother and for as long as I am alive and well, I shall make sure that my granddaughter marries our chief, despite her religion."

Nyake noticed that Kigba was sweating as she spoke. He said, "No, Hindowaa has never told me about this situation. I am being honest with you. I understand your concerns, but what are you expecting from me, if I may ask, my wife? Also, when you spoke to my brother and friend, your late husband and Hindowaa's grandfather, what did they say?"

"They promised to look into the matter. I shall be visiting them again to hear the result."

"My wife, I am now in the picture. Let me ask you seriously, did you tell them the truth, nothing but the truth? They will know, and if they feel that you have not told them the truth and just want them to take a decision favorable to you, they will be very angry with you. I am going to state my own opinion based on what you have told me."

Kigba began to feel slightly uncomfortable as Nyake was well known in Talia and beyond for his brutal honesty. In fact, it had taken her a long time to decide to consult him. Each time the idea had occurred to her, she had hesitated for fear that Nyake might not agree with her about Kunaafoh marrying the chief and would let her know what he thought in no uncertain terms. As he began to speak, Kigba stared at him as if she were in a courtroom in front of a judge about to give a verdict on a matter of life and death.

"My wife, I understand your concern about principles and credibility. They are very important in our dealings with people both inside and outside the family. On this I wholeheartedly support you. However, what is at issue here is this. Who is Kunaafoh to you? She is your granddaughter, not your daughter. The responsibility for deciding who or if she should marry lies with her actual parents, not you. Her mother is dead, so, it is the father who has that responsibility. He can consult family members, but a final and binding decision is his responsibility. I, too, have grandchildren but I would never say I should be responsible for deciding whom they marry. That is the responsibility of their fathers and mothers," Nyake insisted.

"You know, Nyake, I saw Nyamakoro recently," Kigba said with an incredulous shake of her head. "In fact, I am coming from her house. I mentioned the story I was told about the madness that once visited this community and affected many people. Apparently, it happens once in a lifetime. The people afflicted laughed or ran till they fell down and died. Some of them went about naked and many began talking rubbish for hours on end. If you of all people can support my son on this issue, then that madness is here again. Only God and the ancestors will save this town."

Nyake began to reply but could not get a word in before Kigba got to her feet and walked away in anger. In his characteristic way, her behavior did not bother him. What he had told her was his sincere conviction. He was also sure that wherever Kigba went, she would be told the same thing. Silently wishing her well, he continued enjoying his hammock savouring his pipe and the beauty of the night through which Kigba was navigating her way home.

■

CHAPTER FOUR

Hindowaa was sitting on a granite boulder under the big mango tree behind his house. It was early evening and he could hear the boisterous voices of people hurrying from their farms. Most of the early arrivals were men, carrying machetes and various other items on their tired shoulders. Stars had started coming out which meant that, for a change, the rains were in retreat. Hindowaa recalled that the last time he sat on the boulder, the floodgates of heaven suddenly opened and he was soaked to the skin before he could reach his house. This time was different, for which he thanked God and his ancestors.

Two things were troubling his mind as he sat there. The first was the argument he had had with his mother over her determination that Kunaafoh should marry the chief. That was the first time in his life that she had been so bitterly angry with him. He decided that he needed to seek further guidance from the ancestors as well as the elders who were still alive, before referring the matter to the entire family, even though he had quite made up his mind that Kunaafoh would not marry the chief. Threats of a maternal curse, notwithstanding, he was not prepared to change his mind, though he wished there was a way to avoid another confrontation with his mother. He wondered whether she had already spoken to his sisters about the situation and whether either of them would support him.

The second thing on his mind was the amount of money he owed some people in Talia. None of his creditors had approached him yet, but he dreaded the moment they would start demanding payment. He had started to have sleepless nights over the debts, knowing that if his creditors started asking for their money, he would be in trouble. He did not want to appeal to the chief again, but who else could he appeal to? He had mentioned the debts to his father-in-law, but doubted that Ndomawaa would be in any position to help.

Of his six creditors, the two he dreaded most were Lahai Gbapi and Kapindi Pumui. He had been kind to them at a time when they desperately needed help, yet they were the people who once incited others to torment his life when he needed time to sort himself out. Lahai Gbapi was the ringleader. He was a tall, thin man but, despite his slight frame, was known to be a fearless wrestler in the chiefdom and beyond. Hindowaa recalled that when they were boys, Lahai Gbapi used to beat them all in any fight. He talked very little, preferring to use his muscles instead, so Hindowaa and others quickly learned to behave themselves around him. He decided that Gbapi would be the first creditor he would repay when he had some money to spare. Kapindi Pumui, meaning 'white man', had acquired that nickname because, though illiterate, his great desire was to visit England and see the Queen. He had wanted to become a seaman and disappear when his ship arrived at Liverpool. Though he never made it to sea, the nickname had stuck, but he had no quarrel with that. Unlike Gbapi, he was short, fat and talkative. Hindowaa found it strange that the two men had become such close friends.

A boy suddenly appeared and greeted Hindowaa, addressing him as 'maada' (grandpa).

"Eeem, biwah, biseh. Kahun yeenaah?" Hindowaa replied.

"Maada, Kinie Ndomawaa sent me to find out if you are in the house."

The boy looked resentful as he delivered this message, which made Hindowaa say to himself, ah, my in-law, why didn't he just walk over? It's not raining.

"Go and tell him that I am here," he said to the boy, who was already turning away to leave.

Hindowaa's mind returned to his debts and his creditors. He came to the comforting conclusion that time was on his side since it was the rainy season. No reasonable person came asking for debt repayment during the season of hardship. He could therefore relax until the dry season, the season of plenty which followed the harvest.

Ndomawaa never turned up that evening, and Hindowaa concluded that he must have been prevented from doing so by one of his peers who always looked forward to his visits to Talia. The dry weather continued into the next day, but Ndomawaa seemed unaware of the pleasantly sunny afternoon when he finally arrived at Hindowaa's house. He looked as morose as he had been on his previous visit and the reason for his unhappiness surfaced as soon as Hindowaa mentioned his mother-in-law. Kigba had left the house in anger following a slight quarrel with Boi-Kimbo and on hearing this, Ndomawaa remarked,

"Daemia, it is a well known that, more often than not, wives do not get on with their mothers-in-law. That is why we men are advised to live independently of our mothers when we marry. Mothers-in-law always try to bully their sons' wives because they want to control the household. When they live with their sons, the problem becomes worse."

His father-in-law's observations made Hindowa so uncomfortable that he said,

"I understand, daemia, but let us not talk too loudly, Boi-Kimbo is inside the house and she may be listening to our conversation. I tell you, she has sensitive ears."

"Daemia, what difference does it make if she is listening?" Ndomawaa answered irritably. "What difference does it make if what we are saying is true? People are afraid of the truth, tnat's the trouble. Let me say this, never be afraid to speak the truth. It may offend someone, but it will never harm you, because truth is eternal."

Silence enveloped the veranda for a moment before Ndomawaa continued his lecture.

"When mothers-in-law take over their children's households there is bound to be trouble. Having your mother in your home causes all sorts of problems and even makes people question your maturity and independence. In my own town, I have seen households fall apart when they are dominated by the mothers-in-law. That situation can bring immense pain and suffering to the couples concerned as well as their children."

Hindowaa sensed that Ndomawaa's comments were leading somewhere in particular, for he detected a certain amount of venom in his voice. To delay the moment when he would be cornered, he excused himself and went to the toilet where he spent some time. On his return, he further delayed the moment of truth by suggesting that such a beautiful day required that they share a gourd of palm wine. Ndomawaa, however, refused the offer, saying he had already had some before coming to Hindowaa's house.

Hindowaa was not pleased that his father-in-law had refused to share a drink with him. He was now convinced that Ndomawaa wanted to put him in a cage from which escape would be difficult and longed for his mother to return from wherever she had gone.

"Daemia, you know that it is not our custom to refuse a drink when you visit someone" he persisted. "Just take a cupful and I shall drink the rest."

"Okay, I shall have a cup, just to please you because I am not in the mood for drinking right now. Drinks are to be enjoyed, not endured."

When Ndomawaa made those remarks, Hindowaa recalled what his father-in-law had said before about discussing something else at a later date. Again, he wished his mother would return, for he believed that her presence would make a difference if Ndomawaa decided to unleash anger on him that afternoon. He kept glancing in the direction from which he thought his mother would eventually emerge, but Luck was still not on his side.

"Boi-Kimbo, waah."

When his wife answered his summons, he asked her to bring the palm wine to the veranda with cups.

Boi-Kimbo's twin girls assisted her, each bringing a cup while their mother brought the gourd of palm wine. The smell of the wine filled the veranda even before it was poured.

Ndomawaa observed the whole procedure with a certain amount of disdain. Hindowaa continued to watch him closely, still unsure what to expect. Kigba remained absent, much to his dismay.

"Daemia, we were talking about the presence of mothers-in-law in their children's households. And we had not finished before you interrupted and said we should drink. I am returning to this subject because it is relevant to the relationship between you, your mother, and myself. I want to alert you to the fact that in Talia and beyond you are considered a willing victim of your mother's domination. People are wondering what happened to your manhood, and your status in the Wunde fraternity. I agree with them, because I know that I have suffered in this family as a result of your mother's dominance of this household. "

Hindowaa felt as if a razor blade had sliced through his spine, but he tried to sound unruffled as he said,

"So people talk about me in this town. I know that they gossip a lot, but this is the first time I am hearing that they say my mother controls my household. And it has come from my father-in-law. Daemia, please don't listen to what people tell you outside this house. They don't mean well for our family."

Ndomawaa refused to accept that explanation.

"Daemia, do you know how long I have known you, your late father and your mother? A long time; and I share the views that people have expressed about you and your relationship with your mother. I also had a mother and you knew her very well. She never had the last say in my life with my wives. You know that. If there was anyone who had influence on me, it was my father, but even he left me to take care of my own household. That is how it should be."

"Daemia, you people don't understand my situation," Hindowaa protested. "You just don't understand. If you did you would not be saying all these things about me. All of you know that I am my mother's only son. If she had other sons, she would have behaved differently; but I am her only son. It is normal for mothers in her situation to be possessive. This is what people misinterpret as her dominance over me. Not that I am trying to defend her, but I want people to understand her behavior. Why don't they just mind their own business? Why?"

Ndomawaa had still not taken even one sip of his drink and the foam of the wine was almost overflowing. In the continued absence of his mother, Hindowaa helped himself to more wine to give himself courage to face his father-in-law's attack. Ndomawaa carried on.

"Daemia, I think that you are missing the point. The fact that you are an only son does not justify the way your mother controls you. We know several women who have only one son and yet those sons are independent of them. Your own situation is unique, especially so because you are a Wunde man and a Lawaa. You have a big title in the fraternity."

"Daemia, I don't want to go into history, but you know my family history, I mean on my father's side. You know that I come from a family of distinguished warriors. It is in our blood and runs deep," Hindowaa said.

Ndomawaa laughed contemptuously and spat on the floor. Hindowaa noticed that he had still not tasted his drink.

"I know, daemia, I know your family history. And the truth is that you are not behaving like a warrior, even though you come from such a family. You are the exception, which explains why your mother controls your life as if you are a baby. To be honest with you, in your position I would be ashamed to tell the world about my warrior family background. Tell me, and this is very serious because people have been asking the same question, why is it that since your father died, your mother has not remarried? After all she is not that old. All the other women in Talia who were widowed remarried except Kigba. Don't you find that strange? Have you not thought about it? You would have been better off with a stepfather. Anyway, what I want you to know is the general feeling in town. People are asking why Kigba has not remarried."

Ndomawaa had touched a nerve and Hindowaa felt as if his entire body had received an electric shock. Nobody had ever asked him such a question. He concealed his anxiety with a show of indignation, actually pointing his finger at Ndomawaa.

"Daemia, do you expect me to know why my mother has not remarried? That is not a matter children raise with their parents. If you were in my position, what would you say to your mother or father? You people are being unfair to me, daemia. To tell you the truth, I have a feeling that you have come here for another reason. If that is the case, rather than beating around the bush, come clean and talk to me man-to-man."

"Daemia, please do not point your finger at me, I beg you. I consider that an act of provocation."

At that warning, Hindowaa quickly returned his offending right hand into his pocket and looked straight ahead. He was still hoping desperately that his mother would turn up.

"Daemia," he said, now adopting a cool, formal tone, "we have spent a long time together this afternoon and you have been insinuating all sorts of things. I beg you. Please come clean."

Delighted that his confrontational approach had finally yielded results, Ndomawaa now began to expose Kigba and did so deliberately and with relish.

"Let me inform you about another rumor circulating in Talia and beyond concerning your mother. People believe that you are aware of this matter, but you don't have to admit or deny it to me. They believe your mother has a relationship with a djinn. They are also saying that some members of your household believe she has a djinn because it is known that she hardly sleeps at all. She knows all that happens in this town at night. Are you not aware of that, daemia? Be honest."

The atmosphere between the two men had grown toxic and in the long silence that ensued, Hindowaa felt stifled. He realized that Ndomawaa believed that Kigba had had a hand in Giita's death and was taking his revenge.

"Daemia, I hope you realize the seriousness of what you have said about my mother," he said at last. "Why would my mother have a djinn? I could take you to court for this, you know. I hope you are prepared to provide evidence for making such a serious allegation against her."

Though Hindowaa sounded quite agitated, Ndomawaa remained calm and, for the first time, took a sip of his palm wine.

"Hindowaa, you know as well as I do that possessing a djinn does not necessarily mean anything evil. Of course, there are people who acquire djinns for evil purposes, but others have them for constructive reasons. Daemia, you know this very well. Some people have made their fortune because they possess a djinn or have a connection with the mermaid; so why are you worried if people speculate that Kigba might have a djinn? If she has one, it could be because she is aware of the impending calamity in the Hindowaa household and is trying to prevent it. Who knows? But if you want to take me to court, I shall be ready to defend myself. You know as well as I do that there are people in our community who can prove whether or not a person possesses a djinn. They can also determine whether or not the djinn is evil. So before you decide to take me to court be prepared, because the truth will eventually come out…You see, daemia," he went on in the same reasonable tone, "we have known each other for a very long time. Between my daughter, Giita, and you there are five children, and all of them are my grandchildren. I don't mean you any harm; but I want you to know that the general belief in this town is that your mother cannot remarry because of her djinn, that he is her real husband and both of them conspired to get rid of your late father. Oh yes."

In his dismay, Hindowaa rose abruptly from the hammock and walked some distance from his father-in-law who continued his bitter criticism of Kigba and himself.

"Your mother was very instrumental in pressuring you to have more children because she wanted more grandsons. You, in turn, put pressure on my daughter. Giita almost went mad trying to satisfy your mother's craving for more grandsons. I know exactly what happened, daemia. I remember that at one time you went to see a soothsayer, you and your sister. You were told that the ancestors had given Giita her own share of children and that if she were to have more sons to fulfill her husband's desire, it would be at a cost. So you knew what would happen. Daemia, be honest and own up in this matter. You were aware of the consequences, but all you and your mother wanted were more sons at any cost. I do not have to go into the details. My daughter died in childbirth, in search of sons."

After this, Hindowaa had to excuse himself again to go to the toilet, for the palm wine gourd was half empty though Ndomawaa had still not finished his first cup.

While he was urinating, he further considered the possibility of suing his in-law but came to the conclusion that that course of action would be risky. As Ndomawaa had reminded him, experts in such things would easily determine the truth of the allegations. And he agreed with his father-in-law that people had djinns for various reasons, so he decided to let the matter rest. On his return, he found that his father-in-law had moved his stool further from where he had been sitting so that they were now facing each other. Hindowa was ready with criticisms of his own.

"Daemia, now I know why you came to Talia this time," he remarked before going back to the hammock. "You have told me all that you have been harboring in your mind against my mother and me. You have said categorically that we were responsible for Giita's death. How could you make such an accusation, daemia? How can a husband be involved in the death of a wife with whom he has had children? And how can a mother in-law be responsible for the death of her daughter-in-law who has given her five grandchildren? I would never have dreamed that someone like you would pronounce on these serious issues in the way you have done today. I could take this matter to higher authorities, but I will not pursue it beyond the walls of this house. I will not let outsiders know about the problems in my family. As our people say, when you are in doubt, when you are in trouble and you cannot solve problems, leave everything in the hands of the ancestors. This is exactly what I am going to do, daemia. I shall only tell my mother what you have said so that I can have her opinion on the issues you have raised this afternoon. How sad to think that people in Talia smile at us, talk to us in the open, yet hold the same views that you have expressed today."

"Daemia, it is unfortunate that you have decided to cheat nature by evading reality," Ndomawaa replied bitterly. "I mean, you know very well that it was as a result of the pressure your mother put on you for more sons that you yielded to her wishes and subjected my daughter to taking measures detrimental to her health. She went into debt, traveling from one medicine man to another, all in an effort to please you and your mother. Daemia, as a Wunde man, a Ngombuwaa at that, don't tell me you were not aware of the situation. I have known you for a long time and I never entertained the idea that you were a person who tried to evade the truth. You and your mother could be charged with murder. Both of you committed murder, nothing but murder."

Hindowaa did not say a word, and his father-in-law went on berating him.

"You know as well as I do that you even had to ask your mother to give you and Giita time because after you had been married for only three months, she had already started asking why her daughter-in-law was not pregnant. You know, daemia, as well as I do that your mother even told you that she became pregnant not long after she married your father. Yes, daemia, you know that what I am saying is true. So you now begin to see how your mother's desire for grandchildren, particularly grandsons, became a burning issue with her. She was consumed by it. I am happy, daemia, that you have decided to refer this matter to the ancestors. They will deliberate on it and I am positive they willl give their verdict at the appropriate time. I already know what it will be. One day, I shall remind both you and your mother. It will be a day of victory for Giita and me."

Hindowaa was deeply troubled as he listened to his father-in-law. He knew the area Ndomawaa came from had some of the most powerful medicine men in the country and he was afraid his father-in-law might hire them to challenge himself and his mother over their suspected role in Giita's death.

"Daemia, I did not believe, that we would come to a point in our relationship where one of us would curse the other's household," he said, his voice heavy with pain. "That is exactly what you are doing now. You have cursed the Hindowaa household. How can you possibly do that when I have children from your family? It is very rare for such a thing to happen. I shall tell my mother about this sad development. Perhaps this is the calamity you were talking about when you said something bad would befall the Hindowaa family. It is a grave situation. Very grave indeed."

It was on one of the most pleasant afternoons in the rainy season that the in-laws had that hostile meeting. Hindowaa was eager to tell his mother all that had transpired with his father-in-law. Ndomawaa left the house with a sense of satisfaction that he had successfully accomplished his mission. He was confident that the ancestors would vindicate him. It was just a matter of time.

When Kigba finally returned to the house, it was late and Hindowaa was already fast asleep. The amount of palm wine he had drunk, coupled with the emotional pain his father-in-law had inflicted on him, had taken their toll.

■

CHAPTER FIVE

In the darkness of the early hours of the morning, Kigba left the house to start on a journey which would take one and a half days. Hindowaa was not aware of her plan to travel and only Boi-Kimbo heard her leave the house. She was going to consult Madam Yegbeh, one of the most renowned women in the chiefdom. People said Madam Yegbeh could predict the future and communicate with the dead, and such was her fame that it was believed that she was herself a reincarnated being because when she was born, she had all the previous birthmarks on her body. It was believed that she had acquired her magical and spiritual powers from her great-great-grandmother. Kigbah had never met the woman, but she knew and believed in the efficacy of her skills. She had met and talked to people who had consulted her and had had their problems sorted out. These people, and they were many, would swear by anything about the truth of the wonders performed by Madam Yegbeh. She was unable to walk but overwhelmed her clients with her supernatural powers. Some said she could travel to other places by flying in her own aeroplane made of peanut shells. That was why no one saw her after midnight. It was during those hours that she undertook her travels to mysterious places.

Since visiting the graves of her husband and Hindowaa's grandfather, Kigba had wondered about their failure to respond to the situation she had complained about. She had had sleepless nights and even lost her once healthy appetite over the matter. She kept wondering why the ancestors were taking such a long time to come to a conclusion. Their delay in getting back to her through her dreams continued to trouble her. She wondered whether they had not appreciated the emergency surrounding the Hindowaa family. She had no doubt that she had eloquently informed her husband and Hindowaa's grandfather about developments in the family and she felt angry with them for taking such a long time to respond. Were they conspiring against her, she wondered? Were they not concerned anymore about what was happening to members of their family on earth? Or was it that they were angry with them for having unknowingly breached some family taboo?

As she went along the footpath to the river, she ignored the barking of the dogs. In fact, it was almost becoming music to her ears. She knew that she and the ancestors were awake and going their separate ways. It pleased her to think that the spirits of her husband and Hindowaa's grandfather would be observing her as she set out on her journey. Perhaps they would be wondering where she was going so early in the morning and without an escort. Yes, she said to herself, they probably needed an incident like her traveling without an escort to jolt them into action.

Women did not usually venture on long journeys without a male escort or several female traveling companions. However, people who knew Kigba would say that they were not surprised that she was undertaking such a trip alone. It would only confirm their long held suspicion that she had a djinn which would guide her on her journey.

When she arrived at the river, she stood in front of an empty canoe. It was a big one with a paddle. Though it was still dark, Kigba knew the river well because she had ferried herself across it many times. She scooped water from the bottom of the canoe, then rested her bundle inside before sitting down to paddle herself across. The water was calm, for which she thanked her ancestors. The stillness of the morning and the solitude of the river brought a sense of safety and peace to her troubled mind. As she rowed across the river, only the sound of the paddle cutting through the water disturbed the calm atmosphere. No birds had started chirruping yet, and the toads and frogs at the waterside were still at rest.

When she had crossed the river, Kigba washed herself again before continuing her journey. She began to wonder whether she would find the medium she was going to meet, then remembered that the woman was disabled. People came to see her, not the other way around. But what if, what if, after she had put her case and Madam Yegbeh had summoned all the ancestors concerned, she did not get a favorable response, she asked herself anxiously. She wanted to sing a comforting song, which her mother had taught her, but in her troubled state of mind could recall neither the song nor the words. She cursed herself many times over as she went along.

She had still not thoroughly digested her son's behavior in respect of his refusal for Kunaafoh to marry the chief. How could a child she had suckled just the other day dare to defy her? How? What had gone so painfully wrong with this world? Would she have had the nerve to challenge her father when he had decided whom she would marry? It was disgusting that her own son could challenge her in that way. She had already started believing those who said that an only son, unlike an only daughter, could prove a disaster. She recalled her labor pains during Hindowaa's birth, and the sleepless nights she had had when the child would wake in the middle of the night and cry for a long time. She used to stay awake, singing to coax him back to sleep. His father did not stir, not knowing that she and the child were awake. In the morning, she would get ready to go to the farm with Hindowaa securely tied to her back. When Hindowaa was sick, she used to run around to find medicine for him. Hindowaa, the only son was a problem child that tormented her life. His sisters were unlike him, the son. Now as a grown up man, Hindowaa was challenging her. She would not hesitate to curse him if he failed to relent and make amends in this matter. She sucked her teeth loudly and spat on the wet road, then cleared her throat, fidgeted with her wrapper and brought out a kola nut which she started eating. The next village was less than a quarter of a mile away and she could hear the muezzin calling the believers to prayer. She loved the voice of the muezzin. It sounded spiritual and above all, musical. It was beautiful.

If only her granddaughter were a Muslim, she thought. Yes, if she were a Muslim she would have married with no problem whatsoever. In Talia, she knew Christians who went to church on Sundays. She knew others who went to church on Saturdays. Those who attended church on Sundays never went to the farm afterwards. They rested until Monday. Those who went to church on Saturdays rested, then went to the farm every day till the next Saturday. The Muslims went to the Mosque on Fridays and rested. Since she was born, and that was a long time ago, she had never heard that the women who belonged to these religions could not marry. Only the Catholic nuns and priests had this strange idea that some women should not marry and her granddaughter was its first victim.

Kigba felt sorry that she had never discussed this

problem with anyone. Perhaps it was too late to ask the chief whether he was aware of such a practice. The chief would be better placed to find all the relevant information concerning it. She knew that she was not educated enough to know about many things, but so were the chief and Hindowaa. They were all illiterate. She knew of no other person who had preached about such a practice in the chiefdom. She was most surprised by her own son. If this strange idea had come from someone else, maybe she would have been courageous enough to accommodate it, but not from the son she had struggled so laboriously to bring into this world. She was really worried. She had told her husband, Hindowaa's grandfather and the ancestors about the situation and expressed urgency but they had not yet responded. What was happening, she continued asking herself.

Through the early morning mist she realized that she had arrived at the first small town on her way. She saw people hurrying to the mosque and increased her pace. No one seemed to recognize her as she crossed the town and she was happy, knowing that if she were recognized, she would be stopped and questioned. She dreaded such encounters. She finished her kola nut and licked her mouth to remove the bits and pieces stuck between her teeth. Her tongue kept up the licking exercise long after she had cleansed her mouth. When she came across a stream, she stopped and drank some water. After the kola, it tasted sweet.She lifted her wrapper and walked across the water. She had decided that she would spend the night two villages away from her destination, having been been told that that would be her best course of action. That way, she would arrive at her destination reasonably early the next day, have a good chance of seeing Madam

Yegbeh, leave that very afternoon and arrive at Talia the following day. To her relief, she arrived at another small town at midday. She knew she was making good progress and everything was going according to plan. The weather was unpredictable that day, but that did not bother her because she was carrying a bamboo umbrella.

"Nya'nde, biwah, biseh," Kigba greeted as she entered the veranda of a house she stopped by. There were two elderly ladies seated and an elderly man who was lying in a hammock. They all greeted Kigba in a chorus, looking curious.

"Heeh (Be seated)," one of the women told Kigba.

Kigba took the bundle from her head, put it on the ground and sat on the only empty stool on the veranda. She leaned the bamboo umbrella against the mud wall as she made herself comfortable.

"Thank you, good people, I just want to rest a bit. I am on my way to Taninihun and still have a long way to go."

The people on the veranda became even more interested in the stranger because they knew that most people who passed through their town going to Taninihun were going to see the only woman everybody traveled there to see. But why was this womantraveling alone, they wondered.

"Nyahapui, I admire you. Even I as a man would not venture on such a long journey alone. I could do that when I was a young man, but not now. It must be an urgent matter. If my sons had not gone to the farm, I would have asked one of them to accompany you and he would take one of our fiercest hunting dogs. Old age does not allow me to accompany a beautiful woman traveling alone on a long journey," the old man teased. The women, who were all his wives, burst out laughing, knowing he was a joker.

Kigba appreciated his concern but made no comment.

"You will not get there today," said one of the wives. "Why don't you sleep here and continue tomorrow?"

"I know that I cannot get there today, so I was told, but I shall continue until there are only two more towns to my destination, then sleep and proceed the following day. That is how I have planned it. I just want to take a rest before going on. Thank you for allowing me to rest in your house

The old women looked at each other and nodded approvingly. One of them said, "Then, my dear, you must eat before you proceed. You still have a long distance ahead of you. We have food and even some palm wine. It will help you to challenge the rest of the journey." Kigba smiled at the mention of palm wine, for the distance she had covered had made her thirsty. "I have traveled from here to Taninihun and know how far it is even from this end. You are coming all the way from Talia, so it is even longer. But then you are a young woman compared to us. Let us bring food for you."

"Thank you very much, but I really don't want to bother you," Kigba replied. "I came with kola nuts and when I was crossing the last river to this village I ate some and drank water. I feel full." She was not able to convince them, however, and the food was brought to the veranda with a gourd of palm wine which gave off a delicious aroma. Kigba was more interested in the palm wine than the food. The old man also eyed the palm wine eagerly.

"You know, if you rest here for a while, you might be lucky enough to get some other people on their way to

Taninihun. It often happens like that here. This is the middle of your trip which is why people usually prefer to rest here before they continue their journey. You may just be lucky today," one of the women told Kigba who was eating with the steady concentration of someone who was famished. She had yet to take a cup of palm wine.

"Which family do you come from in Talia?" the old man asked.

"My husband died a long time ago. My son is Hindowaa and I have two daughters who are married. My daughter in-law died not very long ago, Giita."

Silence ensued because they had heard about Giita's death and the circumstances surrounding it. After a while, the women chorused,

"We are sorry. We are very sorry." The old man's jaw dropped and he exclaimed, "Kooh, nyabondaah! It is destiny that has brought you to this house. Your husband and I were Wunde initiates many years ago. We went to the Wunde society at the same time and we took title together. Yes, it was a long time ago. I fell ill and could not travel and so lost all my friends. As you can see, I can barely walk from here to there. I was bewitched because people said I danced better than anybody during that session. Ask my wives, Lombe and Katumu. They took good care of me, which is why you have found me alive. I have twelve children and all of them are alive - seven boys and five girls. All the girls are married. I have fourteen grandchildren, so I am a happy man even though I am not well. Had I known you were coming, one of my sons would have stayed behind and accompanied you to Taninahun."

One of the wives elaborated further. "What he has told you is true. He was bewitched, but thank God and our ancestors, they were not able to kill him. He fought them. He went to the woman you are now going to see. You will not believe it, nyahapui, those who bewitched him were all close family members in this town. But you know, most of them are dead. We fought back and our husband prevailed. Do you know that before they died, some of them confessed in broad daylight to what they had done? Yes, it happened in this town of ours. Today, they cannot look us in the eyes, those who are still around."

"My dear, they are everywhere. If I did not have to travel, I would have told you similar stories about Talia," Kigba said. She had finished eating and had drunk her first cup of palm wine. She thanked them and expressed her satisfaction and appreciation for their impromptu hospitality. The weather had not changed and after eating, she felt energized enough to continue her journey. She continued to express her gratitude even as her hosts told her to wait because they saw from a distance a man and two women approaching. The man, who was in front, was carrying an Aladdin lamp and a machete, while the women had bundles on their heads.

As they were passing the house, the women on the veranda greeted them and asked where they were going. The man and the two women stopped and exchanged greetings with Kigba and her hosts. "We passed here a couple of days ago. We are going back home in Ngolahun," the man answered. Ngolahun was the last village before Taninihun, less than two miles away. Like Kigba, they would have to spend the night at a convenient place before continuing their journey the following day. Kigba's hosts were happy that she would have company on the last leg of her trip. The old man said,

"On your way back, do not forget to stop by. We would like to know the outcome of your mission. I would also like to give you a message for one of my old friends, Kinie Joba. Like your late husband, we were good friends during that famous Wunde initiation and I have not seen him for a long, long time."

Kigba joined the group - women at the back and the man leading. He still had his Aladdin lamp and his machete. As they walked away, the old man and his wives watched them go. It had still not rained even though the clouds were dark.

"Nyahapui, do you know anyone in Ngwabu?" the man asked Kigba as they went along. It was the village where they would have to spend the night.

"No, I don't know anybody there," Kigba responded.

"Well, you are in luck. We shall be staying at a relative's house and she will put you up. She has been to Talia many times and likes the town. She will be glad to have a guest from there."

"What is her name, maybe I shall recognize her when I see her?"

After a short silence, the older of the two women said, "She is called Manja Hotagua, and she is a famous woman. She has connections with the chief in your town."

"In fact, there is a rumour that Manja and the chief are very good friends," the man added, slyly. "One wonders why the chief would be involved with someone else's wife when he has so many of his own. I really don't understand it. I have never questioned Manja myself because it is a sensitive matter."

For some time nobody said a word as they continued on their way, then one of the women decided to challenge what her husband had said.

"I am surprised at you. Are you suggesting that chiefs never have other women besides their wives? Don't you know of cases where they have taken wives from their subjects? Of course you do; there have been many cases in our own town. The chief in Talia is no different from the others; they are all the same. Why can't they choose women who are not married? Every year there are Sande initiates and they can have as many of the girls as they want. Taking another man's wife is not nice."

"I will not pass judgment on anyone," the man replied. "What I don't understand is why Manja's husband does not do something about it."

"Oh, my husband, you are assuming that he knows that something is happening between his wife and the chief," the woman remarked.

Kigba listened to this exchange with interest. She was beginning to develop a mental picture of the woman they were discussing and somehow, the image she conjured up was not of a beauty. She herself had heard a number of times about this mysterious woman who sometimes visited the chief. Apparently the chief's wives were aware of the relationship but had never complained about it openly.

The other woman in the group was much younger than both Kigba and her mate. She was the last wife of the man, so she just listened to her elders, merely smiling occasionally.

"But tell me," the man went on. "If Manja's husband had conclusive proof about the relationship between his wife and the chief, what would he do? Could he take the chief to any court for woman damage? It is a delicate matter when the Chief is involved in such matters." This made the woman challenge her husband again.

"So, if the chief were to do the same thing to you, you would do nothing, eh?"

Even the younger wife joined in the laughter that comment provoked; but if the older wife had hoped to annoy her husband, she did not succeed. He replied with calm confidence.

'I am an influential Wunde man, my dear. I'll know what to do. But you see, the chief is a very smart man. He won't do that to everybody. He knows how to choose his victims." He made all the women laugh more heartily by adding, "Don't forget the saying that dogs always sniff the garbage they scavenge so as to avoid anything with hot pepper."

By this time, they were passing through thick forest and a light rain had started to fall. They exchanged greetings with a man coming from the opposite direction. He paused to ask where they were coming from and they went their separate ways. The older woman returned to their previous conversation.

"Even if you are a chief, if you chase certain men's wives, they will fight you in one way or another."

"Yes," Kigba agreed. "In our own town, people have several ways of taking revenge on the chief. Haven't you heard how badly the rule of some them ended? Even an ant can torment an elephant if it knows where to bite." Her own proverb caused more laughter.

Not long afterwards, they reached the town where they were going to pass the night. It was almost evening and still drizzling. The man spotted a flicker of light coming from the house where Manja lived and headed straight there. The other houses they passed had no lights flickering from their verandas, an indication that the people who lived there were already indoors, eating.

"Ahwuyaah bayh (Good evening here)," the man called out as they entered the veranda and put down the various items they were carrying.

There was a chorus of greetings from the women sitting there. "Aaah,wu waah,ah wuseh." They rose to embrace the newcomers, even Kigba, who was a stranger to them. Manja, had not appeared and the man asked where she was.

"She has traveled out of town," one of the women informed him, quickly adding, "But there is no problem. We knew that you were coming and we have arranged a place for you. You will sleep in the house over there because we already have some visitors who came in last night. They will be going away tomorrow."

"Our friend, Kigba, also needs a place to sleep. She is going to Taninihun and we shall all be leaving tomorrow."

"No problem, I shall share my bed and room with her since it is only for one night." The same woman collected Kigba's bundle and bamboo umbrella to take to her room. On her return, she said to the man and his wives,

"I shall prepare water for you and food will be served after you have finished washing. Meanwhile, follow me to the other house so that you can secure your things before you come back here to eat."

"Where did Manja travel to, and where is her husband, if I may ask?" the man said as they walked to the other house.

"My brother, it is a long story. We shall talk later. Manja went to Talia. Things are not easy between them these days. They hardly see each other. In fact, we don't even know when she is coming back. The husband, too, did not say where he was going and when he would be returning. It has been like that for some time now."

The man made no further comment as they walked towards the house in the growing darkness. People tended to retire early in the evening after a hard day's work in their farms.

The following morning, the man, his two wives and Kigba started on the last leg of their journey. It was still raining, but only lightly so, as was usually the case, people were going about their daily business. Only a few carried umbrellas.

"As if we knew the situation between Manja and her husband would be like that, "the man remarked. "How can they both decide to live such a life? And you know, they have five children. I did not see any of them, but maybe that was because it was night. Just fancy! They have gone their separate ways." He sounded so distressed over the matter that his older wife said, "My husband, why can't they go their separate ways? After all, the children are now grown up. As for the chief, he will pay the price in the future. Do you think the ancestors will forgive him for such behavior? They will surely punish him. He has refused to learn a lesson from his own late father. Maybe he even learned such habits from him. You men should be careful, because these things will haunt you to your graves. The end of man is what matters, but our people never learn. Look how the old chief died. They said for a long time he could neither talk nor walk and had to be fed like a baby.You know what that means, my husband; it means that we should all be like babies; babies do not harm anyone."

They were all silent for a moment, each with their private thoughts. Kigfba was the first to continue the conversation.

"I did not comment on this matter before because I am planning for my granddaughter to marry our Chief," she said at last. "I, too, have heard about this Manja woman who is breaking her marriage for our chief who has so many wives. Ah, women! What is wrong with us? Manja is her husband's only wife yet she wants to break the marriage for the chief. What is wrong with her?"

"My sister, there is nothing wrong with Manja," the older woman said. "The way she sees it is that she will become the wife of a chief. There is no other way to interpret her behavior other than to see it in terms of status-seeking. Her husband is not a chief. He is only a farmer. So that is the way I see it."

Nobody spoke after that for they could already see the town where the man and his wives were going. Kigba was sorry to part from such pleasant companions. She thanked them for providing a place for her to sleep and promised to stop by their house on her homeward journey. As she set off on her own, she was praying that she would find Madam Yegbeh free to see her so she could return home in time to tackle other pressing domestic matters. So far she had been lucky. She had encountered pleasant traveling companions and enjoyed hospitality on the way. People could be so pleasant, she thought, smiling at the memory. Her mind now went to the woman who had condemned the chief's behavior, and she said to herself, who would not want to be married to a chief? If you are married to a chief, your social standing in the community is high; and the same is true for your children and members of your family. Who would not want that status? That woman is a big hypocrite. In Talia, the chief's wives enjoy immense status and attract attention. Even his younger wives attract attention when they go out; and their children, too. Even that sister of his who was a failure when she was ionitiated into the Sande Society is now feared and respected because of her noble connection. They say that when she was in the Sande bush she came last in almost every competition, she was so clumsy. And she could not sing, dance, or cook as well as her peers. If Kunaafoh marries our chief she, too, will enjoy social recognition in the community, and the whole family will benefit. Why should her father want to deny us this opportunity? I won't allow it. Hindowaa is out of his mind. Madam Yegbeh will help me drive out the devil that has possessed him.

Taninihun was now within sight and she was glad. Time was on her side. She hoped she would be lucky enough to see the woman that same day. It was just past midday when she finally arrived in Taninihun. The rain had ceased and the town was almost empty of people, including the last batch of Madam Yegbeh's clients. When she was told that she could see her sooner rather than later, Kigba could not believe her luck; but she was nervous as the moment of truth approached. What if the woman told her something she did not want to hear? Her mind was in turmoil, worrying about the outcome of the consultation.

When she was summoned into Madam Yegbeh's hut, she started trembling as if she were in a trance. She could not recall the last time she had had such an experience. She was still trembling as she sat in front of the woman. Madam Yegbeh looked like an incarnated spirit. Her frame was skeletal and her mouth almost empty of teeth so that her jaws had sunk inwards. Kigba could not look her in the eye. She felt threatened as she waited for the moment of truth.

"I know your mission," the woman told her. "The people who left here just before you came were on a similar mission. Like you, they were impatient with the ancestors after consulting them on an urgent family matter."

Kigba was happy to discover that the woman already knew why she had come to see her. She watched with fascination as Madam Yegbeh assembled her ritual items on the floor. She half filled a large white bowl with water then, mumbling incoherent words, put in four eggs, four kola nuts, and four cowry shells. She also put in a small mirror face up.

"Woman, do you know that I can summon the dead from their abode and talk to them? Do you also know that I can see the dead and they can see me? Do you also know that I can let you see any of your dead family members? The only thing that cannot happen is for you to talk to them directly. I am the medium, the conduit, the contact between you and your dead family members. Do you understand what I am saying to you?"

Kigba nodded nervously, not knowing what would happen next.

"I now need details from you concerning your mission," the woman told her.

Kigba moved her stool closer to the medium and turned her face away from the door of the hut. Still, avoiding Madam Yegbeh's piercing gaze, she coughed slightly and gathered her wrapper between her legs.

"I have a family problem," she told the woman in a low voice. "I am a mother of three children, an only son and two girls. The girls are married and have children. My son had a wife who bore him, first two boys and a girl, and later another boy and girl - twins. She died in childbirth when she was delivering the twins. In Talia, the Hindowaa family has never given the chief a wife, which is a shame. I discussed this with my son and I said his daughter should be given to our chief. At first, he agreed with me, then the girl disappeared for a long time. When she came back we were all happy, but she had gone to the white man's land and learned the white man's book and way of doing things. They said she was a doctor and gave powerful injections; they sang her praises. But they also said that she belonged to a religion that does not allow women to marry and have children. My son now says that because of this, we should look for another wife for our chief. The thing is, I have already told our chief about Kunaafoh and he is looking forward to the marriage." At this point, Kigba paused for so long that the woman had to urge her on.

"Before bringing this matter to the rest of the family, I decided to consult my deceased husband and my son's grandfather to ask their opinion on the matter. I went to their graves and poured the libation and offered food, and then I explained all that I have told you. They promised to communicate their views on the matter, but that was a long time ago and I cannot wait anymore. I thought they would come to me in a dream and tell me their response, but that has not happened so far. In fact, I have not had a single dream since I visited them. That is why I am here - to find out what they have to say about the situation. I am having sleepless nights and I have lost my appetite."

As soon as Kigba finished speaking, to her amazement, the woman brought a white satin cloth from under her pillow. She covered her long, grey, untidy hair with the satin cloth, leant over the bowl of water containing the four eggs, four kola nuts and cowry shells and gazed into it for a long time without speaking. Kigba realized that Madam Yegbeh was now in another world - the world of the departed, and she felt terrified and alone. Finally, Madam Yegbeh said, "Woman, I have in front of me your husband. He is a tall man and well dressed. He is not a fat person and has no gray hair, so he must have died young. He says he is aware of your presence here. Do you understand?"

"Yes, your description is correct," Kigba said.

"His grandfather and father have also appeared now. They all look well. There is lot of resemblance in the family. They say they knew you would come this far to find out about events. They are all happy to know that you are here and well. Do you understand?"

The old woman offered to let Kigba see her departed loved ones, but she was too frightened and declined.

"I only want to talk to them through you," she replied.

Madam Yegbeh was not surprised at her refusal. Many of her clients came with problems and concerns, but when she asked them to come under the satin cloth and see their loved ones for themselves, only a few accepted the offer.

"Woman, I am now talking to your loved and departed ones about the subject of your mission. We are in conversation and this will take some time. Do you hear me?"

Kigba's apprehension was now making her sweat as she waited for the old woman to finish her conversation with her late husband and father-in-law and relay their messages. There was an ominous silence in the hut.

"Woman, your loved ones are in good spirits. They send their greetings to all the family. They know everything that is happening and they never forget you on their side of the divide. They will fight any evil to protect you. They say you are to go back and agree with your son. His opinion on the matter is what should prevail. This is a matter for the father and mother, if she were alive. They can consult you, but the final decision remains with the father, not the grandmother. That is their view of the matter and they wish all of you well."

The old woman removed the satin cloth covering her hair.

Those were not the words Kigba wanted to hear, so feeling miserable and angry, she fished out money from the knotted end of her wrapper and remarked bitterly as she paid the required fee,

"I have come to believe the story of the strange disease that afflicted people in Talia and the chiefdom many years ago. I shall not bore you with the details, but it seems to have come again, and I believe and the first victims are my son, my daughters and some other members of the Talia community. This is the only reason why they now believe that women who have acquired the white man's religion should stay unwed and childless. It seems that the disease has also affected the other side of the divide. How else can I explain this response from the ancestors?"

Madam Yegbeh took her money without further comment.

When Kigba started on her homeward journey, the weather was still pleasant. She was alarmed when a cat crossed her path as she started out and for a brief moment stood as if rooted to the spot, wondering what it signified.

At various times in her life, she had had a very strong feeling that she, too, was psychic and thought the cat crossing her path must signify events to come. The incident occupied her mind as she continued her journey and met other people coming to consult the revered medium. Her trip, she thought, had created more problems than it had solved. However, she was determined not to become infected with the madness that had affected members of her family. She journeyed homewards with a firm determination to keep her promise to the chief. Kunaafoh would marry him; it was only a matter of time. And she would do anything necessary to cure her son of this infection with foreign values.

■

CHAPTER SIX

Sister O'Connor was known to everyone in Talia as 'Sister Kono'. She, the priests, Kunaafoh, and Kunaafoh's twin siblings, lived in the mission compound. The people of Talia found the mission compound a strange environment. Sacred, almost. They went there only when it was strictly necessary - for business, for church services, for prayers and to attend the health clinic. The atmosphere in the compound was serene and the place kept scrupulously clean and tidy. 'Sister Kono' continued to gain respect and had become a venerable presence among the people of Talia and beyond. She continued her relentless efforts to recruit more girls into the ministry by training them and sending them to Ireland so that they, too, like Kunaafoh, could return to help their people and promote the Catholic Church. She was proud of Kunaafoh and happy that the young woman had succeeded in adopting her twin siblings. The children had now started going to school.

Hindowaa's relationship with the Catholic mission was good, though his access to the area was also limited to official business. He had confided in 'Sister Kono' and the priests about his problem regarding Kunaafoh's proposed marriage to the chief, and they had taken a great interest in the situation. They knew that it was Kunaafoh's grandmother who was pushing for the marriage, so every Sunday during mass they prayed for the devil to lose his influence over her. Hindowaa had assured them all that, as long as he remained Kunafoh's father, she would never marry anyone. He had taken an oath on his Wunde Society that Kunaafoh would remain a nun for the rest of her life, so as far as he was concerned the issue of her commitment to her vocation was signed, sealed, and delivered. Nothing would change that as long as he was alive and breathing.

In Talia itself, he got along well with most people, though he remembered Giita telling him that people smiling at you, eating at your place and drinking your palm wine, did not necessarily mean that their friendship was genuine. She had cautioned him on many occasions about what she considered his naivety, and wished he would be more discriminating with regard to his so-called friends, peers and acquaintances in Talia and beyond. Giita had not even made an exception of the chief. At the time, Hindowaa had not appreciated his wife's critical assessment of people's characters, but on reflection, his instinct or sixth sense supported her observations, especially those concerning the chief. Now he was faced with a critical situation which was causing him sleepless nights - how to tell the chief that because Kunaafoh had become a bride of God, a longstanding promise that she would marry him could no longer be fulfilled. He would have to appeal to the chief to consider taking another wife from the Hindowaa family. Delivering such a message was a serious challenge and he wondered how best to go about it. He wished he could have gone with his mother but had ruled her out, knowing how divided they were on this issue. He was unhappy that she had traveled without telling him where she was going and why. His wife, Boi-Kimbo, was not aware of her mother-in-law's destination either, though she was aware that she had left the house early in the morning while others were still asleep. He continued to view his mother as the main obstacle in this matter, because she refused to accept his reason for insisting that Kunaafoh could not marry. He was getting more and more troubled by her stubbornness and had even begun to take more seriously the rumors Ndomawaa had told him about,that people were saying that she had a djinn. The fact that people in Talia believed his mother wielded undue influence over him was a concern, as was the knowledge that they were questioning why she had never remarried. He wanted to bring the rumors to her attention, but knew it was considered inappropriate for a child to raise delicate or sensitive issues with a parent. Perhaps he could approach the matter indirectly by expressing curiosity as to why she had not remarried after his father's death. The more he thought about the situation, the more uneasy he became. However, Hindowa realized that dealing with the rumors concerning his mother was not as urgent as the challenge of informing the chief that Kunaafoh would not be marrying him or anyone else. How to do it? He recalled that when he was an initiate in the Wunde Society, they had had long discussions about how to influence chiefs. One thing he clearly remembered from those discussions was that one should always try to tell chiefs what they wanted to hear, look for their weak points and try to exploit them. For instance, he knew that even though the chief's father had been a wicked man who oppressed his subjects, the incumbent loved to hear people refer to him in a flattering way. Hindowaa had had no unpleasant encounters with the chief so far because he was one of those who always told him what he wanted to hear about himself and about his late father. Hindowaa was painfully aware that that situation was now likely to change. He wondered whether he should lead a delegation of notable townspeople to present his case, or whether he should approach the chief by himself. If he decided on a delegation, which of all his friends should he take along with him? He also wondered if a precedent had ever been set in Talia, where a chief had been promised a certain woman, was later denied that one and offered a replacement. If so he could use that as a defense. It was something he needed to investigate.

In the end, he decided to see the chief alone, but that before doing so, he would seek out certain people whose judgment he respected, and discuss his problem with them. One of the first people he thought of consulting was the chief's half-sister, Maa'ngayaa. She was among the few educated members of the ruling family and highly respected in the community. She and her brother,were not on the best of terms. People said that was because the chief accused her of putting on airs since acquiring a little education at the famous Harford School for Girls in Moyamba. He had never gone to school. She was never afraid of challenging her brother on sensitive matters, so Hindowaa felt that she would support his position regarding Kunaafoh. He wished the chief had many more siblings like his sister. His second choice was Nyamakoro, the woman who had become rich by selling cakes and who, some people believed, had become prosperous through shady business practices. Though Hindowaa knew her quite well and had visited herself and her husband several times, he had never discussed family problems with her. However, he believed that she was a woman of character who would give sound advice when she was well informed.

Next, he began to consider his male friends. The first to come to mind was Nyake who, though he was a controversial individual, would look at this matter objectively and would not hesitate to tell him painful truths. If Nyake supported his position, he would be able to approach the chief with confidence. Another suitable confidant was 'Chief' Lamboi. Lamboi was not a chief, but had acquired the nickname and it stuck. He never took offense when he was called (Mahei) chief; in fact, he loved it, declaring that, "Chief will decide any case. Chief, will pass any judgment, Chief's verdict is final." He was a man of average height and nursed a thick beard which he cherished, believing that thick beards signified wisdom. Lamboi and Hindowaa looked so much alike that there was a standing joke in Talia that one of their fathers must have engaged in some hanky-panky at one time.

All these people came from the part of Talia known as 'up town'. Hindowaa decided that he would also consult people from 'down town' or 'old town', as some preferred to call it. Down town, there was an old woman who had been widowed twice. She was called Mamie Tonya, meaning 'truth'. She was a respectable woman and lived by the riverside. Many people believed that she was the queen of all the female witches down town because she never fell ill, or at least, no one had ever known her to fall ill. However, just as many people disputed her alleged witchcraft connections because she was the mother of ten children and countless grandchildren, and it was generally believed that women who had children did not engage in witchcraft or any other dirty deeds. Whatever views people held about her, she remained one of the most respected women in the town. She was the only woman the chief occasionally visited. They would sit and chat and people said she even advised him on delicate chiefdom matters. She was Hindowaa's fifth choice. Kinie Musa Tokowaa, meaning 'Big Hand' was his sixth and final choice. Kinie Tokowaa's hands were not all that large, but that was his surname. He lived not far from Mamie Tonya and they were good friends. He was not as old as she was but had, nevertheless, acquired enormous influence in the Wunde fraternity. His views, on serious chiefdom and family matters carried much weight in the community.

****

Hindowaa had sent a message to Maa'ngayaa, the chief's half-sister, saying that he would be coming to see her that evening and she was expecting him. She wondered about the purpose of this visit since Hindowaa usually visited her without sending to inform her about it beforehand. She had just finished cleaning up in the kitchen and had come out to the veranda to rest in a reclining chair, so she was in a relaxed position with her legs crossed when Hindowaa arrived. Her husband, Kinie Moiwo Lavali, whom she had told about the impending visit, had gone out. He knew Hindowaa very well and also knew how his mother bullied him, but he was a man who could not be bothered with other people's business and seldom took anything seriously.

"Nya'nde, bi waah, biseh," Hindowaa greeted his hostess as he entered the veranda. There was no light, which was deliberate because Maa'ngayaa wanted to maintain a certain degree of privacy. Her two children were also out and were not expected until much later. She had no idea when her husband would be coming back because she did not know where he had gone. It had been the same with her late husband, so it did not bother her. He often left the house unceremoniously and returned either a few minutes later or after midnight, drunk.

"Nyahawa biwah, biseh, kahun yeenaa." Hindowaa always addressed her as 'big woman'.

"Muu gowuu, (welcome)," Maa'ngayaa responded as he chose a seat.

" What have I done to deserve this visit?" she inquired playfully after he had made himself comfortable. "I cannot recall the last time you paid me a visit. Oh, yes, I remember now. It was when Kinie Sandi came to complain that he was convinced someone was having an affair with his younger wife. He wanted to sue the man for woman damage, but his wife had not confessed to an affair with the man he suspected. He was so jealous he was almost in tears. I thought he was such a foolish man."

"That was not such a long time ago," Hindowaa pointed out.

"Yes, but you used to visit me more frequently. These days, I hardly know what is happening to you. That young wife is keeping you busy, eh. Just be careful; I know your mother also keeps you busy. It is almost as if you have two wives."

By now it was dark, so Maa'ngayaa did not notice Hindowaa's pained expression when she mentioned his mother. He said, "My sister, I am here for a very different reason. I have a serious problem and I don't know how to handle it. That is why I have come to see you. Maybe you can help. In fact, you may have heard about my problem already, since there are no secrets in this town..."

"Before you start, let us have something to drink," Maa'ngayaa interrupted. "Someone was supposed to bring us some palm wine today but he has still not arrived. What I have is not all that fresh, but let us have it while we wait for the new one."

As they sipped the palm wine, she said in a serious tone, "Hindowaa, before you tell me what you have come to see me about, let me tell you something that has been bothering me. At first, I thought it was none of my business, but now it concerns me as a woman. It concerns me because I, too, have children; I mean girls. It also concerns me because it has to do with my brother and your family."

Hindowaa's heart beats accelerated, but before he could say anything, Maa'ngayaa went on,

"What is this I am hearing about Kunaafoh marrying my brother? I hope it is just a rumor and will stay that way. Kunaafoh is a nun and a medical doctor. I have never heard about nuns marrying anyone. Kunaafoh is a model for our children, especially our daughters. Look at the good work she is doing, her name is known all over this town and chiefdom. Hindowaa, please do not make that mistake. As for my brother, if he wants more wives, he can have as many as he wants, without running after nuns. He can even marry all the Sande initiates during the next session. I am so fed up with him! How many more women does he want? I beg you, please don't allow this thing to happen."

Hindowaa could not believe his ears. Maa'ngayaa had taken the words right out of his mouth. He felt as if the matter had already been resolved and congratulated himself for choosing the chief's sister as one of his advisers. With a deep sigh of relief, he inhaled the fresh evening air.

"My sister, I cannot believe what I have just heard," he gushed. "I cannot believe it. Because of all the goodness you have shown me, I came to you to tell you about this very matter; to seek your advice; and it is as if you read my mind. I have to tell your brother that because Kunaafoh is now a nun and a doctor, she cannot marry him and we are prepared to give him another wife from the Hindowaa family. My sister, this issue has almost divided my family because my mother is fiercely supporting Kunaafoh's marriage to your brother. We are hardly on speaking terms because of it. That is my problem."

"Talking about family problems, we also have ours." Maa'ngayaa said after acknowledging his appreciation. "My brother thinks I oppose him too often. But that is only because I try to make him realize that being the chief does not entitle him to take matters of interest to the people lightly. This question of marrying so many girls has been one we don't agree on. You see, Kinie Hindowaa, I try to convince my brother and other elders here that girls should be allowed to go to school and even on to college. Learn a profession. Be independent and become useful members of the community. That is all I ask. I have told them that their own generation is not the same as the present one. I have pleaded and pleaded with my brother and other members of the family. So far, I am alone in this vast forest; but I have made up my mind not to give up the fight to convince them of the importance of educating girls."

"Ah, my sister, I agree with you. You see, me I am not educated, but now I feel a great sense of satisfaction because of my daughter, Kunaafoh. The respect I get in this town and beyond is great. What else does a parent need?"

He was deeply disappointed that his two boys, whom he had sent to school in Freetown, had refused to complete their education. One of them was only a seaman and the other, a motor apprentice.

"That is just what I am talking about," Maa'ngayaa exclaimed, interrupting that regretful thought. "What more does a parent need? Kinie Hindowaa, never hesitate to send all your children to school, both boys and girls. Don't be like my brother who does not send his children to school. Instead he sends them to the farm to work. When I try to talk to him about it we end up quarrelling. People say it is because he himself did not go to school, but that is not the reason. There are many people in this town who did not go to school, but they have sent their children, both boys and girls to school.The man is just not progressive. He is living in the dark ages, thinking only of marrying many women. Every Sande session whets his appetite and he acquires more wives. Just look at his compound, it is full of women; some of them are the same age as his daughters. It is a disgrace. Let me tell you once and for all, do not, and never give your daughter, Kunaafoh in marriage to my brother. If you do, God will punish you here on earth and after you die. You have my full support."

"My sister, I thank you. I am so glad I thought of consulting you before we have a family meeting on this issue. That is why they say it is good to know book. When you know book, you see things differently from those who don't. I realize this whenever I have time to talk to Kunaafoh. The way she thinks and talks about life and her experiences in the white man's land are so interesting. I thank God and my ancestors for this."

With that, Hindowaa rose to take leave of Maa'ngayaa. The expected palm wine never arrived but he was feeling buoyant with happiness as he set out for

Nyamakoro's house. Being able to count on the support of the chief's sister was a huge achievement. He hoped he would find Nyamakoro's husband at home because he had great respect for him and wanted to hear his views. Even though he had married a rich woman he asserted his authority in their home and, despite her wealth, Nyamakoro never challenged him.

Hindowaa was trying to avoid people coming his way because he was not interested in roadside chats that evening. He was therefore dismayed to hear someone say, "Kunaafoh, ngikeeh (Kunaafoh's father)." The woman was too close to be avoided.

"Biwaah, biseh," she went on and asked where he was going -- exactly what he had been trying to avoid - unwanted conversation.

"I am going to visit Nyamakoro and her husband," he told her, pretending to be in a hurry. Undeterred, the woman insisted on joining him so as they walked side by side, he asked, "Where are you are going tonight without your husband?"

"My husband left the house as soon as he had eaten and did not tell me where he was going; but I am sure he is drinking palm wine with his friends, near that big mango tree on the way to the small river."

Hindowaa made no comment and, to his relief, the woman left him soon after that without ever revealing where she was going. From a distance, he spotted a light in Nyamakoro's house which pleased him because he had not given her prior notice of his visit. Apart from the chief's sister, he had not notified any of his selected advisers that he would be visiting them. Usually, he just dropped in unannounced, and if he did not find the person at home, left a message that he had been there and would come back another time. When he arrived, he was greeted by a woman, who offered him a seat on the veranda. In his eagerness to consult at least three of his chosen advisers that evening, Hindowaa asked, without responding to her greeting,

"Are Nyamakoro and her husband in?" The woman took offence at this lack of good manners, for she answered grudgingly,

"Mama Nyamakoro is taking a bath. Her husband has gone out and I don't know when he will be back. I will go and tell her you are here."

As he waited, Hindowaa wondered what advice Nyamakoro would give him and what would be the likely reactions of Nyake, Lamboi, Tonya and Tokowaa.

"Biwaah, Kinie, biseh," a passer-by called out, jolting him back to the immediate present.

"Biwaah, biseh," he responded automatically as the woman returned to say that Nyamakoro would soon join him.

He waited several minutes during which he thought about Nyamakoro. She had told him about the behavior of some of the people who owed her money. After taking her cakes on credit with promises to pay her the next day, they avoided her house.When she sent messengers to collect her money, the debtors started calling her a mean woman who was always harassing people over money, even threatening to take the matter to the chief. Human beings are so complicated, Hindowaa thought with a smile. It widened when Nyamakoro finally appeared.

"My brother, good evening, I am sorry, I did not know that you were coming." She sounded as if she had come rushing out. "I took a bath because I left the kitchen late this evening. My husband has gone out but I hope he will find you here when he comes back. We spoke about you just today. I'm sure he would like to see you....But my dear, what brings you here tonight and where is your mother?" Without waiting for Hindowa to answer, she went on, "I haven't seen her for some time. Last time she was here, we had an unfortunate encounter; but such is life. People should learn to disagree without being unpleasant about it. You should tell her that times are changing and we should be prepared to adapt. Even with my own children, I sometimes have to give in when we discuss various things, especially when I know they are talking sense. In our own days, it was impossible to sit with your parents and exchange ideas, but today, we all sit down and talk, and we benefit from each other's ideas. Your mother is not like that, which is why people in Talia think she is a big bully."

Hindowaa had listened attentively to Nyamakoro's comments about his mother because he realized that she was leading up to something.

"My sister, did you have any misunderstanding with my mother?" he asked when she paused. "I hope she did not insult you or any member of your family."

"No, it did not come to that," Nyamakoro assured him. "Honestly, she did not insult me, nor did I insult her. God forbid! She is an elder person for me, so I always treat her with respect. It is just that she always wants to impose her views on other people...But here I am, doing all the talking; and I haven't even asked why you have come to see me. If my husband had been here, he would have scolded me for talking too much... "

"No, please carry on," Hindowaa said. He was not in the least surprised when Nyamakoro told him that the disagreement with his mother was about Kunaafoh and her proposed marriage to the chief.

"Your mother came here one day and told me she wanted my opinion on the matter, saying you both did not see eye to eye on it. Then when I gave her my sincere opinion, she became so furious that she walked out on me without saying goodbye."

"What did you tell her?" Hindowaa asked, though he had a good idea what the answer would be.

"I told her that the decision as to whether Kunaafoh should or should not marry to the chief or anybody else lies with her father not her grandmother.Your mother was very unhappy with my opinion. I won't be surprised if she refuses to talk to me next time we meet."

Hindowaa felt enormous relief and excitement that he had found another supporter.

"My sister," he exclaimed, "this is a great day for me! I just cannot believe what is happening. Eeem, God is great! Our ancestors are great and they are all with me. You won't believe it. I came here to seek your opinion on this very matter because my mother and I are split down the middle over it. I am opposed to the child marrying the chief now that she is a nun and a doctor. I am completely opposed to it, and I have even received the support of the chief's sister, Maa'ngayaa. From what you have said so far, I think I can count on your support and I feel doubly blessed. Thank you very much."

"I wish you had met my husband here, but I can assure you that he has the same views," Nyamakoro replied. "Your daughter has made other towns respect us. She is a good and caring doctor and people speak very highly of her everywhere. How can the chief marry a nun? If he wants to to marry yet again, there are many other women available. Don't listen to your mother."

Feeling even more elated, Hindowaa headed for the last adviser he had planned to consult that night. He was surprised to see the two most senior of Nyake's three wives seated on the veranda with him. Most times when he visited Nyake, they were either still at the family farm or else they had come in tired and retired to bed early. On this particular night, however, they were with their husband to sort out some family problems, which was unusual. More often, Nyake summoned them into his bedroom, shut the door and addressed the issue. The present problem was a minor one, which was why Nyake was dealing with it on the veranda.

"It is a long time since we saw you here, Kinie Hindowaa," the senior wife said in mild reproach when Hindowaa had made himself comfortable.

"I have been busy lately trying to sort out many of things in the family," Hindowaa apologised.

"All right, I understand," the woman said, but Nyake defended his friend, "Many times when Hindowaa comes here, you are at the back of the house, and I call your young mate to serve us palm wine. But since you have complained, from now on, whenever Hindowaa comes, I shall ask you to come and greet him and to bring palm wine for us. Is that okay?"

"Yes, it is all right," Nyake's wife laughed. "I shall do it, provided we all drink the palm wine together."

"I shall give you that privilege as the first wife," Nyake agreed amiably. "In fact let us start right now. There is palm wine in the room. Go and bring it."

The senior wife obliged without further ado.

"Where is your mother and how is she?" Nyake asked while she was fetching the palm wine.

"Mother has traveled, but don't ask me where she

went because I don't know," Hindowaa replied.

"That is very strange, Kinie Hindowaa," the second wife remarked. So far, she had kept her mouth shut.

"No, it is not at all strange," Nyake said. "Kigba is capable of doing things like that. She is a very tough woman. Everybody knows that in this town and beyond. Now you go and bring the cups," he added, noticing that his first wife had emerged with the gourd of palm wine. "You sit here and watch your senior mate struggling without giving her a helping hand."

"But she was the one that volunteered, why don't you leave her to finish the task she has started," the second wife told him in her spirited way. She, however, went into the house to fetch the cups.

"You see, what I tell you about her, Hindowaa," Nyake complained, "She has no manners. Of the three of them, she has the sharpest tongue. I wish I were younger; she knows what would happen. Her mother, is just the same. Her mouth is sharp and she fears nobody. By the way, the last time your mother was here, we almost came to blows on this veranda. I am telling you the truth," he added when Hindowaa expressed surprise. "A Wunde man like me, and a Lawaa for that matter."

"But I thought you both were good friends," Hindowaa said. His mother often visited Nyake and would go back home saying how enjoyable the visit had been. What could have gone wrong? She had told him nothing. Nyake's first wife had already served the first round but his concern made drinking the palm wine less pleasurable than usual.

"Kinie Hindowaa, thank you, for coming. If you had not come and found us here, we would not have had access to this palm wine," the second wife joked. "Please come more often; and let us know ahead of time so that we can come here and wait for you."

"You see what I'm saying? She has confirmed it herself. That mouth of hers. She just opens it wide and lets the words flow freely. She is not afraid of anything," Nyake remarked. The second wife did not respond and her senior simply smiled because she supported what her mate had said.

"Why should you and my mother have a quarrel, ndakei Nyake?" Hindowaa asked. They had not yet finished their first serving of palm wine and the gourd was fairly large.The two wives were determined to stay around until they had emptied it, for this was an opportunity that came all too seldom.

"I shall tell you in the presence of my wives because I have already told them what happened. It is not a long story. And it is also not anything new... After she visited the graves of her late husband and your grandfather, and informed them about the situation in your household concerning Kunaafoh, she wanted my opinion. You can be sure that I gave her my candid view of the matter which was that the person with the final say in this matter was the father -- or mother. Ndakei, at that moment, I can tell you, If Kigba had had a gun, she would have shot me dead. She walked away from my house saying that I was now a victim of the madness that had reappeared in Talia. For the first time, she left this house without saying goodbye and since then, I have not seen her."

The first wife rose to serve another round of drinks without being asked. They had not gone even half way into the gourd and the wives were enjoying themselves. They wanted Hindowaa to stay until they had drunk all the wine.

"You have to go to the farm tomorrow morning," Nyake remarked.

"My dear, we are not children," the second wife reminded him. "We can stay up late and still get up early to go to the farm. After all, this is not the first time we are staying up late."

Nyake did not respond to this tart remark and they stayed on. Hindowaa said, "My brother, you don't know how relieved I am by what you have just told me. I came here this evening to ask for your opinion on this issue. I have already visited the chief's sister and Nyamakoro, and they both told me exactly the same thing. I am so grateful to all of you. May God and our ancestors guide you so that you can continue to give wise counsel in this community."

"But, ndakei, tell your mother, she should be careful," Nyake replied. "She does not have a good name in this town anymore. Why has she changed so much? I am warning you; talk to her. Let her calm down. Talia is a small community. We should all be our brothers' and sisters' keepers. I shall also talk to the chief when the opportunity arises so that he counsels her."

The two wives hoped Nyake's comments were not signalling the end of the visit because they knew that once Hindowaa left, their husband would bring the enjoyable drinking session to a close. They were therefore sorry to hear Hindowaa say,

"Let me go. I also want to hear the views of Lamboi, Tonya and Tokowaa on this matter." .

At the mention of Lamboi, both wives sniggered, and the younger one, made even more cheeky by the drink, said, 'Chief' in a mocking tone. Nyake put her in her place by sharply reminding her that Lamboi was the same age as her father.

"When I decided to seek advice, you were the first person I thought of," Hindowaa went on, ignoring this flash of irritation. " Then I thought I should bring in some women, because this whole thing concerns my daughter's marriage. So far I have had no regrets about any of my advisers. I decided to leave out the imam and the pastor."

There was more chuckling from the two wives when Hindowaa mentioned the pastor, and the younger wife remarked, "Pastor, nyaha gula (Pastor woman wrapper)." She was referring to the pastor's reputation as a womanizer. This time, even Nyake joined in the laughter.

All the palm wine had been drunk by the time Hindowaa took leave of Nyake and his wives. He was delighted with his first round of consultations. All these distinguished people supported his position. He began to feel more and more confident that all would be well when the time came for his meeting with the chief.

****

Lamboi and Tokowaa were well known in Talia as drinking partners and they always reserved Saturday evenings for their binges. People said that they had become friends in Tiama when they were initiated into the Wunde Society in the same year. On this particular evening, they were not satisfied with the palm wine they had drunk and even scolded the man who had sold it to them. Since the evening was still young, they decided to drop in on various people uninvited and chose Tonya's house as the first port of call. Of all the women down town, Tonya could be relied upon to have a supply of palm wine and she was always willing to entertain visitors. Moreover, they felt that they would be doing her a favour by going to keep her company.

On their way to Tonya's house, they decided that after they had exhausted her palm wine, they would go up town and visit Nyake and Hindowaa in turn, as they had done a number of times before. They always enjoyed visiting Hindowaa, and Nyake was also good-natured, though too inclined to lecture his visitors. The two men had become tired of it and had agreed that if he started one of his lectures on moral philosophy that evening, they would pretend to be drunk and give him a sound telling-off.

Tonya had just finished her evening meal when the two friends arrived. Her veranda was as big as a small court room and contained many chairs as well as two hammocks, one of which she jokingly referred to as the royal hammock because it was the more elegant of the two. She actually preferred the less elegant one but said that was only for sentimental reasons. It was the one her late father had used all his life.

"Tonya, we are going to be your guests tonight," Lamboi declared . "We passed by the river, but tonight the palm wine was not fit even for a jailbird to drink.. You are our sister. That is why Tokowaa and I decided to come and visit you instead... Do you know what I did? I put my finger down my throat and all the bad wine came out. Now I am ready to drink." When Tonya looked incredulous, he said. "Ask Tokowaa. He will confirm it. I told him to help me get the bad palm wine out of my body, since his name is 'Big Hand', but he declined. He was afraid I would bite him."

They all had a good laugh at this remark, Tonya so heartily that she began to cough.

"You people, please don't kill me with laughter," she said when she had caught her breath. "My head is already aching. Make yourselves at home. I have plenty of good palm wine and, since you have had a good clean-out, I have food too, if you feel hungry."

"I did not clean out my own system," Tokowaa informed her. "Lamboi refused to put his hand into my mouth, and he was right not to do it. Had he agreed I would have taught him a lesson. I would have closed my mouth hard, like a crocodile, so that when he withdrew hand, there would have been less than a full hand left."

"Tokowaa, I beg you," Tonya teased him. "We know that you people, who originate from across the big forest, practice cannibalism, but please don't introduce it here."

As they were enjoying their jokes and teasing, they were surprised to see Hindowaa approaching the house. He was whistling and appeared jubilant. He himself was taken by surprise because he had planned to see all three of them that evening.

Lamboi and Tokowaa suddenly burst into song - a composition about witches who could smell wine and food and also trace people's whereabouts from any distance because they had long noses and big eyes. Hindowaa soon joined in, and the three men sang away merrily while Tonya, who was lying in her not so elegant hammock, looked on, enjoying the entertainment. Hindowaa finally broke the festive mood by saying,

"If you will allow me, my sister and brothers, before we settle down for the evening, let me tell you why I am here. Tonya, I planned to see your first then I go to see Lamboi and Tokowaa in turn. I have already seen Maa'ngayaa, Nyamakoro and Nyake, in that order. It is about my daughter, Kunaafoh."

They had not started drinking yet , so their mental faculties were still functioning well. There was an attentive silence.

"You all know that before Kunaafoh disappeared, there was a proposal in the family that she should marry our chief; then, as you know, she became a nun and a doctor..."

"And a very good doctor, too," Tonya interjected. "She has treated me many times."

"And she cured my sister's goiter, "Lamboi added. "She was miserable for years and people called her a witch until Kunaafoh came. Now she is no longer considered a witch; people marvel at her."

"Hindowaa, before you go on, let me say something, " Tonya interrupted. "Talia is a small town and all of us here have heard about this matter, and the chief visits me from time to time. In fact, if he were much older, people would have said that something was happening between us. I thank God I am now too old for that kind of gossip." Amid laughter from the men, she went on,"I have discussed many things with him, but I have refused to bring up the subject of Kunaafoh marrying him or anyone else. Kunaafoh is our daughter; she is the child of Talia and the entire chiefdom. She is doing a good job and God has assigned her a vocation. All of us here know your position on the matter and we support you. The chief can marry other women or girls if he wants to, but not our Kunaafoh. I am not educated, but I would have loved for my children to be like her."

The other two men concurred emphatically, and Tokowaa added,

"So there is nothing more to be said. Let us settle down and do justice to our sister's drink and food."

Unlike Lamboi and Tokowaa, Hindowaa was still quite sober as he walked home in the darkness some time later. He felt as if a heavy load had been lifted from his head for he now had enough moral ammunition with which to challenge the chief if he tried to be difficult over the matter of marrying Kunaafoh. When he was passing through up town Talia, he stopped in front of the chief's compound, thinking, Chief, I shall be coming to see you soon, and you know why. Do not be as wicked as your father. Even though I always tell you that he was a good man, he was a bad man and you know it. One thing I shall tell you, though, for as long as I am alive, you will never marry Kunaafoh. Sleep well, and I look forward to seeing you. He then walked on to his house where his wife, Boi-Kimbo, had stayed up as usual, awaiting his return.

■

CHAPTER SEVEN

Kigba and Hindowaa had been avoiding each other for some time, but it was inevitable that they would eventually come face to face. It happened on a Sunday morning when Boi-Kimbo, the children and other members of the household had gone down town to attend some festivity or other. With the entire house quiet, Hindowaa thought the atmosphere ideal for a meeting with his mother and, using his most submissive tone, invited her to join him in his bedroom for that purpose.

As she entered the room that Sunday morning, he scrutinized her expression. It was not particularly pleasant and she sat down stiffly. Hindowaa sighed inwardly, knowing that his mother was ready for a fight whereas he had hoped to avoid another confrontation. He would have to be very careful in his dealings with her. He had escaped confrontations with his mother until their current quarrel over Kunaafoh, but he had made up his mind not to give in to her over this matter. Even if he had wanted to, he could not break his sworn Wunde oath because the consequences of doing so would be grave. Yet his mother had said repeatedly that as long as she was alive, she would make sure Kunaafoh married the chief. He had no idea how to resolve the matter amicably.

"Mother, you don't look well this morning. Are you sick?" he remarked.

"If I was sick, I would not have come to you," she replied sourly. "You wanted to see me. I am here."

"Mother, first of all, let me say that I am not challenging you over Kunaafoh. I don't think it was fair for you to use that word. God and our ancestors know that I am not challenging you. How can a child challenge his parents?" His tone was cajoling and subdued, but as soon as his mother spoke again, he realized that he had not succeeded in lessening her resentment against him. Her voice dripped sarcasm as she demanded,

"Is that what you called me for this morning? Is that what you and your father-in-law discussed?"

Trying again to soothe her, Hindowaa said,

"Mother, we have all been affected by Giita's death. It is not all that long ago that she died. You know that before the twins joined their sister at the mission compound they asked me almost daily why their mother went away as soon as they were born and when she would be back. Children can't grasp the idea of death. Whenever they asked me that, I became almost completely tongue-tied. I have never been able to tell them the truth - that she will never come back. It is just too painful. My father-in-law, too, continues to suffer almost as much as he reflects on his daughter's death. Mother, the whole family is still suffering as a result of Giita's death."

Kigba had listened attentively, but the mention of her grandchildren, and of the pain and suffering resulting from Giita's death seemed to have no effect on her. She showed little emotion as she asked again,

"Is that what you have called me here this morning to tell me?"

Her belligerent attitude was making Hindowaa so nervous that he was relieved when their conversation was interrupted by a loud knock at the main entrance of the house. He rushed out to see who was there and found a man carrying a large gourd.

"Good morning," he said. "I just came to drop the palm wine you asked me to bring for you."

Hindowaa was glad that the man had not forgotten his request as he was expecting visitors later in the day. And the timing was perfect for he knew how much his mother loved the stuff. He returned to his room with the gourd and the air soon smelled strongly of freshly brewed palm wine. Hindowaa knew that his mother's mouth was already watering at the prospect of tasting it. However, he did not offer her a cupful straightaway, but started to answer her question by launching into a longwinded account of how puzzled he had been when his father-in-law sent to announce a second visit.

"Mother, I had no idea what he was coming to see me about. He had already told me about the possibility of a calamity befalling the Hindowaa household. We had discussed that and decided to do something to avert it, including an appeal to our ancestors. I did not think he would travel all the way from his town just to have another discussion about that. Then I remembered that I had once told him I owed many people money and when the time came for repayment, I might need some assistance from him so as to avoid embarrassment; but I had said I would contact him if necessary, so I did not think he would make that long trip to talk about that."

Why hasn't he offered me any of the palm wine yet? Kigba asked herself as the fresh smell tantalized her nostrils. In the end, she interrupted him sharply.

"Hindo, why don't you come to the point? I have chores I want to finish today. If I have to spend so much time listening to you tell me how you speculated about this and that, I I won't be able to do them all."

Offended by her attitude, Hindowaa said, "Mother, I am sorry you feel that I am wasting your time. When I called you this morning, you should have known that it was because I had something serious to talk about. I know that you are a busy person and I would never waste your precious time over something trivial. In fact, when Ndomawaa said he wanted to see me, I was about to suggest that we should see him together. Then he said he wanted to see me alone. The matters he brought to my attention that day are serious, urgent and significant." For the first time, Kigba showed some unease and seemed more attentive as Hindowaa went on in the same injured tone, "so please bear with me. Some of the issues could affect the entire Hindowaa family, both the living and the dead. That was why I decided that we should meet to discuss them privately, without any third party present. At one point, my discussion with Ndomawaa became so heated that if there had been a third party, he would have wondered whether we had any family connections."

Kigba became even more impatient with her son's longwindedness and let out an exasperated sigh, thinking, What is wrong with this boy? Why doesn't he offer me some wine!

"Hindo," she said when he paused at last,"you have still not told me anything about your meeting with Ndomawaa. "Did he insult your mother or father or grandfather? Did he accuse you of killing Giita or did he say that I killed her? Did he say that he suspects I have a devil; a spirit, or that I am in love with a mermaid? Don't be afraid of telling me what he told you. I shall not hold you responsible. After all, Ndomawaa is our in-law and we have known him for a long time. Only, don't let us spend the whole day over this. Besides, very soon the house will be full again and we shall have no privacy."

In the face of his mother's growing irritation, Hindowaa gave up trying to introduce the sensitive topics he had discussed with Ndomawaa in a tactful way.

"Mother, I am sorry," he said. "What Ndomawaa told me was that both of us, mother and son, played a role in his daughter's death."

There was a tense silence during which his mother got up and faced him.

"Are you sure you did not misunderstand him?" she inquired, looking him straight in the eye? " Are you sure? This does not sound like the Ndomawaa I have known for so many years. Did he really say both of us were responsible for Giita's death? Are you sure? Hindo, I know you. Sometimes when someone is talking, your mind wanders and later you tell a different story. I am your mother and I know you through and through. How could Ndomawaa say such a thing or even speculate about such a possibility?" She began to sweat and felt stifled. Hindowaa's answer only increased her stress.

"Mother, he said that many people in Talia and beyond think that because I am your only son I allow you to control me and that you put pressure on me to fulfill your desire for more grandsons. That this was what eventually led to Giita's death. Ndomawaa told me that people have even mentioned your determination to look for another wife for me because Giita had not had a baby for some time, and I, in turn, put pressure on Giita to have another child even though the ancestors had warned us that she had already received her quota. "

Kigba returned to her seat feeling even more suffocated. She would have gulped a cup of palm wine had her son offered it. Hindowaa, however, seemed to have forgotten about the wine even though the lovely, fresh smell pervaded the room. She managed to say,

"Hindo, ever since I was born, and that was a long

time ago, no one has ever accused me of such behavior. It is as good as accusing us of witchcraft. And that was what Ndomawaa said to you? I think such an accusation should come to the attention of our chief and the elders. My in-law-to-be has to be informed about this. I want to hear his views. I have never before been accused of being involved in killing anybody, let alone someone with whom we have blood ties. So what was your response to such a serious allegation, may I ask?"

"Mother, I told him that his accusation had legal implications and I would consider taking the matter to court. However on reflection, I said I would not do that because it was a family matter and it should be resolved within the family."

"And what did he say to that?"

"Mother, he did not answer that. There was much more he wanted to talk about that day..."

"You mean that was not the end of his attack on the Hindowaa family?"

"Mother it was a very painful day for me. I can swear and take an oath on my Wunde Society; that at that point I wanted you to arrive so that you could rescue me. I was alone and Ndomawaa would not stop talking. What really surprised me was when he said that people in Talia were concerned about the extent to which I had become a victim of your overbearing influence."

Kigba jumped up again, crying, "Ee-eeh, he actually told you that, Hindo?"

Midday was approaching and it had become so hot in the room that Hindowaa pushed the door open and left it ajar. " Talia has not disappointed me," his mother went on, her voice bitter. As she sat down again, she said, "Yes, this town has all sorts of people. They laugh with you.

They come to your house and eat and drink. You meet in social places and they talk nicely to you. Then the moment you turn your back , they stab you hard. Did he mention the names of the people who had expressed such views? Did he say he consulted our chief? He won't do that, because he knows the relationship between our chief and the Hindowaa family."

This was the second time she was mentioning a relationship with the chief through marriage and Hindowaa suddenly felt depressed.

"Mother, no names were mentioned," he said, thought for a moment, then repeated, "No. No names were mentioned."

It was only then that he remembered the palm wine and hastily began looking for cups, apologizing for his negligence as he did so. Kigba made herself more comfortable, her eyes glued to the cup Hindowaa was filling from the gourd. She was so busy drinking the cupful he gave her that she did not notice his dejection. He resumed his account of his meeting with Ndomawaa without sitting down himself.

"Mother, of all the things he told me that day, what disturbed me the most was that in Talia and beyond people think you possess something…something…something. I don't even want to mention what it is."

This information was alarming enough to make Kigba set down her cup and fix her eyes on him once more. To avoid her gaze, Hindowaa turned his back on her. The slump of his shoulders suggested misery deep enough for tears and Kigba hurriedly got to her feet again and gripped him from behind. "What is it, my son, what is it? Tell me."

For several moments, while Hindowaa struggled to speak, mother and son stood as if transfixed. Hindowaa was afraid that if he were to say the word, 'djinn', his mother would collapse, and might even have a heart attack. Then people will say I killed her because she had become too overbearing, he thought, feeling even more depressed. Finally, he came right out with it.

"Mother, Ndomawaa told me that people in Talia and beyond have come to the conclusion that you possess a... a... a...djinn and that is why, since the death of my father, you have never remarried. This is what he said, mother."

This time the silence was prolonged as if, like a child about to burst out crying, Kigba was taking a breath from the depths of her lungs. Indeed, she let out a wail.

"Aaa yeehjooh, Aaa yeehjooh. Nya bondaah yooh, nya boondaaah yooh! (My relatives, my relatives!)." - exclamations people uttered when they were in emotional distress. Hindowaa was alarmed by such a dramatic expression of anguish but at the same time, felt relieved that he had unburdened himself, and moreover, doing so had not resulted in his mother's collapse or even death. As she continued to wail, he held her closely.

"Mother, I'm sorry. Stop crying; it is enough; stop crying."

The last time Hindowaa had seen his mother cry was during Giita's funeral. Then, she had cried so much that her big, rather bulging eyes seemed to double in size, further accentuating their beauty. After a while, Kigba brought a portion of her wrapper to her face and wiped away the tears.

"So, Hindo, what did you tell Ndomawaa when he said these things?" she asked, her voice hoarse from weeping. She continued to mop her face as she waited for his answer.

"Mother, it is difficult for me to tell you how I felt when Ndomawaa said those things about you. I was shocked because I had never heard anyone in this town and beyond say such things about any member of the Hindowaa family. And for me to have heard it from someone so close to the family! Then when I confronted him, he said he was only repeating the views circulating in Talia. Despite this, I was still distressed because he gave me the impression that he, too, believed what he had heard. I am still convinced that is so. He went even further, hinting that people suspect you of having a a love relationship with the djinn, and that is why you have never remarried -- that the relationship existed even while my father was alive so he had to give wa, and that is why he died."

Kigba wailed again, "Ndupui gbeh, gbeh, Ndupui gbeh, gbeh ndupui, gbeh, gbeh (Child,stop, stop, stop…)." The taste of the palm wine lingered in her mouth, but it had become unpalatable. Hindowaa tried to console her.

"Mother, stop crying; it is enough. Please stop crying," By now, the room had taken on the atmosphere.of a funeral. Finally, Kigba regained her composure and said, "Hindo, I hope that you have learned a lesson from this meeting you had with Ndomawaa. I hope you learned a lesson."

"Mother, I don't understand what you are driving at," Hindowaa replied. He felt sick in his stomach when she went on to say, "You see, my son, if Kunaafoh had married our chief, do you think that anyone in this town and beyond would have dared to malign me like this? I tell you, no one would dare malign any member of the

Hindowaa family in this town and beyond if the chief were our in-law; and yet you continue to drag your feet along with your head on this matter."

"Mother, what would the chief do about an issue like this? "Hindowaa asked wearily. He had hoped that the matter of the djinn would have eclipsed that topic; but here it was again.

"Hindo, you ask me such a question?" Kigba demanded, her recent distress forgotten. "If our chief had married my granddaughter, and I told him that people were maligning me, he would put them all in jail. Even though we have still not completed the marriage arrangements, I am sure if I tell him what you have said today, he will take action on my behalf and bring all those concerned in this malicious gossip to court."

"Mother, I'm sorry, but you are wrong. The chief can only do things within the law. He cannot abuse his authority like that. Don't underestimate his intelligence. He knows his limitations. People have the right to appeal their cases if they believe that the chief has wronged them. There is the District Court, it is above the Chiefdom Court, and there is also the Magistrate Court and so on and so forth. Our in-law will never allow the chief to bully him. In any case, we have the means in our community to prove these accusations, so if we were to take legal action, the accused would engage those who can conduct the necessary investigations. You know that if one has a djinn that is evil, it can be proved. Mother you know that more than I do."

"Yes, Hindo, you know it all." Kigba scoffed. "You don't know book, but you know the law. Maybe you also have something which I am not aware of. I mean this djinn thing might be in the family. You don't know book but you know law. It is amazing."

"Mother, even the chief knows law though he doesn't know book." Hindowaa reminded her. " We have our own native law and as an adult you should know it so that people don't take advantage of you. I did not go to school but I know our native law. "

" I still find it hard to understand why you are so hostile to the idea of the chief marrying my granddaughter. Is someone bewitching you on this matter? Like I said, if my granddaughter were married to our chief, I bet you all these malicious speculations about me would not have happened. I would have felt secure and protected in this community. So as long as I am alive and well in mind and body, I shall make sure that our chief marries my granddaughter. As your mother, I shall continue to warn you not to stand on my way. It will not be good for you, today, tomorrow and forever."

Hoping to calm her down, Hindowaa pretended not to know that she had already carried out consultations on the matter. He said soothingly,

"Mother, I want to suggest a compromise, and please listen to me. I suggest you consult some of the wise people in this community and let them give you their opinion about Kunaafoh, a nun and doctor, marrying the chief. Think of all the people whose opinions you respect enough to consult. After you have done that, then we as a family can meet to take a final decision. Also, by the time you finish this exercise, we would have got the views of our ancestors. I believe that if we take this approach, we shall come to a sensible solution to this delicate family matter. That was why I started out by telling you that I am not challenging you. You are my mother and I have never challenged you on anything important. In fact, this is one of the reasons why people think you dominate me. Anyway, this is my suggestion and I would like us to sleep over it."

Kigba said in the same aggressive tone, "So now you are sending me to go around Talia and ask people to tell me whether my own granddaughter should get married to our chief. Where on earth, do you get these strange ideas? Where have you ever heard that when a family wants to give their daughter or son to marry into another family you should go around asking for other people's opinions. Or has Kunaafoh told you that is what happens in the white man's land? Maybe, to make things easier, I should tell the town crier to announce this whole matter to the people of Talia. Yes, that would be much easier, than having to go all around town. Let me tell you, Hindo. I will not consult anyone on this matter. I am telling you again: as long as I am well and alive, my granddaughter will marry our chief. Be careful, my son, be very careful. That is why you children of today run into difficulties. You don't listen to your parents who brought you into this world. Let me remind you that you need blessings from your parents if you are to succeed in this world, and a mother's blessing is very important. It is she who carries the baby in her stomach for nine months. It is she who goes through painful labor before bringing the baby into this world. It is she who takes care of the baby as it grows up - feeds it, and takes care of all its needs until it becomes an adult. If your mother withdraws her blessing and curses you, my son, you are in serious trouble. Doomed, forever."

Hindowaa was dismayed that his mother was showing not the slightest willingness to compromise on this issue, even though no one of substance supported her position. He even began to wonder whether the chief might have bribed her. Otherwise, why was she being so inflexible? However, after the meetings with his advisers, where the consensus had been that he had the final say, he really wanted to resolve the matter amicably.

"Mother, if we go back to where this thing started, you will recall that at first we all agreed that Kunaafoh would be given to the chief as his wife. Even Giita agreed to the proposal because the Hindowaa family had not yet given the chief a wife. We were all in agreement. However, that was before Kunaafoh disappeared... Mother, I want you to see the point I am trying to make. By the time Kunaafoh returned to us, the situation was different. I have told you that was the only reason I changed my mind. We can still give the chief a wife from the Hindowaa family, but not Kunaafoh. I have heard that in some other places in the world, it is common to meet men and women who are obliged to fulfill a spiritual obligation and therefore don't marry and have children. It is the same situation for Sister Kono and the priests. You have said many times how people have approached you and said good things about your granddaughter because she treats them and they get well. People continue to bless her because she has cured them of diseases which had been a curse to them for years. Because of all these things, people heap blessings on the Hindowaa family. Mother, I beg you, change your position on this matter."

Kigba was now into her second cup of palm wine and it was past midday. They would have to end the meeting soon and Hindowaa wanted them to arrive at some sort of compromise before they parted. He believed in the efficacy of parental curses and knew that a maternal one was the more potent. He was fully aware that that was why his mother kept harping on her suffering on his behalf. Each time she mentioned these things he felt a sense of remorse because he knew she was telling the truth; yet there was no way he could change his own position.

"There you go again," she said, "telling me about what people do outside Talia and the chiefdom. I don't even know where these places are. Let them do what they want to do. I have asked you to tell me where in Talia and in this chiefdom you have ever seen girls like Kunaafoh, and you can't. I have been to the white man's compound, yes, I have been there and my granddaughter is the only woman from Talia you see passing around like a ghost. All the others are white men and women. They are always dressed like ghosts. Tell me, since you know so many things about them, why are they always dressed in white?"

For the first time since his mother entered the room, Hindowaa smiled, wrongly believing that she might be prepared to climb down. He took a sip of his palm wine before answering,

"Mother, even though I don't know book, I know that in Freetown, there are other men and women like Kunaafoh. She is the first person from our own community to qualify as a nun. They say that is a very difficult thing to do. They say that some people who are not strong enough to be nuns, begin the training but give up because they can't stand the discipline. Mother, these people have to spend most of their time praying. They don't drink, and they have no business with men or women. The women don't smoke. They live a very clean life. That is what they told me. If Fanday were here she would tell you about the women like Kunaafoh that she has seen in Freetown. So, mother, Kunaafoh is not the only one wearing that white dress every day. There are many of them in this our land."

This information made no impression on Kigba. She said,

"So, tell me, if these people don't drink and smoke like you and me, what happens when they want to gain the favour of the ancestors? What happens? Or don't they pour libation to their ancestors? You just open your mouth and repeat what people told you. So these people don't have ancestors? My son, even if you don't know book, you can at least think like a grown man. Even at your age you accept whatever people tell you as the truth without asking questions. If you think like this, what about your younger sisters? How do you expect them to think? And being a man, you are supposed to know better. I am getting more and more worried about you, my son. I am warning you. Don't be influenced by people from outside. You are a man and you should think like a man. Let me tell you again: our chief will marry my granddaughter. I won't allow people from outside to come and tell me why she should not marry our chief. They might influence you, but not me. For me, Hindo, this chapter is closed until the wedding day."

With that, Kigba drained her cup and rose to her feet. As she left the room, defiant to the last, Hindowaa felt as if a large chunk of granite were hanging around his neck.

■

CHAPTER EIGHT

Whenever Hindowaa wanted to reflect on any serious domestic issue he would disappear without telling anyone where he was going or when he would be back. However, if he was going outside Talia he always told both his wife, Boi-Kimbo, and his mother, if possible. If not, he told at least one other member of his household. He even informed some people in town. As he approached Nyake's house some time after the meeting with his mother, he saw from a distance that the hammock was empty and felt as if something had pinched his heart. The chief had sent his policeman for him and he needed Nyake's last minute advice. He had decided that no matter what, he would introduce the subject of Kunaafoh's marriage that day and tell the chief why it was no longer possible. His stop at Nyake's house was brief because, as he had suspected, his friend had gone out. He hoped he would find Nyamakoro and her husband at home, or at least one of them, and tried to get there as fast as possible. On his way, he saw walking towards hm, one of the people he owed a substantial amount of money. Since he had no news about the debt for the man, he began to feel quite faint at the prospect of meeting him. To his relief, someone came out of another house and engaged his creditor in conversation so he was ble to make a detour and go to Nyamakoro's house another way. Her husband, Foday Tonkara called out to him while he was still a few yards away from the house.

"Ah, ndakei, biwaah, biseh."

"Ndakei, Foday, biwaah, biseh, biseh kaa kaa," Hindowaa replied when he entered the house. They shook hands warmly, each excited to see the other after several weeks.

"Ndakei, it has been a long time!" Foday exclaimed.

"Ndakei, biseh, biseh kaa kaa," Hindowaa said again when they had sat down in two reclining chairs. "How is business? You are always on the move, going from one town to another to buy kola nuts and ginger."

"Ndakei, alhamdulilah, business is good. This year has been one of my best, so I can't complain. Allah has been merciful as well as generous. I am hoping that the dry season will be even better... And you, how have you been? My wife has told me all about the situation in your household and, ndakei, I support you completely. Let me tell you this. As a trader, I travel a lot in this chiefdom and even in far and remote towns and villages, your daughter's name is well known. People admire her dedication to her profession and talk about how many people have been cured since she came from the white man's country. They are so grateful to have her. My wife told me that your mother came to consult her on this matter. She was shocked at the way your mother reacted on when she expressed her views. She said she had never seen your mother so angry and she was sure that if Kigba had the power, she would have beaten her up. In the end, your mother walked out on her."

"Ndakei, biseh, biseh kaa," Hindowaa greeted Foday yet again after listening attentively to his views on the Kunaafoh issue. "But, where is your wife?" he added.

"Oh, she went down town to visit Madam Tonya by the waterside." Foday told him. " She has been gone for a long time, so she must be on her way back by now."

Hindowaa was delighted to hear that. "Ndakei, Foday," he went on, "it has not been easy for me. I tell you as a brother, it has not been easy between my mother and myself on this issue. I am happy that your wife has told you about it. I have tried hard to convince my mother that she should abandon this idea, but she just gets furious with me. She even threatened to curse me if I continue to refuse for the chief to marry Kunaafoh. It is a big family problem. However, I am happy to say that my sisters support me and so do people like you and your wife, Nyake, and even Tonya."

"Ndakei, Hindowaa, what I don't understand is why the chief insists on marrying Kunaafoh. Even if she were not a nun, he is not literate; why does he want to marry a doctor? Is it that he wants potent injections?" Both men laughed so loudly that passers-by heard them and turned to give them curious looks. "Ndakei," Foday continued, " every dry season, there is a Sande initiation. If the chief wants more wives or new wives he can have them. Why should he insist on marrying Kunaafoh, who is a nun? That is what I fail to understand. I am afraid, he is beginning to show that he is almost as bad as his late father. He was so bad that when he passed away some people rejoiced. If it were not because my wife advised me against confronting him on this matter, I would have approached him and asked him to make another choice from the Hindowaa family. But, it seems that his mind is set on marrying Kunaafoh, the doctor. That is what I think."

"The person I blame is my mother. It is she who insists that the chief must marry her granddaughter. All my efforts at educating her on this matter have fallen on deaf ears. When I tell her that Kunaafoh should be left to practice her vocation, she just gets furious with me. She is the only one pressing for this marriage; everyone else in the family supports me."

"Hindowaa, tell me; I am just curious," Foday remarked, handing him a piece of sugar cane to chew on.

"Do you know of any illiterate chief who is married to an educated woman, a doctor at that? I'm asking because this is the first time I have come across a chief who cannot distinguish one letter of the alphabet from another yet wants to marry an educated woman. Why he is insisting on this I don't know. My fear is that he might not be too different from his late father. This type of stubbornness suggests a hidden motive. Otherwise, why would a father not think the way any parent would, under similar circumstances."

Hindowaa concurred. He was glad to hear Foday's views, but still hoped Nyamakoro would arrive soon. He was still apprehensive about going to the chief alone, and had begun to think that perhaps he could ask Foday to accompany him. He would have liked to discuss that proposal with both of them but in Nyamakoro's absence, decided to sound Foday out because he needed to be on his way. The chief's compound was always full of people, and he could see himself spending the entire day and even part of the night there, waiting for an audience.

"Ndakei, Foday," he said, "I am here because I am going to see the chief about this matter and thought it might be a good idea if I went with you as a witness. Having someone with me, might make a big difference to his attitude. If you don't agree to come with me, I shall go by myself, but I would really like you to accompany me."

"Ndakei Hindowaa, I have no objection to going with you, but I think you should go alone. The way I see it, this is a family matter and the best person to accompany you would have been your mother. Since you can't go with her, it is better for you to go alone. I know that if Nyamakoro were here she would agree with me... You see me," he went on, seeing Hindowaa's disappointment, " I don't belong to your Wunde fraternity but I respect its values.

Forgive me for saying this, but your real problem is that you have betrayed your manhood and allowed your mother to wear the trousers in your household. That is why you have all these problems. Your entire life is controlled by your mother. This is your problem. You have to make up your mind to put on the trousers like real man. Only then will your problems be solved. Otherwise, my friend, you will drown in problems...Oh, there she is! " he suddenly exclaimed, having spotted Nyamakoro approaching their house.

Hindowaa felt as excited as a boy who had been anxiously awaiting his mother or father. He appreciated Foday's bluntness - not many people would have been as honest - but he was happy that Nyamakoro had appeared at that point in the conversation. However, her arrival delayed his departure further, for she had come with news.

"I now know why the chief wants to marry Kunaafoh," she announced. She had taken a seat close to her husband and had begun to chew on a piece of sugar cane as hungrily as if she had not eaten for the day. Almost in unison, both men inquired how she knew.

" He was at Tonya's house when I was there and I spent some time talking to him because Tonya asked me not to rush away," she explained. "He never mentioned Kunaafoh as such, but I now know why he wants to marry her. You see, he wanted education. He wanted it badly, but their father was not an enlightened man and sent only a few of his children to school. The Chief wants to be married to an educated woman and his first opportunity to do so came with Kunaafoh. He doesn't know that nuns do not marry."

"So! Hindowaa, tell me, do you have any other educated girl in your family?" Foday asked. Hindowaa's face fell.

"Ndakei, we don't; but in spite of that I cannot entertain the idea of the chief marrying Kunaafoh. If he insists on marrying her, thanks to my mother's efforts, then what will be, will be. I have sworn to my Wunde fraternity and as a Ngombuwaa title holder that I shall not live to see Kunaafoh marry him. It isn't my fault that his father did not send him to school. I also wanted to learn book but my father did not send me to school. Is that good reason for me to marry a woman who knows book?"

"Now I come to think of it, I don't even believe what the chief told you," Foday put in. "If his father failed to send all of them to school, why is it that he, too, has refused to send all his children to school? What have the rest of them done that he is refusing to send them to school?"

"I know why, though this is female gossip," Nyamakoro said, spitting out bits of sugar cane chaff. "Don't forget that the chief has many wives. There are those he considers loyal and faithful. These are the ones whose children he has sent to school. He considers the others disloyal and unfaithful, so their own children are punished and remain illiterate."

This revelation angered Foday. He said forcefully, "That is so stupid. They are all his children. Why punish them for their mothers' sins. And who knows which of them will benefit him in the future? Why can't he punish the women he thinks are disloyal and unfaithful instead?"

Hindowaa, whose mind was occupied in considering how best to approach the chief, gave only half his attention to this exchange. Foday asked his wife.

"What was Tonya's reaction when she heard why the

chief wanted to marry an educated woman. I know she has no problem speaking her mind, even to the chief. And I know he respects her."

"I am glad you asked that question," Nyamakoro remarked and then laughed and laughed until she started coughing as if she were choking on the sugar cane.

"That Tonya is a terrible woman," she told her husband when she could speak again. "You know what she asked the chief? she said, 'Chief tell me something, Now that you have this desire to marry an educated woman, have you ever thought of marrying a white woman? And if I may continue to ask you, why do you want to marry the nun and doctor. Allow me to guess on your behalf. Her injections are very powerful. Not so?' " Foday looked a little embarrassed by what his wife said, but he laughed loudly and asked how the chief had reacted.

"He was shocked, I think, but he remained composed. As for Tonya, she was not at all bothered. She told the chief, and I am telling you exactly what she said. She said, ' You see, chief, when you marry a white woman and a woman who has gone to white man's land and learned their book, you will have the same problem.You will not be able to understand them when they talk, because they talk in their noses. How long would you want to deal with that?' That was what Tonya asked the chief. He was amused."

There was more laughter on the veranda at the thought of the chief not understanding an educated woman because she talked through her nose.

"The chief never answered that question," Nyamakoro told them, "but I could see that she was pleased with herself. She is fed up with the way he discriminates against some of his children. She says she has appealed to him about it many times but so far he has refused to listen to her. She is determined to continue to press him about it."

"My sister, I have been here for a long time," Hindowaa interrupted, getting to his feet. " The chief sent for me and I have decided to raise the issue of Kunaafoh today. I thought that I needed an escort for that and called on Nyake, but he was not home so I came here. Foday has advised me that since I can't go with my mother, I should discuss the matter with the chief alone because his proposed marriage to Kunaafoh is a family matter. Did you leave him at Tonya's?"

"We left Tonya's house about the same time, so he should be home by now. If you go right now, he will probably still be alone because while he was absent there was no one in his compound except for the few notorious people who will wait for him indefinitely. Those ones never say, 'Oh, the chief is away; let me go and come back.' Please come and tell us what happened before you go back home. In fact, let us eat together this evening and have more fun. God go with you."

"My brother, may our ancestors guide you," Foday said as Hindowaa was leaving. "Just state your case and don't change your position. Be calm, but firm. Good luck and I look forward to seeing you soon."

Hindowaa walked away, saying, "Nya wamaa, (I am coming)," He was feeling fortified after his meeting with Foday and Nyamakoro. So far, it had not rained and the sky was clear. So was Hindowaa's mind as he walked towards the chief's compound.

■

CHAPTER NINE

Those townspeople who were old enough to remember the reign of the chief's late father had many stories to tell. One of them was that he rarely had to summon his subjects because most of the time they assembled at his compound voluntarily. On the few occasions when he did summon any of them it meant something serious. Hindowaa remembered that when he heard that the current chief had sent for him. It had never happened before, so he was quite apprehensive. It was always wise to take precautions wherever crowds gathered, in case some people had come prepared to test the potency of their magic medicines on randomly selected individuals; so he had dressed in a brownish traditional cotton gown, trousers and cap into whose seams had been sewn several talismans and other protective items meant to ward off witchcraft, witch guns and any other means of doing him harm. And traditional protective shoes encased his feet in case he trod on any creatures of the night sent to attack him by witches. As he walked towards the compound, he wondered whether the chief would take him aside for a private discussion. Unless that happened, he knew he would probably be at the compound until past midnight.

"Ah, Kinie Hindowaa, biwaa, biseh." One of the chief's wives had seen him enter the compound.

"Biwaa, biseh."

"Ah bii lui, Kunaafoh?" the woman went on, enquiring after his daughter, Kunaafoh.

"Taanaa, ngi gahun gbuangoh(She is there and well)," Hindowaa replied, but the question increased his apprehension for he could not recall the woman ever enquiring about Kunaafoh since he started coming to see the chief. He felt even more nervous when all the people sitting on the big veranda turned to stare at him as he entered. However, he felt physically secure in his special clothes. The smell they emitted was immediately detectable and everyone, including the chief, would know that he was well protected. The chief was sitting in a reclining chair and, after a general greeting, Hindowaa went to shake his hand before taking an empty seat some distance away.

"This is where you found us," the chief said, pointing to the big gourds of palm wine and bamboo wine. There were empty cups on the ground so Hindowaa went to serve himself. He decided to drink the bamboo wine instead of the palm wine and poured himself a generous cupful after clearing the froth from the gourd. When he returned to his seat, there was silence as if they were all in a courthouse waiting for the chief's verdict. The person sitting next to him remarked,

"Ndakei, Hindowaa, you are well dressed." The man who spoke was similarly dressed, and was letting Hindowaa know that he, too, was well protected. Hindowaa understood the message and merely smiled as he continued drinking his bamboo wine.

"Ndakei Hindowaa, it is a long time since I saw you," the chief said. Hindowaa sat up and cleared his throat as if there was something stuck in it. He knew he would have to lie.

"Yes, chief, you are right. I traveled out of town a few times; that is the reason. As the rains are coming to an end, I have been looking for land to do my next farming."

"And did you find a suitable place?"

"Not yet, chief, but I shall continue looking. I want

to farm near a river this time to avoid the problems we had last season."

Again there was silence, for people did not talk at will in the presence of the chief. Proper decorum demanded that they look at him first to make sure he was not about to speak himself. Finally, one man said, "Chief, I understand Hindowaa's problem. I am having a similar one trying to find a suitable place to farm in the next season. But I think I am better off, because I have seven wives. If I do not find land by the river, I shall give some of them the task of fetching water, while the others work on the farm. Hindowaa cannot do that because he has only one wife. I would advise him to take another wife during the next Sande season."

When the chief smiled, the crowd laughed, though in a polite manner. .As usual, all eyes were on him, awaiting his comment, whereas he was wondering how to respond to the remark. Hindowaa wanted to refill his cup but he, too, had to wait in case the chief had something to say .

"It is not possible for everybody to farm by the river," said the chief, "but there is a solution to the water problem and all of you know what it is. It has been part of our tradition. I am talking about collective labor. It has worked in the past and continues to work even now that I am talking to you. If you offer labor to one person for two days then rotate accordingly, the question of whether your farm is by the river or away from it can be solved. Our ancestors did that from time immemorial and we should stick to it."

"Yes, yes, chief, you are right." Had Nyake been present, there would surely have been at least one dissenting voice, Hindowaa thought, but since Nyake was not there, everybody nodded in agreement. One man amused the assembly by saying,

"Chief, for my own part, I have never had any problem when it comes to identifying land for farming. We are lucky because our land is fertile - this is the most important consideration for a farmer. You have rightly said that our tradition of collective work has helped us overcome this problem of farming away from the river. Like my brother over there said, we should all marry many wives to solve the problem."

"Which of us, apart from Hindowaa, has only one wife?" another man asked. When there was no response, he went on, "It is people like Hindowaa who make the chief think we are not upholding our tradition of collective work. If you have many wives, the issue of farming by the river or away from the river does not arise. Indeed, our chief has demonstrated this. Let us all act like him and forget about farming by the river or away from the river. As for me, I shall take my fifth wife at the next Sande season."

Hindowaa's heart began to beat faster at this mention of wives and marriage. It was a subject he would have preferred not to be brought into the discussion.

"Chief, as you know, I am now too old to marry anymore," an old man put in. " My knees are not helping me and my hip is also a problem. I have to plan my movements. Bending down and getting up have become major problems for me, so how can I think of marrying? The Sande women are young and very active; one has to be careful, chief. My friends who are younger can go ahead and marry, and have as many children as as they can. I can't do that." Some people laughed but others felt sorry for him.

"Are you therefore saying that you have retired

completely from active service?"

That question came from somewhere in the crowd and everybody laughed except for the old man who said indignantly,

"Ndakei, how can you ask such a question? Are you trying to annoy me? Nobody retires completely from active service. I have served my chiefdom very well in the past and shall continue to do so until God retires me. But inspite of the way you are mocking me, I don't wish my fate on any of you the younger ones. You see, even when you are as old as I am, you still have appetite. You know how some women dress these days, unlike our own time. And look at the way they shake all their body parts as they walk."

By this time, the wine had loosened inhibitions and louder laughter burst from the crowd. Another man barely glanced at the chief before stating his own position on the matter.

"People, my own understanding is that when you get to this age, you need these young ones. They rejuvenate you. If you go for the older ones, well... you know what I mean. My late father had many younger girls and every Sande season he would add another one to the team. He died at an advanced age, so I have decided to be like him."

"Ndakei, I refuse to comment on what you have said in the presence of our chief," the old man answered.

Most people now looked at the chief expectantly, but Hindowaa stared at his cup. It was half empty and he was pleased that the gourds still seemed to contain a good quantity of palm and bamboo wine.

"Well, as all of you know, my father, too, had many wives; but it was not because he liked women," said the chief. "No, it was his entitlement as a chief. During Sande initiations, everyone wanted the chief to marry from their household or from their town. The chief could not deny such generous offers. But things have changed. Now, people even refuse for their daughters to marry the chief. You can see how small my household is. I think I am the only chief around who has only fourteen wives. Am I not right, ndakei Hindowaa?"

Hindowaa felt a pain in his heart as all eyes on the veranda now focused on him. The bamboo wine tasted sour and he needed all his courage to say,

"Yes, Chief, you are right. It is a good custom for our chiefs to be offered wives and we should continue it. As my friend here said, if I had many wives, I would not be so concerned about where to farm. When chiefs had many wives this helped with the labor on the farm so that harvests were big and food always abundant. I favor chiefs marrying many wives. But nowadays, those who know book are asking whether people like me can really afford to have many wives, what with the school fees, uniforms, books, and many other things parents have to provide for children."

The other men on the veranda were impressed by Hindowaa's answer and again waited for the chief's response. When he did not reply, someone else said,

"Ndakei Hindowaa bii maa yiingoh haah.(Hindowaa you are well dressed today." Again it was a message that Hindowaa should not even think of testing the potency of his charms against that particular individual because he would not succeed. Since the chief still did not appear about to speak, another man remarked,

"It is not always that Hindowaa comes up with smart answers, but this time I agree with him. I tell you, sometimes some of my children are sent away from school because of school fees or because their uniforms are old and torn. Sometimes, they are sent away because they do not have the books they should have. They send them away for many other reasons; and it makes me ashamed. I have been embarrassed so many times that now I cannot imagine having more children. Where will I get the money to send them to school? I would like to have more wives, but no more children."

When the chief still remained silent another man cleared his throat and said,

"Ndakei, people like you are behaving like those who have gone to the white man's land and returned with knowledge of the white man's book. How did our parents take care of us? Tell me, how? Don't you know our saying that God will not give you a load that you cannot carry? Don't you also know the saying that, however full a house is, a chicken will always find a place to lay an egg, and the one that says it is God who drives the flies tormenting a cow without a tail. Is it not God that gives us children? If you have only a few children, how do you know they will all be of benefit to you? I feel sorry for you people. Our ancestors must be turning in their graves to hear the way some of you talk."

The chief continued to listen silently to the arguments for and against marrying more wives. One man thought he had wrapped up the debate when he said,

" I have only one question for all of you. Tell me, if your parents had decided to have only a few children, would you have been born and present here today?" However, since no one replied, another man decided to take the debate in another direction.

"What I want to say, and I believe our chief will

agree with me, is that all of us, including the chief would have liked to know book, but education, like every other useful thing costs money. What Hindowaa and others are saying, and I agree with them, is that our means are limited and therefore we should cut our coats according to our cloth. Today, unlike the days of our fathers and grandfathers most of our needs have to be calculated in money. That is what Hindowaa and others are saying."

The man watched the chief carefully as he spoke and was pleased to see him nodding in agreement. Hindowaa was also pleased to see this and wished others would speak up in the same way. He was itching to hear what the chief had to say as only he could give the final verdict.

At that point, one of the chief's beautiful younger wives came in and whispered something into his ear. She made her way back, bowing and curtsying as she went, and the chief finally spoke.

"My people, this has been a very interesting gathering. I have enjoyed every bit of the discussion." Everyone became alert, Hindowaa especially, as it was the moment he had been waiting for.

"You see, whether one has many or few children and whether or not one can afford to pay for their education, for me is not important. To be honest, I would have loved to be educated. Because my father only gave that privilege to some of my brothers and sisters, he put me at a disadvantage. Some of my educated siblings even look down on me now and it is painful. If my father had decided that none of us would be sent to school, I would not have minded; but he was selective. To tell you all the truth, I have never forgiven him for that. Yes, I tell you, it pains me when the chiefs of this district gather for our annual meetings and I see how the educated ones conduct themselves. It makes me feel so inferior. One of my favorite uncles told me why our father discriminated among his children in this way. It is a sad story and I am only telling you because I don't want any of you to behave like that. You see, my father had about twenty wives and considered some of them disloyal and unfaithful. What did he do? He decided not to send the children of those wives to school. That was how, some of us were deprived of education. Unfortunately, we are in the majority."

Amid the sympathetic shaking of heads which followed this story, some of the chief's wives entered the veranda bearing food that had been prepared while the discussion was going on. Hindowaa's appetite for the bamboo wine returned after he heard what the chief had to say on the question of education, and at the prospect of food, his mouth watered. He hoped that after eating the crowd would disperse, but realized this might be a vain hope since there was still plenty of palm and bamboo wine.

Five sets of food had been prepared. One for the chief and four for everyone else. It was a privilege to eat with the chief and four people always ate with him - his Special Adviser, the Speaker and two others, who were his special confidants. This hierarchy was always observed when the four were present. When they were not, which seldom happened, the chief invited anyone he chose to join him. The rest of the assembly separated into four groups and moved towards their favorite sauce, whether it was was saaki tomboi (cassava leaves sauce), njolaa beetii (potato leaves sauce), krain krain sauce, or groundnut soup, which was the only one not cooked in palm oil.

Each sauce had been prepared by one of the chief's wives. That evening, Mendenya had cooked the cassava leaves using some deer meat Hindowaa had sent for the chief. The meat had been smoked and the sauce was absolutely delicious. Nyaha Nynde, one of the chief's younger wives had prepared the potato leaves sauce with goat meat, which had also been smoked. It was also well received by the guests. The krain krain sauce had been prepared with smoked fresh water fish, and shrimps. Like the others, that wife had added vegetables and other spices all prepared in red palm oil. The wife who prepared the groundnut soup was not that young but was also an excellent cook.

There was much merriment as they ate. One of the visitors teased the old man who had said he could not marry another wife because of his physical ailments.

"Ndakei, Joe Bongor, if you are too old to marry again or to marry a young girl, why are you eating so much of this stuff?"

"Ndakei, such jokes are not good when people are eating. You will make someone choke," another man remarked.

The joke was that the some of the vegetables used to prepare the sauces were believed to be potent aphrodisiacs. The old man did not respond to what he considered a provocation.

"Ndakei, Moininah, I see that you are really enjoying this goat meat like a faithful Ngombuwaa.I cannot remember the last time I ate in your house."

"Ndakei saa, I have warned you not to make such jokes. I mean it. Eating is serious business. It is unfortunate that times have changed. In my younger days, when people were eating there was to be no noise and no one was supposed to talk," the previous man commented amid chuckles.

When they had finished eating, the wives came in with bowls of water and started taking away the dishes while the guests washed their hands. They wiped their mouths with their clean hands since there were no towels. Afterwards everybody helped himself to another cup of either palm or bamboo wine and the chief, too, had his cup refilled. After a while, much to Hindowaa's delight, two men got up to go but then no one else gave any indication of being ready to leave, which was hardly surprising though disappointing. It was still early and having eaten very well they were feeling too lazy to move. Besides, there was still an abundance of palm and bamboo wine to be drunk. Hindowaa himself had not drunk much after the meal, thinking that it would be better to approach the chief with a clear head.

Not long afterwards, four other men got up and prepared to leave. They trooped out of the veranda one behind the other after shaking the chief's hand and saying goodbye to the rest of the company. Hindowaa wished the chief would now tell the remaining visitors to excuse him while he had a private audience, but he knew that chiefs did that only in exceptional circumstances. More often they would call the individual concerned into their bedroom without announcing it. That was always a clear signal that the public audience was over. However, the chief did not do that either; but it was still fairly early in the evening when the entire crowd left the veranda and only he and Hindowaa were left. Hindowaa moved his chair closer to the chief's. His anxiety had not entirely vanished because he still did not know why the chief wanted to see him, though he believed that it had something to do with Kunaafoh. There were several moments of uneasy silence before the chief gave a little cough and removed his cap. Perhaps, he does not feel threatened any longer, Hindowaa thought since he knew that the cap, like his own, was there to protect its wearer against any malicious forces. His heart sank when the chief addressed him as "Daemia"

" I sent my policeman to call you," the chief went on, "but he came back and told me that your mother said you were out. To be honest with you, I did not believe that you were out. I have heard rumors that nowadays you tend to hide because of your many creditors. Anyway, that is by the way and not why I sent for you."

Hindowaa's apprehension increased as the chief went on speaking.

"Daemia, you and your mother are aware that you made a commitment to me some time ago. You know what the commitment was; I do not have to spell it out in detail. I have not taken a wife for a while now because I wanted to have Kunaafoh first. Now, it seems as if I shall have to wait indefinitely ..."

To delay the moment when he would have to address the Kunaafoh issue, Hindowaa said,

"Chief, when my mother told me that you had sent one of your policemen to come and call me, I was indeed away from home. I had gone to inspect my traps and it was as a result of that trip that I caught that deer. I don't hide from my creditors; how can I? I owe them money and if they ask me for it and I don't have it, they will not kill me. This is not the first time I have owed a debt and it will not be the last time. They will just have to wait until I have farmed and sold my harvest."

The chief replied in a sterner tone,

"Yes,daemia, but you are avoiding the real issue. Your debts are a legal matter. When the time comes and your creditors demand their money and you refuse to pay them as promised, daemia, you know what will happen. They will issue summons and you will have to appear in court. Failure to pay will land you in jail where you will remain for a long time. That is not what concerns me right now."

Realizing that he was in dangerous waters, Hindowaa now hurried to explain himself over the Kundaafoh issue.

"Chief, if you will recall, it was long ago that the Hindowaa family decided that because we had never given you a wife, we would give you Kunaafoh after she graduated from the Sande session that year. Chief, you know what happened then. My daughter disappeared and was presumed dead. We mourned. Talia mourned. I still recall with appreciation the role you played during those trying moments for the Hindowaa family. Until she died, my late wife never stopped praising you and I am forever grateful to you; but, chief, having said that, you know that when Kunaafoh finally showed up, her status had changed. The whole of Talia knows this. The whole chiefdom knows this. Kunaafoh became a Catholic nun and that religion does not allow nuns and priests to marry and have children. It was not I who asked Kunaafoh to become a nun. It was not her mother who asked her to become a nun. It was God and our ancestors that called her to undertake that vocation to serve her people."

"Daemia, I have heard you," the chief answered, but his tone was dismissive. "Your mother and I have a different understanding on the matter, so I think that from now on, I would rather deal with her and not you. You don't seem to understand what is at stake. You see, daemia, one of the things wrong with our people here in Talia and beyond, is that we like other people's ways of doing things too much. We do. We even change our names because they tell us that if you want to belong to this or that religion you have to abandon the name your parents gave you at birth. You Hindowaa, you know that one of your names was given to you by the white man. Then others say because they go to the mosque, they have certain names from outside this town and chiefdom. We like things from outside. Even the way we dress now is what we are told is better than the way our ancestors used to dress. What is wrong with us, daemia; tell me, what is wrong with us? Now, you are telling me that Kunaafoh is a nun and therefore she cannot marry and have children. Well, as I said, I would rather deal with your mother on this matter."

From the chief's attitude, Hindowaa realized that his mother must have made a solid commitment to him. That explained why she was so inflexible whenever the question of Kunaafoh's marriage arose. He knew he sounded too nervous as he said, "Chief, I understand how disappointed you are, but we have decided that because of Kunaafoh's changed status, we will have to give you another wife from the Hindowaa family. She is a beautiful girl, younger than Kunaafoh, and as usual, a virgin. I have wanted to come and tell you that for some time, but unfortunately, I have been overtaken by events. I beg you, Chief, please allow the Hindowaa family to present the substitute girl to you at a time of your convenience."

He had even considered telling the chief that the proposed substitute wife had specific physical assets - the beautiful black gums, segmented neck and large, slightly bulging eyes favoured by Mende people, but decided against it because several of the chief's other wives were similarly endowed.

"Daemia,' let me ask you one question, only one," said the chief in the same intimidating tone. "You propose giving me another wife from the Hindowaa family. You say that she is beautiful, a virgin and younger than Kunaafoh. Good attributes indeed. But, you failed to mention one thing. Daemia, this other wife you want to give me from the Hindowaa family, is she as educated as Kunaafoh?"

Hindowaa found that question so annoying that his confidence suddenly returned and he made up his mind to stand up to the chief if he refused to compromise in this matter. Why, he asked himself, should he insist on an educated wife? Is he literate? Are any of his many wives literate? Was his father literate? Or his grandfather? The thought that it was his mother who had created this situation strengthened his resolve. She had no right to promise the chief that she would personally ensure that he married Kunaafoh.

"Chief, I can give only one answer to that question," he said."It is no. She is not as educated as Kunaafoh. In fact she is not literate at all."

In anticipation of a real confrontation with the Chief, his heart began to race and he broke out in a sweat. However, that was the end of the discussion, at least for the present, for the chief said, "Daemia, since I have decided to deal with your mother, I don't want to spend the rest of this beautiful evening on this matter. Your mother is more understanding of our culture and traditions whereas you seem to have fallen into a river and , as they say, turned into a fish. One day, instead of turning into a fish, you will turn into a crocodile, then

I promise you that you will be hunted to protect others. You need to understand what I am telling you."

Thus dismissed, Hindowaa rose and took his leave. The chief's hostility left him deeply troubled and as he walked into the darkness that peaceful evening, he wondered what the man meant by bringing up that proverb and adding threats about crocodiles. It was now too late to go back to Nyamakoro and Foday to seek their opinion, so he came to the conclusion that only time would tell.

■

CHAPTER TEN

The next day, a Sunday, the church bell started ringing early to remind Talia's Christian community that it was time to attend service and pray. Indeed, the faithful were already trooping to the church in their Sunday attire with Bibles sandwiched under their arms, even though most of them were illiterate. It had not rained for two days and as a result, everyone was in high spirits especially so because, unlike their experience the Sunday before, they did not have to balance open umbrellas, with their Bibles and other items. Though he believed in God, like his mother, his wife and their two children, Hindowaa was not a member of the Christian community in Talia; so he was still in bed with Boi-Kimbo that Sunday morning.

"When you came in last night you were upset," Boi-Kimbo remarked. "I realized that because you usually look happy when you come in, especially after you have had a few drinks. You looked as if someone had chased you with a machete."

"You are right."

"But where had you come from?" she asked.

"I was with the chief with many other people. In fact, Nyake was one of the few notables who wasn't there; you know how independent he is. He only goes to the chief when he has something serious to discuss with him. Most of us go because we are afraid that if we don't show up frequently, the chief will think we are planning something evil against him."

"Don't you know that it is not good to do things when you are not sincere?"

"You are still a child, otherwise you would know that in life, there are times when we have to do things against our convictions. There are certain unwritten rules in any society and you have to follow them in order to survive. You have to learn to play the game by the rules."

"Even if they go against your conscience, against your religion, and your ancestors?"

Feeling somewhat uncomfortable now, Hindowaa said gruffly, "No one wants to be on the wrong side of the chief. We go there to flatter him and say nice things about his late father. That man was one of the most wicked chiefs that our chiefdom has ever had, but we have to do these things."

"You think this chief does not know that you are not telling the truth? And why do you have to say anything about his father anyway?"

"I have told you that it is a matter of survival. Even our ancestors know this to be the truth. One has to survive in society," Hindowaa told her.

"Then why is Nyake not part of this deception?"

Hindowaa did not know how to reply, so he cleared his throat and forced a cough before speaking again.

"You will always come across people who are exceptions to the rule. Not many, but they are always there."

"Then why are you not one of the exceptions?"

"Because I am not," Hindowaa replied. His irritable tone left Boi-Kimbo feeling confused and, realizing that she would not get an honest answer from him, she changed the subject.

"So, if I may ask, what happened at the chief's place?"

"My dear, the issue of Kunaafoh came up again. Remember he had sent his policeman to call me. I went to see what he wanted but found many people already assembled on his veranda - the usual troop that visits him regularly. It was after they had all left, and only the two of us remained, that he brought up the subject of his marriage to Kunaafoh. To cut a long story short, I reminded him about Kunaafoh's changed status and told him about the Hindowaa family's decision to give him a girl who is beautiful and also younger than Kunaafoh. He refused the offer."

"Did he tell you why?"

"Yes. He wants a woman as educated as Kunaafoh."

Boi-Kimbo sat up and stared at her husband incredulously for a moment before saying,

"But why should he insist on marrying an educated woman when he is not educated and none of his wives is? Me, I don't understand this your chief. So what did you tell him?"

"It is not a question of what I told him. He said he would not deal with me on the matter anymore. That he preferred to deal with my mother because she is more understanding. He even threatened that crocodiles will eat me. He must be assuming that I am going to fall into the river; that is the only way I can interpret the proverb he came out with. So in the end, I left. And you are right. I was feeling despondent and frightened when I came in."

"So, stay away from the river, especially during the heavy rains when it overflows its banks. You see, I did not want to tell you this, but before I came to this your town, what I had heard about this your chief was not good. I never said anything to you because your mother talks as if the man is wonderful. I am warning you now to be careful. Me, I am not educated like Kunaafoh and not old like you, but I have common sense. You see, when a man is desperate for a woman, he can do anything to fulfill his desire. He becomes blind to reason..."

Feeling particularly close to his innocent young wife at that moment, Hindowaa said, "By the way, what happened between you and my mother the day the chief sent his policeman for me?"

"What did she say happened between us?"

"To put it simply, she said that you insulted her. That was what she told me, and she was fuming with acid anger. I told her that I found it difficult to believe that you would insult her. That made her even more angry, and she accused me of not believing she had told me the truth, and that I was taking sides with you. I told her that I wanted to hear your own version of what happened before taking any decision. That was when she accused me of wanting to try her in my own court."

Boi-Kimbo clapped a hand over her mouth and her eyes filled with tears.

"Eeeemmm!" she exclaimed. "I don't have words with which to respond; my mouth is heavy. Your mother...your mother, is a master storyteller. I wish my children were big enough to act as my witnesses because they heard all what their grandmother said to me. They even asked me what I had done to her. Eeeemmmmm! Anyway, since I have no power in this house, I will leave my case to God and our ancestors. They see all that is happening between you, your mother and me. And many people in this town sympathize with me. Sometimes even your sisters ask me how I am coping with your mother. She said that I insulted her? Astergfulai! (God forbid!). My parents did not bring me up to insult people older than me and of their own age. Me? Never!"

Hindowaa listened to this outburst without saying a word, because he knew that Boi-Kimbo had not yet given him her own version of events. She began to sob as she went on.

"You see, your mother continues to ask me when my next pregnancy is coming. She keeps reminding me that I only have two children and they are girls; that she arranged our marriage expecting me to have sons for you and that has not happened yet. On that day she started on me again and I told her that it is God that gives children and that I already have two lovely ones. I said if God wished me to have more, that would be nice, but if He decided that I should only have these two I would still be grateful to Him. It was at this point that your mother exploded, saying I had insulted her by answering like that. That is the whole story. I can swear to my Sande Society if I have said anything that is untrue. I can even swear by my children.If what I have said is not what happened, let them perish in a fire. That is all I have to say."

By this time, she was crying so hard that Hindowaa pulled her towards him.

"Stop crying, stop," he said. "I shall talk to my mother. I understand how you feel. I do. Many of my friends have told me that it is my mother who controls my house and even my life. I have tried to tell them that is not entirely true. I shall talk to my mother again. Let us get up. Don't cry."

Kigba had taken her morning bath, which was a ritual with her. She took a bath in the morning and she took a bath in the evening before retiring. Sometimes, during the dry season when the weather was steaming hot, she bathed three times a day. She was well known in the community for her scrupulous attention to hygiene; and it was a habit she had inculcated in her children, especially the two girls.

When Hindowaa finally went out on the front veranda, he found her having her breakfast which was rice and some leftover cassava leaves sauce. Its well flavored aroma filled the veranda. After they had exchanged morning greetings, she asked Hindowaa to join her, but he declined, saying Boi-Kimbo was bringing his own breakfast. It turned out to be the same rice and cassava leaves sauce. After serving Hindowaa's late breakfast, Boi-Kimbo took leave of him and and her mother-in-law and went down town with the children. As soon as they were alone, Kigba said, "Hindo, when you came in, I was awake. It was so late; where were you coming from?"

Instead of answering her question, Hindowaa said, "Mother, please don't misunderstand me, but just when do you sleep in this house? It seems as if you are always awake when I come home at night, no matter how late it is."

He knew it, was a sensitive question, but he wanted to prove something. Indeed, it did not surprise him when his mother reprimanded him at once, saying, "Hindo, you see, that is why some of you children of today don't live long. You don't live long because you disrespect your parents and your seniors. The way we were raised, I mean our own generation, well mannered children would never dare ask their parents such a question. Is that the way your father and I brought you up? Look how well mannered your sisters are. Everybody in this town speaks highly of their good behavior."

Hindowaa apologized immediately.

Kigba was now busy washing her hands and he did the same. A member of the household, came from inside the house, collected the dishes, and disappeared to the back, where she joined other women sitting under the big mango tree. Its outstretched branches, shielded them from the heat of the sun like a vast umbrella.

"You see, Hindo," Kigba went on in the same reproachful tone, "I am not going to live forever. That is why I have tried to raise you properly. And I have tried my best to guide you so that when I am not around anymore, you can continue to go through life with fewer problems. I am sorry to say that I am disappointed in you. But just you wait. One day you will see that it does not pay to be undisciplined. "

"Mother, I understand your feelings; that is why I apologized. As I said, I did not mean to offend you. I know that when people get older, they don't sleep as well as they did when they were younger. Even I myself I often stay awake for a long time after my wife has fallen asleep. I envy her sometimes because she sleeps all through the night."

After a short pause, Kigba resumed the conversation with a deceptively helpful air,

"I have decided to tell you what I do at night and why I don't sleep because if I don't tell you now, you will ask me again. Then, the next time, your wife will also ask me, and then it will be the grandchildren's turn to ask their grandmother why she does not sleep at night. Yes, I shall tell you now to make sure that you don't ask me again. After I have told you, you should then go and tell the whole town why your mother does not sleep at night. In fact, you can even pay the Town Crier to broadcast it for you. He will do it efficiently. Early in the morning he will tell people why Kigba does not sleep at night. You see, when night comes and all of you are asleep, I have a man that I smuggle into this house. I smuggle him into the house every day. He is the one that keeps me awake. You know that since your father died I have not remarried and it is the talk of the town. So I decided to have this man that I smuggle into my room every night. I hope that you now understand and know why I don't sleep at night. Do you want me also to tell you what the man and myself do that keeps us awake? I am sure you don't want to know that."

Hindowaa was furious with her for talking in that vulgar way and did not reply. Instead, he rose abruptly from his seat and went to lie in his hammock. However, ignoring his angry gestures, Kigba continued, "And now, it is my turn to ask you where you went last night and did not return until late. Your wife, too, was awake when you came in, but that does not concern you. Oh, no. It is me you are concerned about. Your mother who brought you into this world has now become your child to be questioned about why she stays awake. I should be the one to ask you where you were and not the other way around. A different world indeed."

"Mother, it was you who told me that the chief had sent a policeman to find out if I was home because he wanted to see me. I went to see the chief but found many people in the compound. I had to wait for all of them to leave before I was able to find out what the chief wanted to discuss with me."

Kigba listened with keen interest but instead of asking why the chief had wanted to see Hindowaa, she startled him into sitting up in his hammock.

"While you were away, some people came to see you," she told him casually. "You know them. I mean those two ingrates you call your friends, Gbapi and Kapindi. They sat here for a long time, waiting for you. They said they had come to collect the money you owe them. You won't believe that they refused to leave even when I assured them that you would not disappear for good. They said you have owed them the money for a long time and they are not prepared to wait any longer. Next time the other four creditors will come as well. My son, those men you call your friends are the most shameless people I know in this town. They were still here when the afternoon food was ready, so I told the woman to dish some up for them. I was expecting them to refuse it, but you will not believe this. They ate all the food and licked their lips right here in front of me."

"When did they say they would come back?" Hindowaa inquired nervously. That was all that really interested him.

"They refused to tell me. I think they thought that if they told me I would tell you and you would go into hiding. That is my own interpretation of their attitude. They only said that the next time they come they won't leave without their money. Tell me, where are you going to get the money to pay them and the other four creditors?" Since most of the debt was the result of the expenses they incurred by traveling outside Talia and consulting numerous medicine men and soothsayers in their efforts to make Giita produce more sons, she exclaimed, "Chai! Giita's ghost is still haunting this house!"

"Ah, mother, people are too complicated for me," Hindowaa replied. "I would never have believed that Gbapi and Kapindi would be hunting me like an animal for the money I owe them. I know their parents. My father was a friend of both their fathers. Apart from that, we grew up together in this town, went to Wunde Society the same year and became even closer as a result. We spent all our childhood together. You know as well as I do how our house has always been open to both of them much more than to the other four whom I owe money... The fact of the matter is that even if they keep coming here every hour on the hour, day and night, I just don't have the money to pay them yet. Times are hard.They don't expect me to go and steal in order to pay them."

"It is Kapindi that surprised me," Kigba interjected angrily. "Next time he comes here I shall tell him how ungrateful he is, and what a short memory he has. His father almost disowned his mother - may her soul rest in peace. It was only through my intervention that the matter was resolved and they reconciled. If he comes here again and behaves as if I am a stranger to him, I shall remind him about that incident and tell him I shall visit his mother's grave to let her know how ungrateful he is. Stupid man! With that belly of his like a bag of cotton. Anyway, whatever happens, we have to deal with the debts we owe to all these people. What do we do?"

"Mother, the rainy season is almost over. Look at the beautiful weather today. We shall farm, sell our produce and pay off the debts. That is all we can do. Where else can we get money? You know that since my brother, Kortu, died, his witch of a wife, Fanday, has never disclosed what happened to his money. I thought she would come and see me to say, 'your brother died and this is what he left'. Oh, no. She only showed up when Giita died. And your good-for-nothing grandsons, Hinga and Kafo. They don't visit us. They don't write us letters. They don't send us money. Hinga is a seaman. He knows the world; but what good is that? As for Kafo, he does not even have a decent place to lay his head. And we cannot expect anything from Kunaafoh.They say that in their vocation, they are not paid and do not even see money. That is why they get everything free. So we have to look after ourselves."

"I just hope that son of yours, Hinga, who is now sailing all over the world, does not appear here one day with a strange woman. Look at our neighbour's son who went to the white man's country to learn book and came back with a white woman. She and her mother in-law cannot talk to each other. What good is that?...But to come back to the debt issue, Hindo, we cannot rely on the farm alone. You know that there have been times when after farming and selling the rice, ginger and other crops we harvested, we were not able to make ends meet."

"So, mother, what we do is keep paying something towards the debt every year as we farm and harvest. Like I told you, there is nothing they can do to us."

He was so convinced of the truth of what he told his mother that he decided to drop the subject of his debts and discuss another sensitive issue. He began to speak, then, observing his mother's expression of distaste when he mentioned Boi-Kimbo, thought a drink might ease the discussion. He said, "Let us drink some bamboo wine together," and went to his bedroom to fetch the gourd and cups.

In spite of some tension caused by the memory of her quarrel with her daughter-in-law, Kigba was feeling quite happy as she waited for Hindowaa to return with the wine she loved. The weather was still beautiful and, as she greeted passers-by, she hoped no visitors would show up.

"This gourd is small, but I am expecting a bigger one in the evening," Hindowaa said as he poured the wine.

"My friend promised to bring one."

"Yes, mother, as I was saying," he went on, once they had settled down with their drinks, "I spoke to Boi-Kimbo about what you told me had happened between both of you. As I told you, it is not that I am deciding a case between you and her. That is not possible. I am your son and she is like your daughter. Even your younger daughter is older than her. Anyway, she told me her own version and said that there was no insult intended. She said she would never insult you because her parents raised her properly. She said she would never open her mouth to insult anyone older than her, let alone her mother in-law whom she considers her mother."

He had hoped hearing that would soften Kigba's attitude towards his wife; but it did not work.

"So what have you decided to do about it?" she demanded.

Her attitude confused Hindowaa who had hoped his explanation would end the matter. What did his mother mean by asking what he had decided to do about it? Do what about what? How could she be so unreasonable on such a beautiful day?

"Mother, I don't understand your question," he said. "I told you what Boi-Kimbo said about the misunderstanding between you because I promised her that I would talk to you. As I said the last time, I am not passing judgment on anyone."

"Hindo, your wife talked back when I mentioned the fact that she only has two children and they happen to be girls, and so far there are no signs of another pregnancy. That was when she talked back saying it is God that gives children and she has no responsibility for that. Is that not an insult? Is that not talking back at your elder, your mother-in-law. Your mother-in-law who arranged your marriage?"

"But mother, I want to appeal to you to look at this issue reasonably. You said she told you that it is God that gives children. She did not deny saying that to you. Are you saying what she said is not true?"

"So, Hindo, you are asking me again?"

Hindowaa went to pour more wine for his mother, and she did not decline the second offer despite her anger.

"Mother, I have told you in detail what Boi-Kimbo said happened after you told me your own version. I told you that she said she did not insult you and would never do so. I also told you that she did not deny saying that it is God that gives children. If that is what you consider an insult then I am in a difficult position because I, too, believe it is God that gives children and determines their sex. We have nothing to do with it. This is what Boi-Kimbo was saying. Do you really have a differing opinion on these questions?"

"You see, you are on the side of your wife," Kigba declared. "I am your mother but I don't matter anymore. When I tell you that your wife talked back to me, you avoid the issue of insult. Yes, I know that I don't matter anymore to you. Sons always disown their mothers in preference for their wives. Now I know that if Boi-Kimbo and I were drowning and you could only save one of us, you would save her and leave me to be eaten by crocodiles."

Having said her piece, she took a deep gulp of her wine, anticipating another refill.

"Mother, why are you talking like this? It is not necessary," Hindowaa protested, but she kept on drinking her wine in hostile silence.

Hindowaa did not know what else to say or do to convince his mother that he was not defending his wife, though he did not believe Boi-Kimbo had actually insulted her. And he was not prepared to condemn Boi-Kimbo just to please his mother, especially when he remembered the widespread rumors that she dominated him. In the end he silently went up to her and refilled her cup.

He was returning to his hammock when Kigba spotted Gbapi and Kapindi walking in the direction of their house. She was annoyed to see them; first, because there was still wine left in the gourd and she knew that both men would not refuse a drink if offered, and second, because she knew that even after drinking Hindowaa's wine, they would not hesitate to ask for their money. However, she had no choice but to prepare to welcome the men because they were approaching the house menacingly fast.

"I wish we were at the back and under the mango tree," Kigba whispered, and Hindowaa agreed. "I did think of doing that, but we were busy talking and it escaped me."

Turning away from the street, where the two debt collectors were now exchanging greetings with returning churchgoers, Kigba swiftly grabbed the gourd of bamboo wine and their cups, took them into the house, then returned to the veranda and resumed her seat. Hindowaa appreciated her smart operation 'save the wine', and gave her an approving smile. Though he wasn't pleased to see Gbapi and Kapindi, he was glad that their arrival would put the quarrel between Boi-Kimbo and his mother to rest, at least for the time being. He was tired of the way his mother kept on trying to create a wedge between himself and his sweet young wife.

"Awuwaa miakaa," a woman from the church greeted them from the street on her way home. She was one of Talia's regular churchgoers. Everybody knew her for that. They said that her father had been was one of the first pastors from Talia to head a church. Unfortunately, when she married, as the story went, she never had children with her husband and people called her a witch who had eaten other people's children. She remarried after her husband's death and Kunaafoh had cured her infertility, which was why she had devoted her life to God.

When Gbapi and Kapindi finally arrived at the house, Hindowaa was not on the veranda. Both men could tell from Kigba's countenance that they were not particularly welcome. For Kapindi, that was an irrelevant matter; all he wanted was to get his money back.

"Biwaah biseh," they greeted Kigba in a chorus and sat down without being invited to do so.

"Awuuwaa, wuseh," Kigba responded. Both, Gbapi and Kapindi noticed her coldness.

"Ah bilui, Hindowaa (Where is your son Hindowaa)?" Kapindi asked.

"Taawamaa, iyah kulihun (He will be back; he went to the toilet)," Kigba answered just as Hindowaa was emerging from within the house.

"Ndakeisaa, awuwaa," he greeted Gbapi and Kapindi and went to take his usual place on the hammock.

Kapindi noticed that, like his mother, Hindowaa's attitude was unfriendly. "Ndakei, Hindowaa, it has been a long time since we saw each other," he began and rambled on, "I understand that you had traveled. I was also away for a short time. My fourth wife's father was not well in the village so I went to see him. He has improved, so I shall go and bring him to see Kunaafoh at the mission hospital... I was told that you had a big kill not long ago. Unfortunately, I was away, so I did not see anything of it. Anyway, I shall wait for the next time..."

At this point, Gbapi intervened but, much to Kigba's irritation, it was only to continue this gradual introduction to what they all knew was the subject of the day.

"Ndakei, it is not every time that one makes a kill that one has to share it with the whole town. I have trapped animals many times and sometimes I just decide on the spot whom to give and whom not give. Maybe the animal was not that big. So I don't think you should blame our friend and brother, Hindowaa. I also did not get anything this time, but I don't think it was deliberate. The most important thing is that the chief got his share. Let us pray that our brother's next kill will be a big one and that he will remember those of us who did not get anything the last time... But that is not why we are here and we won't stay long. On such a nice day people will be visiting."

Kigba glared at them both, but Hindowaa replied pleasantly enough, "Yes, I was away.My mother told me about your visit when I returned. And she told me why you had come. Gbapi and Kapindi, the three of us have always been more like brothers, not just friends. Everybody in this town knows that. We went swimming, fishing, hunting, and did many other things together. We have always helped each other, so I am surprised that of my six creditors, it is my best friends – my brothers, who are now harassing me over debt. Yes, I understand that when one owes, one should pay. However, one can only pay when one has money. I have discussed the matter with my mother who is present here with us. She is the one who used to cook the cassava leaves sauce that both of you always said was the best you had eaten in this town…" As he had intended, that aside drew slight smiles from the debt collectors, but they grew serious again as he went on. "The truth of the matter is that at the moment, I have no money. I won't have it tomorrow, nor the day after tomorrow, nor next week, nor next month; not before the next harvest season when I sell my rice and ginger. So I appeal to you as friends and brothers to bear with me. Let us not allow this matter to break our friendship. This is all I have to say to you today."

Kigba was pleased with the way Hindowaa had made his case and she smiled at him as they awaited a response from the debt collectors, especially from Kapindi, whom she considered an ungrateful so-and-so.In typical Mende fashion, the two men asked to be excused for few minutes while they went outside to 'hang heads' with each other before responding to what Hindowaa had said.

"Mother, whatever they say, I beg you, please don't make any comment or refer to what you did for Kapindi's late mother. I beg you." Hindowaa told his mother as they waited for the men to return. Kigba had wanted to give Kapindi a tongue-lashing about his ingratitude, but promised to keep quiet.

As if the whole matter was a joke, Gbapi and Kapindi were smiling when they came back from 'hanging heads'. They took their seats and looked at each other before either of them said anything. Kigba had been sure that Kapindi would be the spokesman, but it was Gbapi.

"Hindowaa nginje, ndakei Hindowaa, muu ndiamui kee muu ndee (Hindowaa's mother, Hindowaa, our friend and brother)," he said and paused while both mother and son stared at him nervously.

"Hindowaa's mother and Hindowaa, we thank you

for what you said to us this Sunday," he went on. "We thank you very much. You said many things that are true. We are friends and brothers. It is true. It is also true that many people here in Talia regard us as brothers because we have a lot in common. We do not dispute that also. In fact, we don't dispute anything you said. Yes, we have been coming to your house and have eaten food cooked by your mother, our mother. We drink your wine, talk, joke and laugh. That is true. But it has nothing to do with paying what you owe us. Even within the same family, people owe debts and when the time comes, they pay back. That is as it should be. If you remember rightly, the last time, the chief intervened on your behalf and we agreed. You know why we agreed, yes, you know. It was because your wife had died and you were in a difficult situation. We said at the time that this could happen to any of us. So we accepted our chief's wise counsel that we should wait until you were able to pay back what you owed us. We have waited more than a year now. At least you have been honest enough to tell us the position. Our mother is present and she must be proud of your eloquent performance. So, we shall not make palaver with our brother and friend." Gbapi stopped for a moment and in her anxiety, Kigba could not stop herself from asking about the outcome of their consultation.

"Awuwaa miakaa," somebody greeted them from the street, making Kigba wish they had gone into the house to discuss this matter so as to avoid such interruptions. To her intense relief, Gbapi said,

"When we went to consult, we decided not to fight our brother and friend on this matter. No. We shall not fight with him. He has to pay six people and he has now said that he has no money to pay us. We also realize that we cannot recall people ever fighting each other over debts in Talia and even beyond. We shall consult with the other four brothers, and refer our case to the chief because it was he who counseled us to be patient. We understood then, but the situation now is totally different. No, we are not going to fight with our brother and friend, with whom we went fishing, hunting, swimming and wrestling as we grew up in this town. We have had a wonderful life together and do not intend to spoil it now. Hindowaa nginjee, kee. Hindowaa, this is what we agreed on."

"Kinie Gbapi, biseh, biseh kaa kaa. Ngewo ee mumahu gbeh (thank you, Gbapi, and may God take care of us," Kigba said and took over the rest of the meeting.

"What you have said makes sense. I know our chief. He is a wise man. I think that you are very right. Let us give him an opportunity to give counsel on this matter. Not so, Hindo? Do you want to say anything to your friends and brothers, Gbapi and Kapindi?"

When Hindowaa said he had nothing more to say, Kigba added, with her most charming smile, "Well, it is getting late and we have been sitting here for a long time..." They all left the veranda soon afterwards.

■

CHAPTER ELEVEN

Though she had not yet heard the outcome of Hindowaa's meeting with the chief, Kigba decided to pay a visit to the soothsayer at Gbandama to confirm what the medium at Taninihun had told her. The journey there could be undertaken only by foot, but took only half a day. However, it was impossible to know how long she would be away because once there, it might take one, two, or even three days, before this equally famous woman was available for a consultation. Unlike the last time she made a trip outside Talia, Kigba set off after midday, planning not to return before the following day even if she had immediate access to the soothsayer. Hindowaa, Boi-Kimbo and the children were not at home when she left and she had not informed any of them of her plans. She avoided passing through the center of town for fear people would want to know where she was going and took instead a less conspicuous route behind the houses, which eventually led to the footpath out of Talia.

She had to walk through thick forest but it was a well-frequented route as many people took this once-in-a-lifetime journey to consult the female medium. Her luggage, which she carried on her head, was light - only her bamboo umbrella and the few things required for such a short journey. As she walked along, her mind went first to Gbapi and Kapindi and how they were harassing her son and to some extent, herself. How she wished Kapindi's mother were still alive; perhaps that would have made him behave better. Yes, Kapindi knew he was being ungrateful which was why he had asked Gbapi to respond after Hindowaa had presented his case. Hindowaa had been right to tell them boldly and frankly that he had no money to give them and that they would have to wait. After all, it was the naked truth. Did they expect him to go out and steal to repay his debts? Hindowaa was also correct when he told them that people should not fight over debts and that the matter would be settled when he sold his produce at the end of the harvest season. After 'hanging heads' Gbapi and Kapindi had made the right decision when they said they would take their case to the chief. Kigba chuckled as she thought about that because she knew that, being her prospective in-law, the chief would never take any serious action against Kunaafoh's father and grandmother. The case would end right there.

Her mind then went to her in-law in Freetown. Why had Fanday not given Hindowaa some of the money Kortu must have left? They had no children and owned a house. What would she do with all that money? She could have saved their family from this daily embarrassment over Hindowaa's debts. Perhaps she should put pressure on him to demand something from Fanday; but what if she denied knowledge of any money; how would they prove that Kortu had left her money? She was approaching the only village between Talia and Gbandama, when two big baboons crossed the path, each clutching a big, ripe pawpaw. Though she stopped in her tracks, Kigba was not afraid, for the baboons were too busy to pay any attention to her. They look so much like us, she said to herself as she watched them disappear into the forest. Bitter thoughts about her son soon occupied her mind as she continued her journey. She was still baffled by Hindowaa's daring to challenge her over the issue of Kunaafoh's marriage - Hindowaa, the son she had breastfed, bathed and protected while he was growing up had now become a bone in her throat. Instead of showing gratitude when she told him about the pain she had to endure in giving birth to him, Hindowaa had continued to insist that Kunaafoh was a nun and so could not marry and have children. That reminded her of one of her greatest concerns, something she had never discussed with her son. It was whether Kunaafoh had ever been initiated in the Sande Society. If she had not been initiated, it would be one of the greatest scandals Talia had ever known, an uninitiated woman in the Hindowaa family. Even though it was a very sensitive subject, she promised herself that she would mention it to Hindowaa to hear what he had to say. How did one go about asking an adult like Kunaafoh, a nun and doctor, whether she had been initiated in the Sande Society? A way would have to be found...

She noticed people looking at her as she entered the town with her small bundle still delicately balanced on her head. She knew she would soon have to stop somewhere to ask for water or kola nuts, and as usual, she would be questioned. Of course, if she said she was on her way to Gbandama, then everybody would know she was going to see the famous medium and would then bombard her with further questions. Why didn't people mind their own buisiness instead of always wanting to poke their noses into private matters?

"Your face looks familiar," a young woman said as Kigba entered the veranda of the house she had chosen as a rest stop. Kigba smiled and told her her name, "I come from Talia and was married to Kinie Boima Sandy. He died a long time ago."

The young woman continued to stare at her questioningly, then after several moments, nodded, saying,

"Yes, I know you. In fact, who will not know you here? You are the grandmother of the famous doctor and nun at the mission hospital in Talia. Not so? We have been there a few times. We even stopped at your house once. Kooh; you have forgotten me. You have an only son, Kinie Hindowaa - Kunaafoh's father. Who does not know you people? My mother will be so happy to see you; your granddaughter, cured her of a very big goiter. She used to be very unhappy and people used to call her a chronic witch. Oh, we went through a miserable time until we heard about this doctor in Talia who gave powerful injections and could cure all types of ailments. When you are returning Gbandama, please come and spend the night here."

Kigba's pleasure showed on her face. She knew the other people on the veranda were looking at her with admiration and she cherished the moment.

"Who does not know the nun and doctor in this chiefdom? Tell me, who does not know her?" another woman said. "Muaa, biwah, biseh."

Kigba now became the focus of attention among the people on the veranda. The young woman, who had recognized her, went into the house and a few minutes later, emerged with water, kola nuts and a gourd of palm wine. Everyone's face lit up in anticipation of the refreshments.

"All of you, please don't rush away," the young woman said. "Gbandama is so close that if I shout out to someone there he or she will hear me. So don't rush. Kigba, I want my mother to find you here when she comes."

"I have not met you before, but I have heard all about your granddaughter," a man piped up. "It was my own brother who told us about her. His wife had stopped getting pregnant and everybody said it was because she was a witch. She suffered until we heard about the nun in Talia. My people, you will not believe this. My brother's wife was cured and started having children again."

The people listening were clearly impressed and Kigba basked in the reflected glory. It was another one of the moments she would remember for the rest of her life.

"Ah, I am thankful to Dr. Magay (Dr. Milton Margai, first Prime Minister of Sierra Leone)," another man said. "He was the one who encouraged us to send all our children to school, not just the boys. That was how I sent my children to school. All of them can now write letters for me and I know that one day some of my daughters will be like Kunaafoh and come and help us here so that we don't have to go to Talia. Who would not like to see their children, especially girls, be as successful as Kunaafoh. I never stop thanking Dr. Magay who put the idea into my head."

Kigba wanted to tell them how her granddaughter became a doctor, but not wanting to reveal the problem with her son, decided against it.

"I am also happy to know the grandmother of Kunaafoh," another woman said. "We, too, have been to the mission hospital in Talia. That was my first time of seeing a woman doctor from our chiefdom and what was more, people told me she was a child of Talia. I could not believe it."

The palm wine went round a second time as the woman continued to speak. "But tell me, why she is always dressed in white with something around her neck that looks like a snake?"

The question caused laughter which was followed by

silence because not even Kigba knew the answer. The woman had thought that one of the men among them could provide an answer since many of them traveled to large towns like Moyamba to sell rice and ginger to the Syrian traders.

Kigba said, "What I can tell you is this. Both men and women who dress like that are not supposed to marry and have children. I don't know about the snake thing she always wears around her neck; but it does not bite, otherwise she would not wear it."

As everybody laughed again, an old woman said, "Me, I have never heard about this. How can they stay without marrying and having children? No. I have never heard of this before." She rose abruptly, soon disappeared into the house with her cup, and never came back to the veranda.

"But where is the world going now?" another woman asked. Just then, their hostess's mother emerged from within the house, having entered it through the back. She was of average height and looked well preserved, though Kigba guessed that she was older than herself.

"Mother, look at that woman sitting over there. Look at her properly," the young woman told her mother who then fixed her gaze on Kigba.

"Oh, oh. Of course I know her," the hostess's mother replied after a moment. She went to embrace Kigba, saying, "Nyahapui, biwaah, biseh."

"You are right, my dear, I have seen your mother before," Kigba told the young woman, and turning to the mother, said "How are you? It is a long time since you people came to Talia. Yes, a long, long time. I am going to Gbandama and stopped by to drink water and eat kola."

"I just went to visit one of my friends. I am glad my daughter told you to wait for me... You look well."

"Thank you, and you; you look well," Kigba replied.

"How won't she look well?" one of the men remarked. "Her granddaughter is a doctor. How can she be sick? If your daughters or sons were doctors would you ever be sick?"

Everyone readily agreed with him.

"But my sister, I am curious. Why are you going to Gbandama?" asked the hostess's mother. "A trip to that woman in Gbandama always means that something is seriously wrong. I hope it is not a matter of life and death." Before Kigba could answer, she continued, "Anyway, I would advise you to sleep here tonight and decide whether you want to change your mind about going to see her. Other people have done that. She never sees the same person twice and you don't want to waste your one chance. Life is too complicated."

"My sister, I thank you for the advice," Kigba replied. "It is good, sisterly advice, but I have made up my mind to go on to Gbandama and try to see the medium. On my way back, I shall spend the night with you; your daughter has already extended an invitation to me. Thank you both from the bottom of my heart."

There were only two other people on the veranda who were also going to Gbandama - a man and a woman, both of around Kigba's age. The man said to Kigba,

"My dear, I had the same problem trying to decide whether to go and see the woman at Gbandama. It was not an easy decision to make. But let me tell you this, life is full of risk. If we had a different way of solving our problems, we would not use mediums and soothsayers. I started this journey asking myself, what I would do if another problem came up which was even more difficult than the present one. I asked myself that several times before coming to the conclusion that life is a gamble. That is why I am here."

"It took me and my husband a long time to make the decision for me to come here alone," said the woman, who introduced herself as Nyande. "If husband and wife come together, then they have both exhausted their once-in-a-lifetime chance. This way, we still have one more chance if the need arises again, because then my husband can come."

The three of them set off together. It had begun to rain, but only lightly, and they were protected by the dense foliage of the forest. The man led, followed by Nyande, who had a small suitcase on her head, and a small bundle which she carried on her back like a baby. Kigba brought up the rear. None of them had ever been to Gbandama before or even passed through the village on their way to another town, so they had no idea what to expect except that Kigba had heard that Gbandama was much smaller than Talia and had no houses with zinc roofs. However, none of them was bothered by not knowing anything about the place. All they wanted was to go and see the medium and resolve their problems.

"Nyande, will you be coming back today if you see her?" Kigba asked.

"That is what I plan to do if I am able to see her today. I have many important matters to see to. What about you?"

"If I see the woman today, I too shall return, but I might sleep with our hostesses, then continue my journey home tomorrow. You know, I envy you for having a husband. I am traveling alone because I have not remarried since my husband died. If he were alive, he would not have allowed me to travel alone, or he would have come instead. I could have asked my son to come with me, but he is part of my problem. He has put on big trousers and wants to challenge me. I am coming to see the woman in Gbandama to confirm some information before making an important decision."

The man had slowed his pace and so heard all that Kigba said. He was curious about the problem with her son.

"Nyapui, what happened between you and your son that you have decided to come all this way?" he asked. "It sounds very serious. Me, I have eleven children with three wives. I have eight daughters and three sons; the only problem with the boys is that they are like me. They like women too much and it costs money to provide the bride price these days. It is not like our own days when we paid bride price with bags of rice and goats and little money. Now one has to pay huge sums of money. However, my sons are very hard working in the farms so that helps. I have no problems with them and even hope that I have more sons in the future."

"So, why have you not remarried since your husband died?" Nyande asked Kigba, ignoring the man's self-satisfied comments. "Where I come from there is no unmarried woman."

Kigba had dreaded having to answer that question, but gave an honest answer.

"My sister, when my husband died, rumors spread that I killed him. Can you imagine that? Even today some people in Talia still believe that I killed him. Have you ever heard of a wife with three children from a man killing him? For what? What would I have gained from that? And to make it worse, they said that I killed him with the assistance of a male djinn. The town I come from is full of people with evil minds. Rumors and malicious rumors are a fact of life in Talia; but I don't care what they say. I shall stay unmarried until I die. "

"But tell me, if I may ask, do you have a friend, I mean a male friend?" The man was asking a question Nyande had not dared to ask, though she was just as curious.

Kigba had anticipated the question and had already prepared an answer for her traveling companions. However, she let a few seconds pass before speaking.

"You see, people, my reasons for not getting married again are complicated, so I don't want a male friend. People start gossiping if you are friends for a long time and don't get married, and I don't want anybody to propose to me. Oh, many men in Talia have made eyes at me but I have ignored them - married men, young men and not so young men. Even old men have tried. I have ignored them all."

Nyande, suspected that Kigba's real reason for not remarrying was that she did have connections with a male djinn. She was still good-looking and not that old, and Nyande had heard of such cases in other villages.

"You are unique in this respect," the man remarked. "A woman or man without a male or female friend is almost unheard of in our culture. So, why are you going to Gbandama?"

"I have told you; I am going to confirm some information before making a very important decision." She did not elaborate, and the man and the woman did not probe any further.

"In my own case, I am coming to Gbandama because

a woman in our town, who dislikes our daughter, has claimed that she eats people's children, born and unborn," Nyande told them, and when her companions expressed sympathy for her family's predicament, went on, "Yes, it is a big case. Our innocent child has been accused of witchcraft even though she has four children with her husband - two boys and two girls. Why would a mother want to engage in such practices? Why? Tell me. This other woman is lying. And we have been told that the reason she is telling lies against our daughter is because she suspects her of having an affair with her husband, which is another lie. You see how malicious people can be? But we shall put a stop to it. After I have seen the medium to clear my daughter's name we shall call in a medicine man who has the ngeleegbah (a deadly Mende charm). Before I undertook this trip, we heard that her family had sent a delegation to the chief asking him not to grant permission for the use of the ngeleegbah in the town. Well, we shall see about that when I return. We have to put a stop to these malicious people who go around making life a misery for otherss."

"My sister, I fully support you," Kigba declared. "She sounds like a horrible woman. May she die with fire in her mouth."

That vivid curse made the man roar with laughter, and even the aggrieved woman could not help laughing. She had never heard such a curse in her entire life.

"My own case is different but also very serious," the man now told them. "It is a family matter, but it has gone too far. One of my wives wants to leave me because of a certain big man in our town; but I shall teach him a lesson. What hurts me more is that my wife is doing this with the knowledge of her mother. The big man has been giving her a lot of money. I am going to teach them all a lesson. I shall make sure that man never again touches anyone's wife; he does not know that I come from a family of medicine men. When I get clearance from the woman in Gbandama, I shall then go to my mother's town and deal with him; and when I am done with him, ah, I tell you my people, when I am done with him, he will never touch another woman until he dies. Even if he sees a naked virgin he will run away like a hunted, wounded leopard. Money, I don't have but I have other things that can make money men suffer when they step on my toes."

Both women found the idea of a big man fleeing from naked virgins quite hilarious but they suppressed laughter because their traveling companion sounded extremely bitter.

"Why don't you employ the ngeleegbah?" Kigba asked him.

"No, no, my sister. With ngeleegbah, death is instant, so he will not suffer much. With this other device, you stay alive and suffer. You see, it is like having food, delicious food, in front of you but you cannot eat because someone has cut out your tongue. That is punishment, not instant death. Like you, I am coming to check facts before I go and deal with Mr. Money... What also pains me is that of all the women in our town, it is my wife that he wants. I have had so many sleepless nights over this. Well let him wait for me. I will make sure he suffers endless pain. He has been doing it to other people, but I shall be the last. I am going to clean our town of dirty money men."

"If he has money, why can't he marry a new wife every Sande season? Why does he have to look for another man's wife?" Kigba remarked.

"Indeed. But it is my mother-in-law that I blame. If

your married daughter comes to you with money saying a man gave it to her, can't you tell her that she should not accept it? It is themother who should warn the daughter against such things, but my mothe-in-law did not; instead, she became an accomplice by taking the money. Me, as I said, I don't have money but I have something that will torment that man's life for ever. Not only will he never again touch somebody else's wife, he will also lose the one he has. Let him just wait for me to return with my licence from this woman in Gbandama. I shall return home as soon as she finishes with me. In fact, my sisters, because of the urgency of my case, I am begging both of you to allow me to see the woman first. Please, I beg you."

Nyande turned to look at Kigba and in a chorus they told him that they would oblige. So he was feeling much happier as they entered Gbandama and began exchanging greetings with people and asking for directions to the medium's home.

"Alii miakaa," somebody answered, pointing out where they should go and wait. They were glad to see that there were not many people around because they had heard that sometimes the town was chock-full of people. This medium was known to have less complicated ritual procedures than many others, so they expected to be able to return home that same day. Kigba even began to think that she might go straight back to Talia instead of spending the night with her new friends.

The man was soon summoned for his consultation and as they waited their turn, Kigba said to Nyande, "If he decides to leave us after seeing the woman, we can travel together, not so?"

Nyande agreed and said, chuckling, "My sister, our traveling companion is very angry. Maybe, the woman is his ndomaanyaa (favourite wife). Isn't it better for that big man to die than to suffer the calamity this man wants to inflict on him?"

"My dear, how do I know, am I a man?...I wonder if something like that can happen to a woman," Kigba said. They were both laughing at this bit of naughty speculation when their traveling companion emerged from the woman's hut. His entire face and bearing expressed triumph.

"Everything is fine," he announced. "Justice is on my path. Thank you very much for letting me go in first." Without further delay, he waved goodbye and set off for home, leaving the two women still waiting to be called.

When Kigba finally entered the woman's hut, she was nervous. It was unlike any other soothsayer or medium's place she had seen in that it looked just like an ordinary room, without much ritual paraphernalia visible. Having welcomed her, the woman warned, "You don't come here twice; you know that, don't you? This is your first and last consultation."

"Yes, I know," Kigba answered. "Anyone who comes here knows that this is a once-in-a-lifetime thing. It is like death. You experience it only once. She kept looking around the hut, comparing it unfavourably with the other places she had been to, but began to feel less apprehensive when she remembered that many experienced people had mentioned that the most competent medicine men and women worked faster because they did not surround themselves with a lot of ritual equipment. Their traveling companion had come out in a short time.

The medium wasted no time in delivering her findings.

"I want to assure you that I have been where your late husband and your son's grandfather are. It is a very different place from here. They already knew that you were coming to see me and they are angry that you made the trip."

Dismayed by this blunt report, Kigba asked through trembling lips, "Did my husband and my son's grandfather tell you anything else?"

"Yes, they did. They said that before you came here, you visited another place. They want me to tell you that this consultation will change nothing. Their judgment that you should allow your son to make the decision still stands..." Smiling kindly, the old medium said, "This audience with your departed has been so easy that I shall only ask for my basic fee." As Kigba rose to leave, she added, "Since I shall never see you again, I wish you a safe journey."

When Nyande emerged from the hut, she was smiling so broadly that Kigba knew that she, too, had good news to report. She said to herself. It seems that I am the only one of the three of us who did not get what I came for.

"What was the outcome of your consultation with the woman"? she asked as they put their luggage on their heads to start on their journey home.

"My daughter has been cleared. It was all malice on the part of the woman who accused her, so we shall proceed with the ngeleegbah medicine to teach her lesson. I know that the chief will give us permission to use it because it will also warn others not to be malicious. That woman won't live long enough to regret the damage she has caused us as a family."

"Oh, my sister, I am happy for your family that your

daughter's name has been cleared over this dirty matter. I think people should pay for their misdeeds, but are you sure the chief will allow you to use the ngeleegbah after their appeal? That thing is so deadly. I feel sorry for her children."

"I was going to ask you about your own visit to the old woman," Nyande said, assuming that Kigba had also found her consultation satisfactory. The light rain that had lasted several hours now became heavier, but they were sheltered by the umbrella of the thick forest.

"My sister, my own situation is different," Kigba answered, making no attempt to hide her despondency. "I went to see the old woman for her interpretation of a dream I had about consulting my late husband and my son's grandfather. They say I should allow my son to make the decision about my granddaughter's marriage to our chief - she is the nun and doctor people were talking about."

"My sister, what is the problem? I have been to Moyamba many times and I have seen the white women at the convent school. It is well known that nuns don't marry. They don't marry and cannot have children. The same is true of the men who also dress in white like ghosts. They too don't marry. Don't you know that by now, Kigba? That is what their religion says. Me, all this time I thought it was something else."

"My dear, you don't understand. Before my granddaughter became a nun and doctor, we had promised our chief that we would give her to him as a wife from the Hindowaa family. It was agreed and all we were waiting for was her initiation into the Sande Society. Then disaster struck our house. My granddaughter disappeared. We mourned her because we thought she was dead. Then after many years, she reappeared as a nun and a doctor. I still want her to marry our chief because it was a promise, nun or no nun. Our chief, too, is prepared to marry her. Only my son disagrees, and that is the conflict between us. He is not my father to tell me what not to do. But when I put the matter to my late husband and my son's grandfather, they tell me that my son should be the one to decide whether Kunaafoh should marry our chief or anyone else. It is an affront to my dignity that my son whom I carried for nine months should have the last word in this matter. And it is plain nonsense."

Nyande had listened intently and though she kept her opinion to herself also believed that Hindowaa should have the final say in the matter. Her only comment was, "My dear, you are indeed in a difficult position and I am sure God will solve the problem for you and your son. I believe in our saying that a family tree can bend but will not break."

By this time they were approaching the town where Kigba had promised to spend the night. The rain had ceased, though the atmosphere threatened another downpour. "Muu kpokoh, muu kpokoh, maalooh." The women said goodbye and they went their separate ways.

Even as she was walking towards the house, Kigba had still not decided to spend the night. She was longing to get home but was also considering the possibility of more rain.

"Kigba, biwaa, biseh, kahun yeenaah?" The woman, who had been eager to see Kigba again, greeted her warmly. Kigba had put her bundle and umbrella on the stool near her and they exchanged small talk for a few minutes before the daughter appeared.

"Let me take your things into the room," she said immediately, but Kigba refused, saying that she did not think she would be staying after all

"When I said that I would spend the night with you, I was expecting my mission to the old woman to be successful," she explained. "It was not, and my heart is heavy. So let me go. When I have arranged all my business, I shall come and visit you again and even spend a few days. I hope you understand. My mind is not at rest and I won't be good company."

Neither the mother nor the daughter tried to persuade Kigba to change her mind. They accompanied her to the edge of the town, before saying goodbye. The rest of the journey to Talia passed quickly. Alone with her thoughts once more, Kigba relived her encounter with the medium at Gbandama. She regretted that she had not asked her about the world where the dead resided when she said she had been there. She wondered whether the woman knew any of the people who had died prematurely and then returned to earth. It was believed that such people became famous no matter what profession they practised. It had begun to rain and since she was no longer sheltered by the forest, she opened her bamboo umbrella and walked faster, saying to herself, let me go and hear what Hindo has to say about his meeting with our chief. I was not expecting that his sisters would support his position. They are children; they don't even understand the whole situation. I am sure they will fall in line when they see how I shall deal with their brother. Hindo has surprised me. I hope that it is not people like Nyake, Nyamakoro and husband and others who have poisoned his mind. His thinking is not straight anymore. He never used to be like this. How dare he defy me like this?

The rain was now pounding the bamboo umbrella, but having worked herself into a rage, Kigba was oblivious of it. When she finally arrived in Talia, she thanked God that she made the trip safely and returned home in good time. From a distance, she spotted Hindowaa lying in the hammock on the veranda. Hindowaa also saw her coming and wondered where she had been without informing anyone in the entire house. However, he dismissed that concern, remembering that he, too, had sometimes undertaken trips without telling his mother or Boi-Kimbo. And he also remembered his mother's indignation the last time he asked her where she had been.

"Yeea, biwaa, biseh, kahun yeenaa, biseh." He sat up and greeted his mother who had now entered the veranda. She leaned the bamboo umbrella against the wall and put down her bundle. Her grandchildren, Boi-Kimbo, and the rest of the household, came to greet her but did so without enthusiasm because they were always more comfortable in her absence. She went inside to change her clothes and when she returned Hindowaa greeted her again. Knowing exactly what subject of conversation she would bring up, he was ready for her.

"Mother, welcome," he said again as she settled herself on a stool near the hammock. "I hope you had a nice trip. Welcome." When she did not reply, he continued, "Mother, you remember that the chief sent his policeman for me and I went to the compound in response to the summons..."

"Yes, so what did you talk about?" Kigba answered so curtly that Hindowaa realized that she was in a foul mood. He would have to be careful how he spoke to her.

"We discussed the subject of him marrying Kunaafoh.

I reminded him about Kunaafoh's changed status and that we had decided to give him another woman from the Hindowaa family. I told him that the girl is beautiful, younger than Kunaafoh and above all, innocent."

"And what did he say?"

"He asked me whether the girl was educated, and I said no. Then he dismissed me, saying that he would rather deal with you on this matter. But that did not bother me so much as when he told me that when I fall into a river, I turn into a fish."

Kigba wanted to laugh, but restrained herself as Hindowaa went on.

"The chief said something else that really worried me, mother. He said that one day I will fall into a river and instead of turning into a fish, I will turn into a crocodile and when that happens I shall be hunted down for the safety of others., What do you think he meant by that?"

"I am glad our chief dismissed you the way he did," Kigba told him. "He thinks it is a waste of his time to discuss this matter with you and I fully agree with him. As for the proverb, that is how chiefs talk and they assume that intelligent people will understand and act accordingly. In your own case, since this madness has entered your head, you are not capable of understanding. What the chief meant was that when a crocodile is in the river, people cannot bathe and swim in the water; so to make the water safe, you get rid of the crocodile. You better watch out. He is saying it will only be safe for him to marry Kunaafoh with you out of the way. That is my own interpretation of what he told you. Hindo, I can see you having to run away from this town, so you should listen to people who are older than you. But since you are now crazy, you will not listen to me and behave accordingly."

"But mother, do you think that it was nice of the chief to make such comments?"

"Hindo, it was the chief that made the comments, so go and ask him. Don't ask me. I am not the chief," Kigba answered irritably.

Hindowaa wished he had some palm wine to offer her, but there was not a single drop in the house though he was still expecting a delivery. He was relieved when Boi-Kimbo appeared on the veranda and announced that their food was ready.

Kigba decided to have hers indoors, but Hindowaa waited for Boi-Kimbo to bring his to the veranda. He was still hoping for a gourd of palm wine but, as rain continued to pour down on Talia with a vengeance, a delivery seemed unlikely. He turned his attention to the delicious potato leaves sauce. Boi-Kimbo had prepared it the way his late wife, Giita, had taught her and Hindowaa did it justice that wet evening.

■

CHAPTER TWELVE

Women visitors to the chief's compound were a rarity, and those who came usually had problems they wanted the chief to solve for them. Young men visited the compound in the evenings after returning from their farms. They took their baths and ate at home, before deciding to go and visit the chief; so for the most part, his regular morning visitors were Talia's elderly men. They usually arrived at the compound soon after the younger people had left for the farms, and stayed on, talking and eating with the chief. Some of them went to their farms later in the morning, while others waited for the afternoon meals. The chief's many wives knew his regular visitors well. They knew the ones who ate every bit of food in the bowl, not leaving even a grain of rice or a piece of bone for the children. They knew the ones who always waited until the last drop of wine had been drunk before they left the compound. They knew the ones who sent the chief only strips of meat from their hunt, those whose wives were devoted to them and those whose wives carried on with other men. They sometimes gossiped about the visitors, laughing and joking about them while they were doing the cooking or some other chores. Sometimes, when they were in high spirits, they even composed songs about the visitors.

On this particular day, the six men who came to the compound in the morning were of Hindowaa's generation. They came in the morning and not in the evening because they had something so important to see the chief about that they decided to delay going to their farms. They brought no palm wine or meat for the chief that day though they had done so before and would continue to do so. That day was different. The last time they had come to see the chief as a group was soon after Giita passed away. Then, it was the chief who had summoned them to ask that they wait for a more appropriate time before trying to collect the money Hindowaa owed them. The chief had appealed to them, saying that Hindowaa had had to spend a lot of money before, during and after Giita's death. They had heeded his appeal and waited but since that time, Hindowaa had paid not a single penny, shilling or pound to any of them. These were the men who arrived that morning to see the chief. They had sent him no prior notice of their visit because people didn't usually give him notice; they just came to the compound. Most of the time they found the chief at home, usually on the veranda, either sitting in his reclining chair or lying in his big hammock which was different from all other hammocks in Talia. His father and grandfather had used the same hammock and chair and the only other persons who ever did so were his senior wife and the latest, favourite wife. None of the chief's visitors would have dared to use either the royal reclining chair or the hammock.

"Mahei, biwaa, biseh. Biseh. Kahun yeenaa, (Chief, good morning, how are you?)" The six men greeted him in a chorus, bowing slightly -- a sign of respect accorded the elderly and dignitaries.

"Awuwaah, awuuseh." The Chief returned their greetings collectively. "It has been a while since I saw the six of you in my compound at the same time. What brings you here again today? I hope it is not for the same reason; I remember how hard it was for me to convince you to postpone trying to recover the long overdue debt that Hindowaa owed all of you. I hope that he has now repaid all of you and that you are here about something else."

Delighted that the chief remembered what had brought them all to the compound before, the men glanced at each other and waited for their spokesman to respond. This time, it was Kapindi. He cleared his throat as if it was itching, looked towards the chief, who was sitting directly opposite him, and lowering his head slightly, said,

"Chief , we thank you for receiving us this morning. We met last night to decide on the best time to come and see you. We decided not to come too early because we knew you would be in bed resting."

"Oh, I wake up very early in the morning," the chief interrupted. "The only person who gets up earlier than me is my wife. I wake up early in the morning and pray, and I don't go back to bed after that. No. I wake up early. If you had come even two hours earlier, you would have found me sitting right here. Ask any of my wives; they know that about me. I go to bed late but wake up early... Carry on, carry on..."

"Chief, let me start by thanking you on behalf of my brothers and friends who asked me to talk on their behalf as well as mine. I thank you very much for granting us audience. We will not take up much of your time because we know that our elders will be coming to visit you very soon, and we, too, want to get on with our usual activities...Chief, you will recall that the last time the six of us were here, it was you who summoned us to plead for Hindowaa, our friend and brother, who owed us a substantial amount of money. You asked us on compassionate grounds to give him some more time to pay his debts. Chief, if you had not personally intervened, we would have taken legal action against him. We are here today because we have still not been able to recover our money from Hindowaa, Each time we go to his house to collect the debt, they say he is not at home. Somebody has even said that maybe he has decided to become a ndogbowuussu, and live permanently in the bush. Chief, I am sorry to say this, but the entire household of the Hindowaa family, including his mother, your future in-law, seems to be involved in hiding him from us. We have now lost patience with Hindowaa and we are here to seek your advice since you are our wise chief. I thank you for listening to me and please forgive me for talking so much."

"Thank you, Kapindi. Thank you," the chief replied. "You have eloquently presented your case on behalf of your friends and I have heard you. I can see that in the future, you will make a very good Speaker (Deputy Paramount Chief). Do you know that you are next in line for that post? Yes, you are next in line."

At this Kapindi's friends laughed and clapped, while he beamed with pleasure.

"Let me tell you what I am going to do," the chief went on. "I shall summon both Hindowaa and his mother and tell them exactly what you have told me. I shall tell them that they should come up with the money Hindowaa owes you and within a certain time. If the money is not forthcoming, then you have the right to take legal action. I shall do it soon. How long do you want me to give him?"

The question was unexpected and the six men looked at each other in embarrassed silence.

"All right, go out and 'hang heads', then tell me when you want Hindowaa to pay back all the money he owes you," the chief told them, and they trooped out of the veranda.

Since they did not want to waste any more of the chief's time, they soon returned and Kapindi resumed his seat. Before speaking, he coughed a little and cleared his throat, putting his hand to his mouth each time to avoid saliva escaping.

"Chief, we have decided to give our brother and friend one month to come up with the money."

"That is very reasonable, considering how long it has been since Hindowaa borrowed the money. I shall get in touch with his mother and hope he will agree to come out of the bush."

As they chuckled together, the men prepared to rise to their feet. Kapindi said, "Chief, we must now take our leave so that we can go and inspect our traps and do some work on the farm..."

"But, my people, how can you do this to me?" the chief objected jovially. The men settled down again. "All of you know my morning program. Share my breakfast before you go; you will be able to work much harder, instead of yawning with hunger every few minutes. You know the saying that an empty rice bag cannot stand."

They laughed deferentially and stayed until after breakfast.

****

A woman called Mbalu was one of the creditors' wives. She had been close to the deceased Giita and was one of the few friends who had maintained contact with Hindowaa and his mother, though she was not particularly fond of either of them. She always said she was doing it for Giita's children -- Kunaafoh and the twins.

The next day, having heard the outcome of her husband and his friends' audience with the chief, she visited Hindowaa and his mother unannounced.

"I have come to see both of you secretly," she told mother and son, lowering her voice after the usual exchange of greetings. Kigba and Hindowaa detected a degree of urgency in Mbalu's voice and took her into Kigba's room. Having invited her to sit down on the stool, Kigba sat tensely on her bed while Hindowaa remained standing with his hands on his hips.

"I don't have time to go into the details," Mbalu told them hurriedly. "My husband and the other five that Hindowaa owes money went to see the chief yesterday and they decided that if after one month if you have not repaid all the money, they will take legal action against you with the possibility of jail -- don't rule out having to pawn your house and your farm. My friends, it is just a month from now. The chief will be summoning both of you anytime now to tell you about their decision. I have come to warn you for the sake of Giita's children. I have tried talking to my husband on your behalf, but he says the problem is with Kapindi and Gbapi."

After Mbalu's departure, the seriousness of their situation began to weigh heavily on both mother and son, for the one month deadline seemed menacingly close. Pawning property was tantamount to being regarded as a slave and it was an idea repugnant to any Mende man or woman.

"It was good of Mbalu to come and warn us," Kigba remarked afterwards and as Hindowaa concurred, went on, "This is how I see it. We wait until the chief summons us. We go to the compound and after listening to him, tell him that we cannot repay the money under the present circumstances. Let us be very frank with him; he should understand our position better than anyone else in this town and I believe that he is a wise man. So let us not make any hasty move that could make the situation worse. People are already spreading rumors that you spend half of your time in hiding, as if you have committed murder here. When this is all over, I shall deal with them all one by one. They are all a bunch of hypocrites. Look at that Kapindi, with his belly like a bag of cotton; he is the worst of the lot. What did we did to him, Hindo, that he should behave like that? What did you do to him? Because one can never be sure with you men. Were you rivals over a woman?"

"Mother, I can swear on my Wunde Society and your breast milk in my stomach that I have not done anything bad to Kapindi and the rest of them. I keep my distance and have tried not to involve myself in any of their escapades. One day when all this is over, I shall sit down and talk to them man-to-man. This crisis will end one way or the other. Every problem has a solution."

Temporarily united over the debt issue, mother and son looked at each other in somber silence. This was a serious challenge to the dignity of the Hindowaa family.

Nyake had heard about developments in the Hindowaa household regarding the debt situation. He had foreseen that Hindowaa would one day run into problems, because he knew how much money he had borrowed when he was traveling all over the country trying to help Giita to have more sons. Nyake had not supported Hindowaa and thought he was wasting far too much money. He had told Hindowaa that he should marry more women to improve his chances of having more sons, but his friend had paid more attention to his mother's advice.

Nyake was lying in his hammock, smoking his pipe that evening, when he saw Hindowaa approaching and knew that his friend was coming to see him about the debt issue. Hindowaa looked morose as he entered the house and greeted him.

"Eeeemmm, Ndakei, biwaa, biseh, kahun yeenaah," Nyake responded. "Aah bi'nje (How is your mother)?"

"Taa peelaah, ngi gahun gbuango (She is at home and she is well)," Hindowaa replied as he sat down close to Nyake. He was certain that Nyake already knew the debt problem, but nevertheless told him,

"Ndakei, do you know that Kapindi, Gbapi and others went to see the chief about the debt I owe them. First, Kapindi and Gbapi came to my house. They found my mother and me at home and told me that they had come to ask for their money. I told them that I was not denying the debt but that I did not yet have the money and would pay them when I sell my produce after the next harvest. They both went outside to hang heads and came back to tell me that they were going to put their case to the chief. I understand they have now done so and that the chief intends to summon my mother and myself."

"When?" Nyake asked.

"My brother, I don't know, but I shall not be traveling out until he calls us. He summoned me once before about Kunaafoh and this marriage business. He wanted to know when we would start the proceedings. I told him about Kunaafoh's changed status and that we would give him another woman from the Hindowaa family, more beautiful, younger, untouched..."

"What did he say?" Nyake asked, chuckling.

"He asked me if the girl was educated like Kunaafoh and I told him that the girl was not literate at all,"

Hindowaa replied. "Ndakei, do you know that the chief took offence and told me he would not deal with me anymore on the matter? He said he would only deal with my mother, because I have fallen into water and have turned into a fish. Yes, he said I have turned into a fish. What worried me was when he aslo said that one day when I fall into the river, I shall turn into a crocodile and then I will be hunted out of the river for the safety of others. My mother seemed to agree with what the chief said. And she believed that he was making an indirect threat."

Nyake had not interrupted the narrative to offer Hindowaa any palm wine or kola nuts; he had continued smoking his pipe as he listened. When Hindowaa stopped speaking, he left him alone on the veranda and disappeared into the house for several minutes. Hindowaa wondered what he was up to. Though he knew Nyake could be painfully blunt, he was anxious to hear his opinion on this matter.

"Ndakei Hindowaa," Nyake said as he returned to his hammock, "you have raised two issues. Regarding the one about Kunaafoh marrying the chief, you already know my views. As for the debt issue, you know that you have owed these people money for a very long time. To be honest with you, to ask them to wait until after the next harvest, is not acceptable. You cannot be sure that you will have enough produce to sell to pay all the debts. Think about it; we are all farmers. It is not every year that your harvest is abundant. If they had agreed for the debts to be paid next season and your harvest fell short, what would you do again, tell them to wait for the next season? My own advice would be for you to consult with your mother and come up with a realistic solution to the problem."

"Ndakei, I see your point, but my mother and I have considered all possible means of getting the money. We just cannot find a solution. My older children, the two boys, are no good. When my brother Kortu died, I thought that he had left a lot of money because he was in the army and had fought the white man's war. Later, he worked in the railway and his wife, too, was in business. My sons believed that their uncle and aunt were quite rich, but my sister-in-law, Fanday, never gave us a penny after my brother died. Believe me, we have considered every possibility."

"I have heard you and I am sorry, but I don't support you in this matter. Ndakei, do you know why this debt business suddenly came up with such a vengeance? Let me tell you why. Do you remember when Kapindi and Gbapi went to see you about their money and they found you and your mother at home? Hindowaa, the way you talked to them in the presence of your mother was bad. You did not show any humility. After all, whether you like it or not, it is you that owe them money, not the other way around. It was the way you spoke to them that made them take the action they did. I am surprised that your mother tolerated the way you spoke to them. Is it because Kigba thinks that the chief is going to marry Kunaafoh that she allowed you to challenge Kapindi and Gbapi? I only hope that in the end the matter will be resolved without bringing pain to anyone."

Just then, Nyake's third wife appeared on the veranda with a gourd of palm wine and two cups, and poured them drinks.

"Now, I understand why they have taken such an action. I have to admit that I spoke to Kapindi and Gbapi in a harsh manner. But I had a good reason. I was angry with them. They are very ungrateful, Nyake. You know the bond between those people and me. We grew up in this town together. They have been to my house countless times, have eaten my food and drunk my drink, yet they have been harassing me as if I am going to run away from this town. That was why Ispoke to them the way I did."

"Yes, Ndakei Hindowaa, I understand what you have just said, but the fact still remains that it is you who owe them money. Ndakei, even me, if you had owed me money and talked to me like that I would have taken action even if I had eaten every day in your house and drunk your wine. I would have demanded payment and if my money was not forthcoming I would have taken legal action. Let us be frank with each other."

Hindowaa was not surprised by Nyake's attitude, but he wasn't pleased.

"Ndakei, Nyake, now that I have told you that I have exhausted all means of getting the money, what do you expect me to do? I have been frank. For now, I don't have the money. Can you lend me all of it and allow me to pay you over a reasonable period of time?"

He was actually teasing Nyake and even as he spoke, his friend began to laugh.

"Let me also be honest with you, ndakei Hindowaa," he said. "The only people who could give you that amount of money here in Talia are either the chief or Nyamakoro and her husband, because they are business people. But I understand that business people don't easily part with their money, and besides that, Nyamakoro and her husband come from a Jeelibah clan. They are very stingy people when it comes to money. Another problem is that your mother has already antagonized them over the Kunaafoh affair. If you cannot get the money, then be ready to appear in court. What I advise is that you wait and hear what the chief has to tell you and your mother. That is my advice, my friend and brother."

"Ndakei Nyake, I agree with you. It is better for us to wait and hear what the chief has to say before contemplating our next step. I shall tell my mother that, though I know that until the chief calls us I shall have sleepless nights and my appetite will be affected."

"Ah, ndakei Hindowaa, don't be a coward; remember you are a Wunde man and you also hold a big title. Be brave. So you are not enjoying the wine; and will your appetite for everything deteriorate?"

As they chuckled, Hindowaa said, "Ndakei, Nyake, let me leave you now so that I can report back to my mother. She, too, is worried."

"No, no, ndakei, I will not accept this. We have just started drinking and you want to leave me here alone. I cannot drink by myself and my two wives are not here yet. So this loss of appetite is really serious. No, ndakei don't go yet. If my wives come then you can go and I shall continue drinking with them; but they will be happy if they find you here."

"Ndakei Nyake, please understand my situation. I have to be in my house because now there is this rumor that I am always hiding from my creditors and I stay almost permanently in the bush. I have become the bush spirit, the ndogbowusui. Just imagine if one of them decides to come to the house and he is told that I am not home. That will confirm their suspicions. In fact, my mother and I are expecting Mbalu's husband to drop in because it was Mbalu who told us what happened when he, Kapindi, Gbapi and the others met the chief. Please forgive me, let me go."

Nyake did not press him further, but when he left the house, Hindowaa was not sure whether to go straight home. He had earlier decided to go and see Nyamakoro and her husband as well as Nyake. And he also wanted to see Tonya, the woman at the waterside because he knew that she and the chief were good friends. There was also the possibility that Mbalu's husband might pay him a visit. He was the least difficult of the six creditors and they had since heard that he had not been in favor of taking the case to the chief. He had agreed to go only because he was in the minority.

In the end Hindowaa decided to go home and when he arrived there found Mbalu's husband sitting on the veranda with Kigba. She was happy that Hindowaa had returned because she had had to tell Mbalu's husband that she did not know where her son had gone, though she suspected he might have be visiting Nyake. She had been about to send one of the girls in the house to go in search of Hindowaa because she did not want Mbalu's husband adding to the rumor that her son was in hiding.

"Ndakei, biwaa, biseh," Mbalu's husband greeted Hindowaa.

"I was at Nyake's house, Hindowaa informed them.

"I suspected as much," Kigba replied. "You see, you children of today! He did not tell me he was going out and where he was going and when he would be back. If he had not come, the rumors would have been confirmed that he is permanently on the run in the bush - running from his creditors."

"Yeea Kigba, Hindowaa, I am here tonight just to tell you that I was not in favor of what happened. I tried to reason with them but they told me that we should take up the matter as a team and they even threatened me. I told them that my own money was not that much and that I was willing to wait. That was when, they called me all sorts of names and said I was a big coward and expressed doubt that I am a Wunde man. It was Kapindi who really insisted on us taking action because he said that when he and Gbapi came to ask for their money they did not like the way Hindowaa spoke to them. They said they were surprised at the way Hindowaa spoke to them and also that you supported him."

"My son, thank you very much. We understand your dilemma. We can't blame you. And thank you also for allowing your wife to come and bring us up to date. Thank you. May God and our ancestors bless you and guide you. Nothing lasts forever; this matter will come to an end and we shall continue to live here in Talia."

"Thank you for coming, my brother," Hindowaa put in. "I agree with what my mother has just told you. We live here in Talia and when the matter is resolved, we shall continue to live here where we were all born. We shall all die and be buried in this same town. Kapindi and myself know each other very well. We were born here and we were initiated in the Wunde Society in Tiama the same year. Like my mother said, this matter will rest one day. Now what we are waiting for is for the chief to call us so that we hear what he has to say. Till then, we won't do anything. I thank you for coming, my brother. I was telling Nyake just now that these days I don't sleep well, I have lost my appetite and I don't even enjoy a drink. How can I enjoy food or drink? It is just natural that when you are faced with a situation like this you lose your appetite for everything."

"Let me leave you people," said Mbalu's husband, giving Hindowaa a sympathetic look. "I shall stay in touch. But Hindowaa, don't let this matter affect you so much. You are man. Yeea Kigba please tell him to show more courage. He is not a child anymore and I don't think that this is his first challenge in life."

Hindowaa was dismayed when, as Mbalu's husband disappeared into the charcoal darkness, Kigba said, "When the chief marries Kunaafoh this matter will die a natural death. That is why I am not saying anything until we see him. I also have to see him about making arrangements for the marriage. I shall deal with Kapindi and Gbapi; they are the ringleaders in this matter, pushing the others. I know that, but I shall wait for my turn. I am going to tell that ingrate Kapindi that I shall visit his mother's grave and tell her what he is doing to us, even though he knows that I was instrumental in saving his mother's marriage. I shall tell her how her son is now rewarding me."

Hindowaa made no comment, wanting to take leave of his mother as soon as possible to avoid any further discussion about Kunaafoh's marriage to the chief.

"Hindo, did you hear what I said?" Kigba demanded.

"Yes, mother, I heard you." To his great relief, Boi-Kimbo announced from the doorway,

"Yeea, Kigba, your bath water is ready."

He was glad that his mother would soon disappear to take her bath and the sensitive issue of Kunaafoh would not resurface that night. He believed that she had deliberately mentioned Kunaafoh's marriage to gauge his reaction, given their present predicament. She probably thought he would change his position on the matter.

After she had gone away, Hindowaa said to his wife, "Boi-Kimbo, tell me, was my mother here when my friend brought the gourd of palm wine that is in the room?"

"No, she was in her room when I took the palm wine inside. She did not see me; but perhaps she smelled it - your mother's sense of smell is sharp, and the wine had a big layer of froth. I was smelling it myself while I was inside the house."

"Go and clear the froth and close the door," Hindowaa told her, but she pointed out that the smell was already all over the house.

"Don't you want to share the wine with your mother tonight?" she asked.

"Why are asking me that?"

"I am just interested because it is better to leave the wine outside. In any case your mother is sure to smell it and start asking me questions. Do you want me to lie?"

"What is the matter with you tonight, woman?" Hindowaa asked, raising his voice. Boi-Kimbo disappeared into the house without another word.

Hindowaa did not want to spend the evening drinking with his mother because he knew she would steer the conversation around to Kunaafoh's marriage and he was not prepared to discuss that toxic topic. However, as Boi-Kimbo had pointed out, she was bound to detect the smell of the wine and ask questions about it. What to do? He wished he had stayed longer at Nyake's place. He called out to Boi-Kimbo and when she arrived, asked her to pour half the wine into the empty gourd under his bed and leave it outside his mother's room.

"Why, don't you want to drink with your mother?" Boi-Kimbo asked again.

"Just do as I say and don't bother me with questions," Hindowaa snapped. "My mother knows that I don't have an appetite for anything, and I don't want to sit with her while she is drinking. I shall keep the rest of the wine in case someone drops in this evening."

When Kigba returned from her bath, she was pleasantly surprised to find the gourd, half full of palm wine. She called Boi-Kimbo and asked her to thank Hindowaa and tell him that since she was feeling cold after her bath, she would just drink the wine and go to bed. That message, immediately rekindled Hindowaa's appetite for palm wine. He asked Boi-Kimbo to bring the other gourd to their room and drank the rest of it with great enjoyment.

■

CHAPTER THIRTEEN

Hindowaa preferred to call the woman down by the river by her long name which was, Tonya Njala (Tonya by the river). He was among the few who called her by that name. Though it was a nickname, Tonya never took offence. There were many houses near the river but some people considered Tonya's to be dangerously close. They were afraid that during the heavy rains when the river flooded, crocodiles would gain access to her house. However, this had never happened, and people wondered why. Hindowaa's father had told him the story of the worst floods in living memory that washed away many houses by the river, but not Tonya's. It was since then that she had acquired the nickname. People came to believe that she had a connection with the spirits of the river, which she never denied. Hindowaa believed the story though he had never asked Tonya about it. It was as a result of that story that he developed a friendship with the woman.

It was on a wet morning that he decided he would visit Tonya. He was careful in choosing what he considered an appropriate moment. It was the time of the morning when most people were at their farms and other places of work. He left the house without telling his mother but informed his wife in case the chief sent for him and his mother. He mentioned the possibility of also visiting Nyamakoro and her husband. Since he wanted to dispel the malicious gossip that he was hiding from his creditors, he decided to use the main road leading down town. On his way to Tonya's house by the river, he spotted the only vehicle in Talia. People had already gathered around it to see off those who were traveling. It made him recall the numerous times he himself had used the vehicle, seeking assurances from various soothsayers that Giita would give birth to more sons. That was what had led to his current problem with his six creditors. The vehicle was always a painful reminder of the circumstances surrounding his wife's death.

"Good morning, Kinie Hindowaa," said someone standing by the vehicle and Hindowaa returned the greeting. A flood of greetings then descended on him from people around the vehicle and those who had already boarded it.

"It is a long time since I saw you in this town," one woman remarked.

"Yes, my dear, you are right. I, too, have not seen Kinie Hindowaa for a long time," concurred another.

"I have been keeping to myself, but I have been around," Hindowaa told them. "I did not go anywhere... Where are all these people traveling to this wet morning?"

His question was not addressed to anyone in particular, and he moved on without waiting for answers.

"Kinie Hindowaa, good morning." The voice belonged to a little girl. "My father saw you when you were passing by. He says he wants to talk to you."

"Aah. Please tell him that I have urgent business to attend to down town and I shall pass by his house on my way back. Also, tell him to keep some palm wine for me."

Why does the man want to see me? Why? Hindowaa asked himself irritably as the little girl skipped away to deliver the message. If I had not used this route, would he have sent his daughter to call me? He is not even one of my friends. I won't visit him even for a minute. He now regretted his decision to use the main road because he had wasted too much time greeting people and answering questions; he was barely half way through the town. On impulse, he changed direction and used the back road for the rest of the journey. A woman greeted him from a distance. She was coming from the river with her fishing net, a small container of fish, and a bucket of water balanced on her head. Hindowaa returned her greeting, recognizing her as Nyake's second wife. She continued on her way and he was glad she did not stop to chat. Seeing Nyake's wife reminded him about what his friend had told him. He could try to secure a loan from the chief and from Nyaamakoro and Foday to pay his creditors, though Nyake had warned him about the stinginess of the Jeelibah clan. It was unlikely that Nyamakoro and her husband would part with a penny unless they could secure a guarantee by his pawning property, house or land. He imagined how his mother would react to the idea of pawning their house to secure a loan from Nyamakoro and Foday. Just the thought of it would be enough to give her a stomach ache.

When he arrived at Tonya's house, he was surprised not to find her on the veranda. In fact, there was nobody on the veranda. Oh, he said to himself, why did I not send someone to tell her I was coming to see her; but he had never done so before and could not remember the last time he had visited Tonya and not found her lying in her hammock. Maybe she was in the house doing something, he conjectured. Tonya was too massive and too old to move around the town. Her feet were always swollen, so she lived a sedentary life. She must be around, he thought. He called out a greeting as he entered the veranda and waited for a response.

"Yeemiah?" A woman's voice asked who it was. Hindowaa identified himself and sat on a bamboo chair to wait.

"How are you this morning?" the woman asked, as she emerged from the house.

"Aah, Tonya (My dear, where is Tonya?"

"Taa qoolihun (She is in the wash room)," the woman told him, adding, "It has been a long time since you came here. Did you travel out of town or were you not well?"

"No, I did not go anywhere and I am well. I have just been busy, doing this and that. You know that in the rainy season you don't travel like that, especially if the rains are heavy. This year the rain has been very heavy. Don't you think so?"

The woman did not answer Hindowaa's question because she had heard Tonya's footsteps approaching the veranda.

"Aah, taa waamaa (She is coming)," she told Hindowaa.

Hindowaa greeted Tonya as she emerged from the house and rose to shake her hand.

"What brings you here this morning?" she asked, because it was unusual for Hindowaa to visit her early in the morning. The news had reached her about his problems with his creditors, so she guessed that that was the reason for the visit. She went to lie in her hammock and Hindowaa returned to the bamboo chair which was close to her.

"Have you had breakfast?" she asked.

"Oh, yes, I had breakfast before I came here."

"Well, you are not going to sit here and watch me eat mine. You have to join me. If you refuse, I shall divorce you for another man," she joked. "You know that I have many men in Talia, including the chief. Did I tell you that people once thought we were having an affair? Our Talia is a wonderful town. Instead of minding their business, all they do is gossip."

"Okay. I shall hold the dish for you while you eat," Hindowaa said. It was a polite way of saying, 'I shall join you, even though I am not hungry'. In no time the dish was empty even though Hindowaa was supposedly only 'holding' it for Tonya. The children of the house, who were used to eating Tonya's leftovers, cursed Hindowaa silently and prayed that he would not visit Tonya at breakfast-time again. Unfortunately for Hindowaa, Tonya did not drink palm wine, so there was none to be had after breakfast. He would have to make up for that later.

"What is new in town, or let me say, what is new up town?" Tonya asked.

"Oh, my sister, you know our town, there is always something in the air. People talk about other people all the time. Did you hear about my own case? They are saying that I am now a hermit and live permanently in the bush."

Tonya feigned surprise.

"Yes, my sister. You know that when my late wife was trying to have more children, I was always on the move, traveling here and there to help her to give birth to sons. It cost a lot of money and I had to take loans from friends and brothers, or rather, people I thought were friends and brothers. Among the six men are two of the worst so-called friends and brothers - Kapindi and Gbapi. These people say that they have been trying to collect their debts and I have taken to hiding from them each time they come to my house. That is why they spread the news that I have taken up permanent residence in the bush."

"Hindowaa, you must be joking. You mean to tell me that these people with whom you have spent all your life here in Talia and with whom you went to the Wunde Society could do that to you?"

"And that is not the end of the story, my sister," Hindowaa told her. "It is not the end of the story. They have gone even further and taken me to court because when you go to the chief to complain about your best friend and brother that is taking him to court. We understand that the chief is going to call my mother and me soon. In fact, even as we are here talking, I am expecting someone to come with a summons from the chief. Anytime I want to go out now I have to announce my plans so that people know where to find me. I might as well be under house arrest. My sister, it is painful to be in my situation, but it also has its funny side. Yesterday, I was sitting on the veranda alone when I wanted to go to the toilet. Because I did not know how long I would be there, I had to tell my wife where I was going in case the chief to send someone to call us. She laughed so much. It is the same for my mother; we are both prisoners now. It is very sad, my sister."

"My brother, I don't envy your situation," Tonya sympathized. "But tell me, at one time Kapindi's mother and your mother were good friends; everybody knew that here in Talia. So what has gone wrong with Kapindi? I hope he has not been influenced by bad company."

"My sister your observation is absolutely correct. Many people are surprised at Kapindi's behavior, particularly my mother. Someone told me that he thinks Kapindi wants to marry a new wife but he does not have the bride price so he has become desperate."

"Even if that is true, is it sufficient reason to harass an old friend? Is money the answer to everything? What about all the good times you had together when you were all growing up in this town? Why can't he recall your good old days? I hope he does not make the mistake of coming here because I shall give him a piece of my mind..." As Hindowaa thanked her for her support, she went on. "So, my brother, what are you going to do? Or let me put it in another way, do you have the money to pay all your debts?"

"My dear sister, the answer is no. You see, Kapindi and Gbapi came to my house and found my mother and me. They informed me that they had come to collect their debts. I told them that I had no money then, but that I would pay them everything after the next farming season. Apparently, they were not pleased with that response and that was why they went to see the chief. They said they were offended because I showed no sign of humility towards them. At the moment, there is nothing we can do except wait to hear what the chief is going to say about the matter. After we have heard what he has to say, then we shall decide how to meet the current challenge."

"In our time, a matter like this would never have come to the attention of the chief. We would either resolve it among ourselves, or ask a brother or friend to intervene. Taking a matter like that to the chief would be the last resort. I think they have all misbehaved and if I see any of them, I shall tell them off."

"Kapindi is the ringleader," Hindowaa remarked bitterly.

"My brother, I am sorry to say this, but I think that I am correct. Your generation does not have any respect for the older generation, otherwise Kapindi and others would have come to me or Nyake or any of the older townspeople for advice before going to see the chief. People of your generation have made a mockery of our customs and traditions; that is why so many bad things happen to you. You have made our ancestors angry. Haven't you seen signs of their anger? Look how heavy the rains come sometimes and destroy our crops. The dry season lasts longer than before, and you know the consequences of that. Women now give birth earlier than nine months. That never happened with our own generation. All this is because of the anger of our ancestors. We defy them every day."

"My sister, you are right, and we must do something about it otherwise when our ancestors get to the peak of their anger, they will unleash their collective vengeance in a way that will damage us even more. You are the one who should talk to our elders so that the entire chiefdom does whatever is necessary to regain their favour. This is my own appeal to you."

"All right, but my brother, you will have to pay all your debts eventually. What plans do you have for that?"

"My sister, when I saw Nyake, he told me that my only hope was to ask Nyamakoro and Foday, or the chief for a loan. Well, under normal circumstances this would be a possibility, but the circumstances are not normal. First of all, I am going to deny the chief the prospect of marrying my daughter. Then, Nyamakoro and Foday are not only business people, but as Nyake pointed out, they come from the very stingy Jeelibah clan. They will demand that we pawn our house or farmland to them as security for the loan, I can't do that. It is not dignified, so, for now, the prospects of securing a loan are remote."

"Yes, Nyake is right about Nyamakoro. I knew her former husband. He was a fierce businessman and spent days, if not weeks, traveling from one town to the other buying ginger, kola nuts, rice and cotton to sell. He spent little time at home. That was how he and Nyamakoro acquired their wealth. Those who don't know the story think that she became rich because of her cakes. Foday, her current husband, comes from the same tribe and as you see, they are continuing the tradition."

"My sister, one thing I know is that this matter will be resolved. As I said to Nyake, every problem has a solution. It might take some time, but a solution will be found. In spite of what you said, I believe that the ancestors will not let us down. They are there to help us solve our problems."

"Aah, you see now. When you need assistance, you count on our ancestors, yet you of this generation are destroying what they built for us. You are a defiant, disobedient and undisciplined generation. That is what you are, Hindowaa. All of you, including my own children. May our ancestors have mercy on you."

Hindowaa agreed with Tonya's observations. Indeed, as he reflected on the conflict between himself and his mother, he realized that it was a problem between generations. However, he had made up his mind not to give in regarding his opposition to the chief marrying Kunaafoh, even though his mother had threatened to curse him. When he finally decided to leave, he thanked Tonya once more for the breakfast, though he had eaten reluctantly. He had told Boi-Kimbo that he might go to see Nyamakoro and Foday after his visit to Tonya, so he headed in that direction. On his way, he reflected on the fact that the prospects for obtaining money to repay his debts were remote. The chief would probably tell them to pay back all the debts owed to his creditors after the next harvest season. If that were the case, he would then ask his mother to join him in appealing to Fanday to come to their rescue. Kortu must have left her money when he died. He started thinking of traveling to Freetown to tell Fanday that unless she came to their rescue, the Hindowaa family was heading towards a social calamity that had been predicted. He would also take the opportunity to talk to his son, the younger boy, Kafo, the motor apprentice, about how he and his senior brother, Hinga, the seaman, had been a great disappointment to the family. He would tell him what was happening and how, were they worthy of the Hindowaa name, they would have done all in their power to save the family from a disaster. But would the boy take him seriously? In fact, his son's generation was worse than his own. If Tonya thought his generation was bad, she had better think again. His children's generation was far worst.

It was raining when he arrived at Nyamakoro and Foday's house and he was glad to find them both at home with no plans to venture out. He knew that the couple supported his position on Kunaafoh, but could not predict their reaction to the matter of his debts to Kapindi and others. As Nyake had warned him, when it came to money, one had to be very careful, especially with business people. He decided that he would not raise the issue with them, but that if they volunteered to lend him money and did not introduce the element of pawning his house and farmland, he would consider taking it.

"Welcome," Foday said, beckoning towards the veranda. After they had exchanged greetings he left Hindowaa alone and went into the house. It was apparently to change his clothes, because he re-emerged wearing an impressive brownish gown, made of cotton. No amulets were sewn on it, but Hindowaa wondered what might be concealed beneath it. Not that he was afraid of Foday and his wife. They were good Muslims and only smeared their bodies with protective liquid charms brought by people who had made the pilgrimage to Saudi Arabia. Nyamakoro soon joined them on the veranda and greeted Hindowaa. Neither she nor her husband drank any alcohol, so Hindowaa was not expecting to be served any palm wine though he was longing for a drink. While he was fond of Nyamakoro and Foday, he did not like the fact that whenever he visited them no palm wine or bamboo wine was offered; and they never apologized for not doing so, as if denying people palm wine was normal behavior.

"My dear, you will live long," Nyamakoro said. "You know, my husband and I were talking about you last night and here you are this morning. You will live long, but that doesn't mean you should stand in front of a moving vehicle."

As they all laughed, Foday said,

"Yes, it has been some time since we last saw each other. Well, I have been away on business trips, but my wife told me that she, too, had not seen you for a while. It was just yesterday that we were talking about you. How is your mother? I hope that she is well… and the rest of the family, especially the children."

"My people, I shall be back," Nyamakoro interrupted before Hindowaa could answer. "Let me just check the food on the fire so it doesn't get burned."

"So, Foday, how is business?" Hindowaa asked when she had disappeared into the house.

"To be honest with you, I can't complain. This is the rainy season, but business is fine. I am expecting it to be even better when the dry season comes. You see, with business, especially our type of business, you can't afford to sit at home. If you do that you will not make money. You have to travel, otherwise how can you buy produce?"

Nyamakoro began to serve breakfast when she returned. The potato leaf sauce smelled delicious.

"Nya'nde Hindowaa, food is served. Let us eat. We

woke up late which is why we are only eating now. You know when it rains at night, sleep is good and you just go on sleeping. To tell you the truth, I love the rainy season, because you can sleep well."

"Thank you, but my stomach is full. I had breakfast at home before I came," Hindowaa said. He did not mention the other breakfast he had had at Tonya's house.

"But how can you sit here and watch us eat? That is not done in our culture. I would never do that to you in your house."

As Hindowaa continue to protest, Foday said, "Well, just come and hold the dish for us?"

So Hindowaa went to sit with them and soon began eating his third breakfast that morning.

"Ndakei, this is my favourite sauce, believe me," he said, licking his fingers, "and it tastes even better when you eat it like this - warmed up in the morning. My late wife knew how to cook it well. It was her specialty. How I loved her for that!"

They ate up everything. Fortunately, all the children in the house had gone out so there was no one there to grumble because of the extra mouth. Afterwards Foday patted his stomach with satisfaction, saying,

"It is good to have breakfast in the morning. For me, it is one meal I don't miss. After that, I can stay for most of the day without food and go about my business. For us business people, before you leave the house in the morning, it is essential for you to have something in your stomach. Otherwise, the stomach will complain. I try never to miss breakfast. When I go on my business trips, I always tell my hosts that all I want is a good, big breakfast before I hit the road. They don't have to bother about an evening meal for me."

"Well, for me, the meal I don't like to miss is the one in the evening. That is my main meal, because after that I can relax with my palm wine."

Good Muslim that he was, Foday did not take the hint about palm wine.

"How is your mother?" Nyamakoro asked. "I told my husband what happened the last time she was here...Remember, I told you the story. To be honest with you, your mother seems to have become difficult overnight. She used to be a very sweet person, but now many other people have seen an unpleasant change in her. She does not respect other people's views on issues, and it's not good; we should all learn to be tolerant."

"You know, my sister. You are right. Many people ask me what has happened to mymother? Indeed they are right. This is the first time I have known my mother to be so stubborn and, I am sorry to say, so unreasonable. It worries me a lot and I even wonder whether somebody is responsible for the change in her character. Take this issue of Kunaafoh and the way she is making my life miserable about it. I have the total support of all those who are aware of the situation, so you see, she is the one who is wrong on this matter. But she will have to accept it in the end. Kunaafoh will only marry the chief over my dead body."

Nyamakoro had offered the two men kola nuts but since they declined, she was eating one on her own as she listened. At that solemn declaration, she said, in a jocular tone,

"Yes. Now, Hindowaa, tell me, what is this we are hearing about you spending most of your time hiding in the forest and living with animals. Do you want to change yourself into an animal, a ndogbowusu or a leopard? Tell us." As they all laughed, Hindowaa replied,

"My sister, I am glad that you are joking about this matter. Indeed, it is a big joke. I tell you, my people, I am just coming from Tonya and she mentioned the same rumor..."

"How is she, by the way?" Foday asked, "I should visit her one of these days when I am in town. How is her foot? Has the swelling gone down? Has she seen Kunaafoh at the mission hospital?"

"Tonya was in good spirits when I visited her this morning. Yes, the swollen foot is improving and it is Kunaafoh who is treating her. I have told her that she is not helping the situation by not taking exercise. Her body is already too heavy. I told her she should try to walk from down town to up town once a day, but she dismissed that suggestion. If she had remarried it might have helped because the husband would have put pressure on her; but she was all right when I saw her this morning."

"Yes, Hindowaa, my husband and I wondered why these six friends and brothers of yours had to rush to the chief on this matter. Why didn't they see one of our contemporaries instead and try to resolve the matter? Once a matte goes to the chief it becomes serious."

"My sister, I know that this matter is now all over Talia. My friends and brothers, led by Kapindi, took the matter to the chief even though I never denied owing them money. I had to take the money from them when I was running up and down trying to make sure that my late wife would have more sons. Now I am being hunted as if I am a criminal. I do not sleep, eat, or, drink well and even when I want to go to the toilet, I have to announce it in the house so that if any of my creditors comes for his money they will tell him that I am in the toilet and not hiding in the bush. Yes, my people this is now my fate. When I was coming here, I had to let my wife know in case the chief sends for us today."

"So you don't know when the chief is going to summon you and your mother," Foday remarked.

"No, he will summon us at his pleasure, and meanwhile, I am a prisoner. He is the chief and I suppose he is not in any hurry. But he should be aware that the more he keeps me and my mother waiting the more we suffer the mental pain that comes with speculating about just what he is going to tell us."

"Do you then think that this delay is a stealthy way of punishing you?" Foday asked.

"That is a good question, my brother. It is possible that that's what he is doing. You see, my brother and sister, I have been told certain things about this our chief and his past. People have told me that we the younger generation don't know him. I now believe that they are right. They say he is like his late father who was known in this chiefdom for his tyranny. Have you not heard about his father? "

Hindowaa had aroused the curiosity of the couple, who originally came from a distant place to settle in Talia and carry on their business.

"So exactly what did his father do to his subjects when he was chief?" Foday asked.

"My brother, I told you earlier that the man was a brutal tyrant. They said that he was cruel, just like his son is now being cruel to me. He has made me lose my appetite"

Nyamakoro and Foday looked at each other and smiled, knowing how much Hindowaa used to love to eat.

"So when did the father of the chief die; how long

ago?" Foday asked.

"Well, the current chief has been on the throne for almost twenty years. My brother, what made news when the former chief died, was that he died twice"

"What!" Foday and his wife exclaimed together, for they had never heard of anyone dying twice.

"Hindowaa, how can you say that? Foday asked. "How can somebody die twice?"

"Well, that is the story," Hindowaa told them. "The chief knew that many people disliked him while continuing to flatter him, so he wanted to find out just how many of his subjects were sincere. The only way he could do this was by pretending to be very sick and make them believe that he had died. That was precisely what he did. In accordance with tradition, he was rushed to the Wunde bush where after some time news started circulating that he had died. The people were very happy and decided to make merry. They even sang and danced. Then, not long afterwards, they were told that the chief had suddenly come back to life. Well, many people who had celebrated were so brutally punished that they regretted doing that before the chief had been buried. When he finally died the people waited for a long time after his burial before they dared to celebrate his demise and proclaim their freedom from tyranny... That was a long time ago."

"Are you sure that story wasn't just a joke?" Foday asked.

"Perhaps, but, my brother, there must be some truth in it, otherwise, why would people keep repeating it? And this chief seems to have his father's character. Let me tell you why I say so. You see, people go to his compound every day. They go there to gossip and tell him what they think he wants to hear. For some of them, it has become a full time job - going to the chief and telling him stories that will please him. They say that he knows all those who frequent his compound just to pay lip service. They also say that if he does not see you or me for a long time, he will ask for you and if he asks for someone twice, that person will be summoned to answer whether he has developed a large hernia of the scrotum that is preventing him from walking. He asks that sort of question even of someone older than him. What does that tell you about him? What do you make of such a chief?"

"Hindowaa, I am confused," Nyamakoro said when Hindowaa stopped speaking. "If this is the type of chief we have, tell me, how is it that you once agreed for him to marry your daughter?"

"My sister, you have asked a good question," Hindowaa replied. "Well, I will tell you the reason. If a daughter of mine were to marry the chief, I and the entire Hindowaa family would be more protected from his domineering behavior. He would regard us as one family, especially if there were children. My mother actually believes that if Kunaafoh had been married to the chief, my creditors would not have dared to take me to his court. And I think she is right. What would they have done in that case? They would have tried to resolve the matter in another way. They would probably have come to you and other older people to ask for your help."

"So, you are going to have to repay the money, especially since the chief will not be marrying your daughter anymore. Am I correct?" Foday said.

"You are correct. That same question came up when I was with Tonya. It also came up when I was with Nyake yesterday. However, I keep saying that no matter how difficult a problem is, there is always a solution to it. Indeed, our people believe that God will not put a load on your head if you are not able to carry it. And it is also true that however tight a house is, a chicken will always find a place to lay an egg. You see, my people, God can work wonders. Someone advised that I seek another loan to pay my debts, and even suggested two possible sources I could try."

Here Hindowaa paused to gauge the reaction of this couple from the reputedly stingy Jeelibah clan.

"And which are the two sources from which you might secure a loan to pay the debts?" asked Nyamakoro innocently.

Hindowaa hesitated at first, then summoning up his courage, said,

"Well, the person suggested the chief himself; but that source is closed because my daughter cannot marry him. The second source is closer to home. The person suggested that I go to friends who are business people like yourselves."

Once again, Nyamakoro and Foday looked at each other and smiled. Then, they laughed with artificial heartiness, as if they were acting in a play.

"Whoever gave you that advice is very smart," Foday remarked. "Yes, it is possible to secure a loan to pay your debts. Business people lend people money all the time, but what the same business people do is to secure a guarantee for the loan - something of the same value as the money being borrowed." Seeing Hindowaa's face fall, he went on, "My brother, this is business we are now talking and when it comes to business, we put friendship aside. Let me give you an example of the kind of guarantee I am talking about. The money you owe the six people is substantial, so if you came to me for a loan, I would need something like a house or large farmland which I could use to recover my money in case you fail to repay the loan. It is called business..."

Nyamakoro nodded her concurrence and asked, "So do you have something like that to guarantee the loan?"

"Aah, my people, I am surprised at you," Hindowaa replied. "We have been friends for a long time. Now that I am in need you say I have to pledge my house? In my tribe, that is an insult. If I were tell my mother this she would not believe it. I am really surprised at both of you - faithful Muslims who pray every Friday and don't touch palm wine. Can't you assist a friend in need to please Allah? Isn't that what the Muslim religion preaches - kindness to those in need? And Allah will reward you ten times over, and more."

"Hindowaa, Hindowaa, you are our friend and brother, but please do not confuse religion and business. Like I said, this is business and we have to deal with you strictly on business principles, and it will preserve our friendship," Foday answered, but Hindowaa had already got to his feet and started walking away.

He left Nyamakoro and Foday that rainy morning feeling very angry with the couple, whom he had considered friends but who had done nothing to help him solve his problem. He wished the chief would call him and his mother that very day so he would know where he stood, instead of having to endure this painful uncertainty. The weather did nothing to ease his mental torment, being humid and uncomfortable. Why, oh, why, he kept asking himself, had the chief not yet summoned them for a meeting?

■

CHAPTER FOURTEEN

Unexpected sunshine after rain always had a soothing effect on Hindowaa's mind. That was the feeling he experienced as he walked home reflecting on the encounter he had had with Nyamakoro and Foday. The outcome of his visit to the couple had been exactly as Nyake had predicted. If there had been the least bit of hope of securing a huge loan to repay his six creditors it had lain with Foday and Nyamakoro; now that hope had to be abandoned. He reconsidered the possibility of obtaining some sort of contribution from within his own family, the best hope being Fanday, his late brother's wife; but Fanday had never been forthcoming about any wealth her husband had left with her. As for his sons, Hinga and Kafo, they were a collective disaster in this regard. Ndomawaa, Giita's father, was not in a position to assist him either, even though at one time, he had hinted that he might be able to help. Inspite of the apparent hopelessness of the situation, Hindowaa's mind remained temporarily soothed by the sunshine. He still believed that God and his ancestors would come up with a solution to his problem.

Kigba, meanwhile, was sitting on a stool on the veranda, staring into space with her chin cupped in her right hand. She was furious because it was Boi-Kimbo who told her that her son had gone down town to see Tonya and would subsequently visit Nyamakoro and Foday. Was Boi-Kimbo now the woman of the house even though she, Kigba, was still alive? she fumed. Hindowaa was becoming too independent for her liking; and she did not understand why he would go down town to see Tonya Njala first and then come up town to see Nyamakoro and

Foday when it would have made more sense for him to visit the people up town before going down town. She was becoming more and more convinced that Hindowaa was mentally unstable. She even compared his behavior to that of a well known mad man who used to travel long distances to go and buy snuff when better snuff was available a stone's throw away. When she spotted Hindowaa approaching the house, she got up at once and went to meet him. Hindowaa saw her coming and from the way she was walking, thought that there had been some development regarding the chief's impending summons. He also sensed anger from the determined way in which his mother was approaching him. She seemed to be scolding him already, though they were still some distance apart. When she drew nearer he heard what she was complaining about and sighed inwardly. It was the same old issue.

"You have demoted me to a second place in this house," she accused him. "Yes, that is why you don't tell me where you are going and when you will be coming back. It is Boi-Kimbo and other people in the house, including my grandchildren that you tell when you are going out. Well, Hindo, I have told you several times that when I sort out Kunaafoh's business, I shall leave you in this house and go away. And I shall not tell you where I am going, so don't be surprised. I have told your sisters that. Unless you change you behavior, I shall move from this house. I have given you advance warning."

She was talking so loudly that some of the neighbors could hear what she was telling her son. However, Hindowaa decided to ignore her complaint and said quietly,

"Mother, is there a new development? Did the chief

send his policeman to come and call us?"

Instead of answering the question, his mother harangued him all the way to their house. Even as they entered the house, she continued to scold him.

"You see now. You see Hindo what I am saying? When you woke up this morning and left the house, did we see each other? Now, instead of greeting me, as children should do first thing in the morning, you are asking your mother questions. Ah, Hindo, what have I gained from all the tribulations I have had to go through for your sake? All I continue to get from you is heartache. You, Hindo, you, my only son; look what you are putting me through in this town. It is now an open secret that you have challenged me about my granddaughter marrying our chief. Yes, it has become common knowledge because you have chosen to tell people what is happening in our household. We have been washing our dirty clothes in public thanks to you, my son, thanks to you. But, Hindo, you will see the result of your behavior. I shall curse you and I have repeatedly warned you about a mother's curse. Yes, I sent Boi-Kimbo to go and look for you. She told me you went to visit Tonya and after that you would visit Nyamakoro and her husband. I wondered, why you decided to begin from the end of town. Does it make sense to you? Is that a normal way of doing things? Would it not have been more sensible for you to have visited Nyamakoro and her husband before going to visit Tonya down town? The way you did it was as if you were walking backwards. Think about it. I am getting more and more worried about your sanity because you are my son and we have never had a case of mental illness in our family. That is my worry..."

Hindowaa had listened to this diatribe in silent

frustration, wondering when his mother would get to the point which was why she had been looking for him. Finally, she said,

"While you were out, our chief sent his policeman to say that he would like to see us today."

"What time of the day would he like to see us?" Hindowaa wanted to know.

"Hindo, wait for me to finish," his mother replied. "Why are you so impatient these days? I was going to continue when you interrupted me. We can see him right now. If you had been at home, we could have gone with the policeman he sent to come and call us. I did not tell him that you had gone to Tonya and would later visit Nyamakoro and her husband. I told him that I sent you somewhere and we would come as soon as you returned."

Hindowaa immediately went to his room and reappeared soon afterwards dressed in his charmed cotton gown, trousers and hat, as well as his charmed shoes. He felt confident about attending the meeting with his mother and the chief. He knew that it would be a meeting with just the three of them in the special place where the chief had his most private and secret meetings with his subjects. They would not be interrupted. If visitors came, they would be told where the chief was, and would immediately conclude that he was having a private meeting. They would sit down and wait for as long as necessary and while they waited, would be served food and palm wine or bamboo wine, depending on their preference.

"Hindo," Kigba said as they made their way to the chief's compound, "Why are you dressed as if you are going to war? Do you think our chief is going to send his witch gun on you to test you? Why would he want to hurt you, his future father-in-law? It is now too late otherwise I would have asked you to dress normally, not as if you are going to enemy territory. I am very uncomfortable about going to visit our chief with you dressed like this. I can understand if we were going to visit Kapindi, Gbapi and the others, but not when we are going to visit our chief."

"Mother, I am sorry to say it, but from the experience I have had in this town, I am not prepared to take chances. I do not know who is a friend anymore and who is not a friend. When you have friends and brothers, people you grew up with in the same town, went to the same Wunde initiation session with, went hunting together, swimming, wrestling, playing together, and they take you to court, I don't know who my friends and enemies are anymore. Then look at Nyamakoro and Foday. There is no time now for me to tell you what happened when I went to see them about this problem of the debts I owe. This is why I have protected myself. I just don't trust people anymore. From now on, when I am going out of the house, I shall arm myself with my protective charms - even if I am only going to the toilet."

"What rubbish!" said Kigba, who refused to believe that the chief harbored sufficient ill will towards Hindowaa to want to harm him. "I understand your fears about other people, and I support you; but tell me why would our chief want to test you? He is not like that. Have you ever heard that he has tested anyone in this town? Or have you ever heard that he hurt any of his subjects? So why should you be armed from head to toe?"

"Mother, we don't have time now. I shall tell you later why I am protecting myself. But don't you remember the story about his father dying twice and how people danced and rejoiced?"

"What has that got to do with the present chief, my son?"

"Mother, haven't you heard the saying, 'an orange tree doen't produce limes'?"

"That is not always true," Kigba replied. "Are you trying to say that you are exactly like your father?"

"Yes, mother, I have all his good qualities, and you know that?"

For the first time in a long time Kigba smiled during a conversation with her son.

"Our chief, too, took his father's good qualities," she said.

"Mother, I am sorry but you don't know this chief. Why does he make enquiries about his subjects who don't visit him as frequently as others? Why should he want to know which of his subjects have more money than him? Why does he want to know how many wives each male subject has? Those are personal matters and no business of his. Such prying is not a characteristic of a good chief. When his father died, people rejoiced."

"Hindo, this chief is the best one we have had for a long time. All the stories about his father are history, and he himself is different from his father. When a chief asks about his subjects, it is because he has their interests at heart. Only a good chief would want to know the whereabouts of his subjects. Why do you interpret that as interference?"

"Mother, I have told you that we don't have enough time to discuss our chief now, but let me also tell you how he has refused to face reality. I told him that, due to Kunaafoh's changed status, the Hindowaa family would give him another girl who is pretty, younger than

Kunaafoh, and above all, a virgin. He does not want her because she is not educated. Yes, this chief, who is as illiterate as you and I, wants an educated woman, a nun and a doctor. This is the chief that you are praising with passion. I beg to differ."

Kigba was not amused.

"Hindo, you never cease to surprise me," she said. "Tell me, my son, tell me, where did they say, even in the white man's book that you should not marry an educated woman unless you, too, know bookj? I have never heard this. So, tell me, Hindo, even now, if I meet a man who knows the white man's book and he says he wants to marry me, what will happen? Will they take him to court because he is educated and wants to marry someone who is not educated? Oh, my son, I have never heard this," she told Hindowaa.

"Mother, Kunaafoh, is a nun. That is the most important point... Anyway, the chief's compound has ears and we are almost there. Let us continue this conversation after our meeting with him."

Yeea Kigba, biwaah, biseh, Kahun yeeanaa." Greetings came almost spontaneously as Kigba and Hindowaa entered the compound. The chief's wives greeted her first.

"Awuuwaah, Awuuseh. wugahun yaenaa," she replied and enquired after their health. She always felt welcome at the compound, and indeed some of the women there went up to her and shook her hand. However, the chief's wives were not particularly pleased to see her because they knew that she was the person in the Hindowaa family who was championing Kunaafoh's marriage to their husband. They had all come to the conclusion that if Kunaafoh were to marry the chief, they would be painfully marginalized because they were all illiterate and they knew that their husband would be partial to a literate woman, especially a medical doctor who had become renowned in Talia and the entire chiefdom.

The chief had instructed his policeman that when Hindowaa and his mother arrived, he should usher them into the meeting room which was one of many little round huts with thatched roofs. They saw many people on the veranda of the chief's main house as they passed it.

"Please, while you are waiting for the chief, would you like a drink?"

The question was asked by one of the wives. Mother and son glanced at each other questioningly as the woman stood waiting for an answer.

"I think it would be better for us to wait until we have seen the chief," Kigba said, looking at Hindowaa who nodded agreement. As the chief's wife left them, she asked,

"Have you been here before; in this particular hut?"

"Yes, mother, but only once. It was when my father died and the senior Wunde title holders had to 'hang heads'. This was where they met and Kortu and I were present. It was from here that we went into the bush to organize the funeral."

When the chief finally came into the hut, he was accompanied by one of his official escorts, a policeman. He left as soon as the chief was seated. Hindowaa rose when the chief walked in, but Kigba remained seated for the formal greetings. Mother and son looked nervous as the chief welcomed them because though they knew why he had summoned them, they were not aware of the details concerning the summons. Hindowaa moved his seat closer to his mother when he sat down again. There was a charged silence as they waited for the chief's next statement. To their surprise, when he spoke again he did not immediately mention the summons.

"Hindowaa, do you remember the last time you were in this hut? This particular hut?" heinquired.

"Yes, chief, and it was the first time I came into this hut," Hindowaa replied. Kigba became more interested when the chief went on to say,

"Come to think of it, it is not so long ago that your father died and his burial and funeral ceremonies were discussed here. I still remember your late brother, Kortu. What about his wife?"

"She is doing fine; as a matter of fact, chief, I was thinking about her just yesterday."

"You know, Hindowaa, life is very interesting. Your father was a great man in this town and chiefdom. Many people only realized it after he had died. I had great respect for him and while he was alive, he was one of my senior advisers. I relied much on his wise counsel and wish there were many more people like him in this chiefdom." Turning his attention to Kigba, he said, "Your late husband was a great friend of mine."

"Thank you Chief," Hindowaa said. "Thank you very much for those kind comments about my father. He left us all at a time when we needed him most. But what can we do? It was the will of God and our ancestors. We are also thankful that in his absence from the family we are blessed with having a good chief. That is how God reveals his wonders. We lose in one area and gain in another. We never lose everything at once."

Pleased with her son's remarks, Kigba decided to make her own contribution to what they all knew was merely an introduction to the matter of the day.

"And chief, many people never knew my husband, which is why when they ask why I have never remarried, I simply ignore them. They would never understand that I could never have found another person like him. He was a special person and I do not regret that I have not remarried. I know that the few of you who knew my husband well will understand why I have decided to stay away from other men. Even my son understands, because he knew his father. My late husband was a great family man."

"But Kigba, to be honest, I think that you should have given someone else a chance. There may be other men who are as good as your late husband, but when any man has tried to catch your eye, you have always averted your gaze. When we men want a woman, we look her in the eye to guage her reaction."

Kigba looked flattered, but not embarrassed.

"By the way, would you like something to drink?" the chief went on to ask. Again, mother and son glanced at each other questioningly, and again it was Kigba who replied.

"Thank you, chief," she said. "One of your wives offered us a drink earlier and I told her we preferred to wait till after our meeting with you. Thank you very much."

"In that case, let us start," said the chief, immediately becoming more formal and businesslike. "Kigba and Hindowaa, I have called both of you today about a very important matter. I should have called you earlier, but I have been very busy with chiefdom matters. At present, there are several land cases between and among people in the chiefdom. As you know, this is the time when they go about identifying pieces of land for the next farming season. That is why I have not been able to see you as early as I wanted to. I hope you understand my situation and don't feel that I was deliberately keeping my in-laws waiting."

He smiled directly at Kigba when he referred to them as his in-laws. Kigba returned the smile, but Hindowaa felt slightly sick.

"Hindowaa, you know that I have been involved with you even before Giita died; when you were concerned about having more sons. And I know all you had to endure when Giita died. You know also, and I am sure Kigba was aware of it, that when Kapindi, Gbapi and others wanted your debts to them paid, you came here and appealed to me to intervene on your behalf because of the special circumstances in which you found yourself. I agreed, and summoned all of them to the compound to plead for you. I asked them to be kind enough to wait until you had fully recovered from all your problems in connection with Giita's death. They complied with my request and everybody was happy, including Kigba..."

"Chief, everything you have said so far is correct and my mother would agree with me," Hindowaa responded.

"Chief, Hindo is right," Kigba put in. The chief went on.

"I was not aware that your creditors had been visiting you, collectively and individually, demanding payment of the money you owe them. From the information I have, they experienced great difficulty trying to isee you. They said that for over a week they never found you in your house and the whole exercise had been reduced to a game of hide and seek. It was because of their frustration that they sent Kapindi and Gbapi to ask me to demand payment of your debt on their behalf."

"Chief, please allow me to make just one small correction," Hindowaa interrupted. "Most of what you have said is correct. However, I never went into hiding. My mother, who is a Sowie, can testify to that, even under oath."

"I believe you," said the chief, "but I was also told that when Kapindi and Gbapi went to your house and demanded payment, they took offence because of your unacceptable behavior towards them in the presence of your mother. That was the main reason they decided to come and see me. They came and told me the whole story, reminding me that I was the one who had initially pleaded with them to give you more time, which was true. They told me that they were again appealing to me so that you would make good your commitment to them. Failing that, they intended to bring the matter formally to court."

"Chief, please allow me a few moments to make an observation on this matter." This time the person who spoke up was Kigba. "All you have said is correct, apart from the point Hindo made when he intervened briefly. We never dreamed that Kapindi, Gbapi and others would bring this matter to your attention. I was present when Hindo told Kapindi and Gbapi that we would repay them when we sold our produce after the nest harvest. He was only being honest when he said that at that moment he had no money. I think that they took offence only because my son was so honest with them. Both Kapindi and Gbapi left us on the veranda and went out briefly to 'hang heads.' I was very surprised when they came back and said that they would appeal to you for redress. I was surprised, because I thought all the six of them were Hindowaa's friends and brothers in this town. I can't understand why they behaved like that."

Having allowed Kigba to say her piece, the chief said,

"I don't want to spend the rest of the day on this matter. Let me tell you straightaway what was agreed between your creditors and myself. Hindowaa should come up with the entire amount owed to them within one month. If he fails to do that, they will take the matter formally to court and allow the law to take its course. That could lead to imprisonment for Hindowaa and after his release from prison he would still have to make the repayments. Can you make them within the one month period?"

His eyes moved from mother to son, waiting for an answer, but there was no immediate response from either of them. Then Kigba said in a typically combative manner.

"Chief, let me tell you one thing. We don't have any money now, but I can assure you that I shall tie my wrapper tightly around my big bottom and make sure we pay all the debts within one month. I shall show all those who want to humiliate the Hindowaa family that they will not succeed. I know all those who are fighting my household and all the evil things that they are saying about me in this town. What have I done to them that they are so determined to ruin my family? They have come to our house singly and in groups, eaten our food and drunk our palm wine yet they have been malicious enough to try to ruin my family. Well, I shall show them that I am not only a woman but also a Sowie in this town."

Hindowaa's mouth almost fell open when he heard his mother make that firm commitment knowing that there was no possibility that they could produce such a large sum of money within a month. He noticed that the chief had a strange expression, but did not try to analyse it. Instead, he said to himself, What has got into my mother? Is she suffering from the same madness she keeps accusing me of, or did she drink palm wine before we came? Perhaps the rumors about her having a djinn are true.

When Kigba paused for breath, the chief said mildly,

"So, can I summon the six creditors and tell them what you have just told me in the presence of your son, or should I ask you to repeat it in front of witnesses? This is not an informal matter anymore. It is now a legal matter."

In spite of the warning, Kigba sounded quite lighthearted as she said,

"Chief, you can go ahead and summon witnesses, but I can assure you that what I have told you will happen. The matter is now in your hands. You are the chief and, by the grace of God, our future in-law."

Feeling more confused and alarmed than ever, Hindowaa said to himself, Now what does she mean by that? Why is she taking such a risk at this critical time when I could end up in prison if I default? She knows the chief will never marry Kunaafoh, so we can't expect any money from him; she knows that... He continued to worry about his mother's sanity as they made their way home, but realized that if he dared to question her about the rash commitment she had made, they would never go to bed that night.

For her part, Kigba, expected Hindowaa to raise the matter when they arrived at the house, so she went straight to her room to avoid any further discussion. Hindowaa stayed on the veranda and continued to reflect on his mother's behavior till Boi-Kimbo came to deliver messages for himself and Kigba from people who came to visit while they were away. Some palm wine had also been delivered during their absence, so Hindowaa asked his wife to do what she had done before and take some for his mother in the gourd under their bed in case Kigba decided to stay in her room till the next morning.

"How did your meeting with the chief go?" Boi-Kimbo asked when she returned from her errand. The rest of the household had already gone to bed and the house was quiet. This was one of the few times Boi-Kimbo had come to the veranda to be with her husband. She had served him the fresh palm wine and he took a welcome gulp before answering her.

"My dear wife, I don't have words in my mouth to tell you what happened," Hindowaa began. "I am now so confused. First of all, the chief said that if I don't pay the debts within one month I will be sent to prison and I will still have to find the money to pay the debts when I am released. That is justice for you. Then - you won't believe this - my mother promised to repay all the money within one month. Her confidence baffled me because she did not say where the money would come from. I know that if I ask her that, I shall open the floodgates of heaven and the whole of Talia will drown."

Equally puzzled, Boi-Kimbo said, "But how could Yeea Kigba make such a promise?"

"You ask her tomorrow. Don't ask me. I am too confused."

"My husband, something tells me that your mother knows something she's not telling you. Let me whisper something in your ears," she added, pulling her stool closer to her husband's hammock. "There is only one possible way that she could get that big amount of money - from the djinn. You know the rumors in town and beyond that she has a djinn. Everybody knows that a djinn can perform miracles and that that is how many people have risen from poverty to sudden and unexplained riches. This is my guess."

"My dear wife, you are so clever!" Hindowaa said, adding untruthfully. "It never crossed my mind. No. It did not. No wonder mother was so confident. Yes, my wife, you are absolutely correct. And you know, my mother has never actually denied the djinn rumors. No wonder she was so definite about being able to clear the debt in one month. Now I can enjoy my wine. Fill up my cup, let me drink."

Boi-Kimbo, who seemed to be familiar with the djinn phenomenon, now mentioned a serious concern of hers. She told Hindowaa that when people who had connections with a djinn were desperate, they willingly sacrificed members of their family to achieve their desires. She was afraid that her children might become Kigba's sacrificial targets and wanted to take them to the safety of her parents' distant town. Once there, she would take further steps to protect the children. Hindowaa thought his wife's idea was brilliant and agreed for Boi-Kimbo to take the children far away until all his debts had been paid; and he would not say anything about it to his mother.

The following day, having summoned enough courage, he decided to ask her just where she intended to get the money she had promised during their meeting with the chief. He called out, "Boi-Kimbo-o-o-o," and his wife came immediately. "Please see if my mother is in her room. If she is there, tell her I would like to see her."

Boi-Kimbo did as she was asked, went to her mother-in-law's door and called out a greeting.

"Yeea, biwaa. Kahun yaenaa?" then waited to be invited to enter the room.

"Jookooh (Come in)," Kigba told her. She found her mother-in-law sitting on a stool with both legs comfortably outstretched.

"Have my grandchildren gone to school?" she asked. When Boi-Kombo told her that they had, she said in reproachful surprise, "And they did not come to say good morning and good-bye? I kept something for them to eat during their lunch break. Aah, I know what must have happened. I was still asleep when they came to greet me and say goodbye. I only fell asleep towards morning and the sleep was so sweet. I didn't even hear the the muezzin calling people to prayers."

That was because of all the palm wine you drank last night, Boi-Kimbo said to herself with bitter amusement as she waited to deliver Hindowaa's message.

"What can I do for you this morning, my young and only wife?" Kigba said feigning warmth. "I shall keep reminding you that my granddaughters are looking for brothers."

Ignoring what she realized was another deliberate provocation, Boi-Kimbo told her coldly,

"Yeea Kigba, your son would like to see you. Should he come to your room or will you meet him on the veranda?"

"I am hungry. Have you prepared our breakfast?"

"Yes, Yeea Kigba, breakfast is almost ready."

"Alright. Tell your husband to come and meet me here. If we sit outside, we won't have any peace because people always pass by and either spend minutes and minutes greeting you or else they just come and sit down and talk and talk and talk. So let him come to my room. Do you know why he wants to see me?"

Boi-Kimbo shook her head.

"Okay. Tell him to come here," Kigba repeated.

When Boi-Kimbo went back to the veranda, she found her husband already deep in conversation with someone who had just dropped in.

"Your mother says that she is waiting to see you in her room," Boi-Kimbo informed him and Hindowaa left his hammock at once,

"In that case, let me leave you," the visitor said, taking the hint. "We shall talk some more the next time I pass by your house. Please greet your mother for me and tell her it is a long time since I saw her. Is she well?"

Already at the door of the house, and intent on going to see his mother, Hindowaa did not answer.

"Good morning, mother, how did you sleep last night?" he said brightly as he entered his mother's bedroom. He was in a good mood, thanks to Boi-Kimbo who convinced him of the likely source of the funds that will be used to clear the debts.

"Good morning, Hindo," Kigba answered in like manner. "I slept well. I hope you also had a good night."

She was still sitting with her legs outstretched and Hindowaa thought her obvious relaxation augured well for their meeting. He was glad, because it was a long time since he had seen his mother in such a good mood. To make it last, he began the conversation by saying.

"Mother, I have come to thank you for your contribution during our meeting with the chief yesterday. I was happy when he spoke so kindly of my late father, your husband. It was very kind of him."

"Hindo, I have always told you that you don't know our chief and you are wrong to associate yourself with those in this town who malign him. I am happy that you have seen for yourself how kind he can be. Yes, your future son-in-law is a good man. I am glad you realize that now. You are beginning to learn. Don't allow people to think for you and follow them like a tail - always behind. It is not good; you are an adult. Use your head and think for yourself and you will always be in front. If you behave like a tail, people will lead you into all sorts of trouble."

When Hindowaa decided to come and talk with his mother that morning, he knew he was taking a big risk, but he thought the risk would be worth it. Now, going straight to the point, he said,

"Mother, I have come to see you because I am feeling anxious. I want to ask you something. I have told you that I went to see Nyamakoro and Foday. It was to see if I could raise a loan from them to pay off all my debts. They said that they were business people and they would need a guarantee so I should pawn my house or the Hindowaa farm land. I rejected it outright. They were my own last resort, so I wonder where you intend to get the money you promised the chief will be available within a month. I am completely baffled and I want you to put my mind at rest."

He looked at his mother expectantly and saw her countenance darken.

"Hindo, I am your mother and you are my only son," she said, "but I shall not tell you where the money is coming from. I have declared in the presence of our chief that I shall tie my wrapper around my big bottom and get the money to shame our enemies in this town and beyond.

Just believe in your mother and don't come asking me questions this morning. I am not a child. I said what I said because I believe in our ancestors. They will provide for us when the time comes. That is all I have to tell you. Don't ask me about it anymore. When the time comes, I shall provide the money and you can pay all your debts. As usual, the whole of Talia and the entire chiefdom will know about it and all those who have slandered us will have to shut their doors when they see us coming because they will be ashamed. I beg you, leave everything in my hands now and go about your business. That is all I have to tell you this morning."

Hindowaa was now convinced that Boi-Kimbo's speculation was the truth. There was no way his mother could come up with such a large amount of money without the help of a djinn. But he could not condemn her because he, too, longed for the day when all the debts were paid and he could confront his so-called friends and brothers, Kapindi and Gbapi.

****

The news that Kigba had given the chief an undertaking to repay Hindowaa's debts within a month was the fastest ever to spread around Talia. By the day after their meeting with the chief, everyone had heard about it. Kapindi and Gbapi and the other creditors could not believe their ears and immediately went to the chief to confirm the news. They were jubilant when he told them it was true. As the townspeople gathered in small groups to gossip, speculation grew that Kigba must have a connection with a djinn. Many of them also recalled rumors about her in-law, Fanday. Had it not also been rumored that Fanday had a djinn connection? There were those at Ginger Hall in Freetown, where Fanday and her late husband Kortu lived, who were convinced that it was she who had killed him. They said that even Hindowaa's two sons believed it. How could a man die in his sleep in broad daylight? A man who had never even complained of a headache! Kortu's death remained an unsolved mystery, but nobody had dared to accuse Fanday to her face.

Nyamakoro said to her husband, "I now believe that Kigba has a djinn. Before, it was just a rumor, but now I believe it. Don't forget that we also have people rumored to have a djinn in our tribe. It must be through the djinn that Kigba got the money, otherwise how would she and her son come up with such a huge amount. The djinn comes to your rescue at critical moments in your life. I think that when Hindowaa came to us yesterday, he already had the money."

"Then why did he come to us asking for a loan?" Foday asked. "Perhaps it was to test our sincerity as friends."

"That is possible, but I still think he already knew how they could get the money when he came here. Perhaps, the djinn made some tough conditions for giving them the money and they were trying to get a loan without conditions. They say that sometimes the djinn asks you to sacrifice something precious to you, like a member of your family, perhaps even your child. Foday, don't tell me that you have never heard about these things; now, you are behaving like a white man. I think Kigba only decided to accept the djinn's offer after we gave Hindowaa our own terms. As I said before, I definitely believe that she has a djinn. Why has she not remarried since her husband died? Is it not strange that she is still not married?"

Foday agreed.

Another person who was astonished by the news was Nyake. He was disappointed that Hindowaa had not come to tell him about it at once, when he had been his chief confidant for a very long time. At first, he decided that he would give Hindowaa a piece of his mind the next time they met, but on further reflection, decided to forgive him. He understood Hindowaa's problem; he was firmly under the thumb of his domineering mother and Kigba might have told him to keep his mouth shut.

The Hindowaa family's immediate neighbours were not as surprised as some other people in Talia. Kigba was such an extraordinary woman that they had always firmly believed that she must be keeping a djinn in a bottle in her room. They were actually afraid of her because they thought that she might have sacrificed one of their children to the djinn. The baby had died suddenly just seven months after birth, having shown no prior signs of illness, and the soothsayer they consulted told them that an immediate neighbour was responsible. So Talia and the surrounding towns were abuzz with excitement, convinced that it was through the djinn that Kigba had managed to solve the family's huge financial problem.

Since other members of the household had also made clandestine travel plans, Hindowaa was alone in the house with his mother while he waited for her to clear his debts. He was glad that Boi-Kimbo had gone away with the girls because he also believed that if the djinn demanded some human sacrifice in exchange for the money, she might be tempted to use one of them instead of a grandson. Thanks to Boi-Kimbo's quick-wittedness, the children were now out of harm's way. When Kigba wanted to know what had happened to Boi-Kimbo, the children and the rest of household, he had his answer ready.

"Mother, first of all let me thank you again for undertaking to pay all my debts. I am sure that all our ancestors and my late wife, Giita, will appreciate what you have done for the family. You have saved the family name. My mouth doesn't have enough words to tell you how grateful I am."

"I have heard you," Kigba replied. "Now, how about answering my question? The whole house is deserted and I don't know why."

"Mother, let me be honest with you," Hindowaa said. "Boi-Kimbo and the children have gone to her parents and the others have left for various destinations. The reason is that although you assured me that you would get the money to pay my debts, I wasn't convinced. I did not want my children and other members of this household to witness my humiliation when the police came to put handcuffs on me and take me to prison. It was because of this uncertainty that I decided that they should all leave Talia until the situation was resolved. I did not know how you would react if I told you, so I decided not to mention it before they left. Forgive me. I did it with good intentions."

Kigba surprised him by saying, after a moment's reflection, "Alright, I understand. When we have made the payments to your creditors, please let them know that we have resolved the matter and make arrangements for them to come back. We shall also make sure that Fanday is informed that we have made the payments and she can keep all the money that Kortu left. We should also let her know that she has not been of any help in our difficulty and we shall let her late husband know about it.

■

CHAPTER FIFTEEN

When Kapindi and Gbapi heard that within a month, their pockets would be full of money, they decided to celebrate by joining friends down town for a drink. It was raining when they set off, but not too hard. On their way, they spotted Nyake lying in his hammock smoking his pipe and, knowing how close he was to Hindowaa, decided to make a detour to avoid him. Nyake had also spotted them but pretended he was not looking in their direction. He planned to talk to both Kapindi and Gbapi about the way they had treated Hindowaa. He knew all of them in Talia and was disappointed by their conduct.

"Ndakei Kapindi, when this case is finally over and our debts are paid, what do we do next?" Gbapi asked Kapindi as they walked along, side by side.

"I don't understand your question, Gbapi."

"What I mean is how do we behave towards our friend and brother, Hindowaa?"

"I have been thinking about that myself. We were too sure that Hindowaa would not be able to come up with the money. The whole thing boils down to the fact that the chief was angry with Hindowaa because he refused to allow his daughter to marry him. It was the chief who called me and asked me to bring the case up again. He believed that if Hindowaa and his mother could not pay us, the marriage matter would be easier to pursue. I am sorry I did not confide in you before, but the chief swore me to secrecy and wanted me organize the whole thing without bringing him into it."

Shocked by what he his friend told him, Gbapi stopped in his tracks and glared at him with one hand over his mouth.

"Ndakei Kapindi, that was bad," he said shaking his head in disgust, "If you had told us that the chief had asked you do that to frustrate our friend and brother, I, for one, would not have agreed to it. You duped us."

"That is true; but Gbapi, look at it this way. We are talking about our chief. I am sure if he had approached you instead of me, it would not have been easy for you to turn him down."

"I don't know the chief as much as I know our friend and brother, Hindowaa. We were born in Talia, went to the Wunde Society together, went hunting and swimming, and did many other things together. I don't know the chief and the same goes for our other friends and brothers. You have embarrassed us all to please the chief who wants to marry a nun and an educated woman when he cannot neither read nor write. Kapindi, our friend and brother could have ended up in prison or as a result of what we did? Who knows how this whole case will end? Believe me, we shall all be very unhappy if anything unpleasant happens to Hindowaa. And do you think the chief will care? No, my brother, he will not care, and it is well known that he can be ruthless when his interests are threatened. Kapindi, I am so upset by what you have told me, that I can't continue this trip down town to go and drink. I won't enjoy my drink now that you have revealed the facts to me. I won't even enjoy the company. My heart is really heavy."

With that Gbapi headed back up town. He was planning to go and tell the other four creditors what Kapindi had told him, and ask their opinion about what they should do to make amends when Hindowaa had made the payments - how they could repair the broken relationship with him. Nyake would probably be best the person to start the process of reconciliation among wounded friends and brothers, Gbapi thought. They would have to go to him and explain how Kapindi had allowed the chief to use them. He hoped their big brother would understand their dilemma and help them out of it.

Meanwhile, ever since she and her son had been summoned by the chief over Hindowaa's debts, Kigba had started paying more frequent visits to the compound. The chief's wives had remarked on these frequent visits and came to the conclusion that Kigba's behavior was rather strange. They also wondered why she never came with her son. She had meetings with the chief morning, noon and night and always in the special hut while the other visitors waited on the veranda.

"Yeea Ballay, tell me, since you are the senior wife, what do you make of Yeea Kigba's frequent visits to our husband lately?" asked one of the chief's younger wives one night. "She has never visited him so often. Don't you suspect something?"

"I, too, have noticed her frequent comings and goings. I have come to the conclusion that it has to do with Kunaafoh's marriage to our husband. What else could it be? The reason the father is not coming is because he is against it."

"So, we are going to be fifteen wives and Kunaafoh will be the favourite," the junior wife remarked sourly.

"But don't forget, she also knows book and she is a doctor. Whenever we get sick, we shall be sure of very good treatment," the senior wife replied, and they chuckled together.

"But, Yeea, as for me, I have never heard of any man who does not know book marrying a woman who knows book. It is the first time I am seeing this thing happening and it will be with our husband."

"Well, you are going to see it now. You see, our husband has a problem. His father refused to send him to school even though some of his brothers and sisters were sent to school. He wanted to be educated, but his father never sent him to school. So now he thinks that by marrying Kunaafoh, some of her education will rub off on him," the senior wife told her mate and they laughed heartily at such a ridiculous idea.

"Let me tell you something that the policeman told me one day about our husband," the senior wife continued in a conspiratorial whisper. "He said that our husband sometimes tries to give the impression that he is not illiterate; so when he receives letters, instead of waiting for his clerk, he opens the mail and looks through it, shaking his head and even smiling. The policeman said that most of the time, our husband turns the letter upside down since he does not know the difference. Many of his visitors are also illiterate so they start expressing admiration as they watch him looking through the letters. Have you noticed that when the court is in session, our husband has a fountain pen stuck to his shirt or gown? The man cannot even sign his name and always uses his fingerprint to sign the papers; so what does he do with the fountain pen? Tell me." The women chuckled again.

On this particular night Kigba was paying the longest visit to the compound that she had ever made. As usual, she and the chief met in the small hut where he had seen her with Hindowaa. That was the night she secured the large amount of money needed to pay back all that her son owed his six creditors - his 'friends and brothers', as they always referred to themselves. The money represented part of the bride price or dowry, which the chief had to pay for his impending marriage to Kigba's granddaughter, Kunaafoh. With this agreement, Kigba and the chief believed Hindowaa would be forced to agree to the marriage because there was no other way he could clear his debts, and if he defaulted, he would land in prison.

Not long after that meeting, all of Hindowaa's debts were paid and again, the event became news in Talia. No one knew that Kigba had secured the money from the chief himself and that it represented part of the bride price for his marriage to Kunaafoh. All they knew was that the debts had been paid in full and within the agreed one-month period. For many people in Talia, that solidly confirmed the truth of the rumor that Kigba had obtained the money from her djinn. People started avoiding her after that, and her unmarried status was again attributed to the djinn. The fact that she ruled the Hindowaa household with an iron fist was also attributed to her djinn. She became an object of fear in Talia, so much so that when people mentioned her name in conversation, some would say, "As for me, from now on, I shall not say a word about Kigba. That djinn has given her very long ears which hear everything, and very big eyes which see everything at the same time. I shall not gossip about her because she will know and see all the people who gossip about her even if they are many miles away." However, many people also continued to admire her as a tough woman who had worked hard to rescue the Hindowaa family name from humiliation. They gave her credit for the courage and steadfastness she had shown in upholding the dignity and honor of her family.

Kigba and her son had agreed that whenever they wanted to discuss family business, they should avoid sitting on the veranda outside because people who passed the house frequently interrupted them. On the evening after all the debts had been paid, they decided to meet in Kigba's bedroom. There was no palm wine and the house was still empty.

"Since we are the only ones in the house, I can talk as loudly as I like," Kigba began. "You see, Hindo, you are my son. Even if you are one hundred years old, you will always be my son and I, your mother. That is the reality. Even if you now put on big trousers, you are still my son. Even if you put on your charmed gown, cap, trousers and shoes, you are my son. Parents know better. This is how God wanted it. You may not believe me but I know it is true. Hindo, I have always told you that our chief is a good man. He is a good man but there are those who don't know him well and go around spreading falsehoods about him and his late father. I knew his father very well. My late husband, your father also knew him very well, and he told you so when we both met him. His father was also a good man. People in Talia like to go around casting aspersions on others. I am a victim of their malicious rumors. But what has happened to me? I am still alive. Some of those who said bad things about me are dead and gone. I promise you, many more will go and leave me here in Talia. That is the world we live in, my son, and I want to drill the idea in your head that our chief is a good man. Do you understand what I am telling you, Hindo?"

Wondering what this long speech was leading to, Hindowaa simply said,

"Yes, mother I understand."

Kigba cleared her throat and coughed. She looked under her bed and took out a bundle containing kola nuts, which she shared with her son, and began to chew before she spoke again.

"You see Hindo, you are my only son. This is why I have tried so hard to make sure that when I die you do not go in the wrong direction. When I die, I want you to be confident that you are capable of being independent and can take care of yourself, your sisters and all my grandchildren. That is what it means to be a man in our culture. That is why we called you Hindowaa (big man). People have been putting false ideas into your head about our chief. I want you to know from tonight that they are wrong and very wrong. Are you listening to me, Hindo?"

Hindowaa still had no idea what his mother was really saying. He wanted her to tell him where she got the money to pay all his debts because he was still convinced that it had come from her djinn but did not believe that she would admit that. People never admitted to having a djinn for fear that they would be accused of antisocial practices.

"I am sure, that after this meeting between us tonight, you will go to sleep, convinced that our chief is a very kind man and that from now on, wherever you hear people talking against him, you will be the first to defend him. Please defend him resolutely and if need be take an oath on your Wunde Society that you are telling the truth, because it is true. He is a good chief... Now, let me tell you what happened when those friends and brothers of yours decided to embarrass our family. After our meeting, I went and discussed the matter further with the chief. I told him that no member of the Hindowaa family had ever seen the inside of a jail. I told him that I would do anything humanly possible to make sure that my son that came from inside my stomach would never see the inside of a prison. He agreed with me; so I told him that if he lent us the money to settle the debts, the money would serve as part of the bride price when he married Kunaafoh. That was how I got the money from him and now we are safe and happy. He asked me to proceed with arrangements for the wedding. This is the only thing you and I have to do now, so please, try to complete all the prepartions within two weeks."

At first, this information left Hindowaa too stunned to speak and a long silence ensued. Finally, he surprised and delighted his mother by saying with all the submissiveness she had longed for,

"Yes, mother, I think that two weeks will give us enough time to make all the arrangements for Kunaafoh's marriage as you and the chief have agreed."

Congratulating herself on having created a situation from which her son could not extricate himself, Kigba wrapped her arms around him as they concluded the discussions and separated for the night.

The next day, which was a Saturday, Hindowaa went to the mission compound, ostensibly to visit his children. The twins were absent, but he was not worried because the real purpose of his visit was to inform Sister 'Kono' and the Reverend Father about the latest developments regarding Kunaafoh, and the predicament in which his mother had put him and the entire family. He spent over an hour with them, during which Sister 'Kono' said to him,

"Hindowaa, I have told you that I always l pray for you and the chief so that the devil will not prevail over you. We shall continue to pray for all of you in Talia and the entire chiefdom. The devil is stubborn and will never give up. That is his nature; but we, too, shall never give up working against him. The mission has a practice of moving its staff to another location every few years, so we shall send Kunaafoh and the twins to our mission in Ghana as soon as possible; and our arrangement will be kept a secret within the mission. A Nigerian sister will replace Kunaafoh here. She is also a doctor so Talia and the chiefdom will not miss much. Don't worry; everything will be fine."

Overjoyed at this simple solution to his problem, Hindowaa heaped blessings on Sister 'Kono' and the Reverend Father. As they parted, Sister 'Kono' whispered, "May the Lord continue to guide us."

Hindowaa felt that, in what he considered a war with his mother, he had emerged victorious. How could she have come to such an agreement with the chief without my consent? he asked himself indignantly. He was now prepared for a final confrontation with her over this matter and decided he would have it on the day after Kunaafoh was put beyond the reach of the chief by her departure for Ghana.

Kigba went around, telling people about the forthcoming marriage of her granddaughter to the chief, saying that it was only at the last moment that she had been able to convince her son to proceed with the arrangements. Again many people expressed their admiration for her steadfastness and courage. Others, however, were not impressed and called her an iron woman who had bullied her son into submission; for how would any normal person want their daughter, who was a nun and a doctor, to marry an illiterate man. Because of this, the belief was reinforced that she was an overbearing mother and had had much to do with the death of Giita by putting too much pressure on her son to have more sons. It was his weakness that had resulted in Giita's untimely death. There were many in Talia who believed in retributive justice and said that in the end, Kigba would pay dearly for all the bad things she had done because she thought she could use her power to overcome others. They said that they had heard of several people just like Kigba - women who had become bones in the throats of other people because they had had some influence or power in the community. They waited for the day when she would receive her just deserts and they could say, 'You see, we told you so. We told you how she would end.'

****

Kigba and her son decided to sit on the veranda because there was nothing in particular that they needed to discuss. The rest of the family had not yet returned to Talia. It had been two days since Kunaafoh and the twins left for Ghana and her replacement had arrived safely. Hindowaa wondered when he would see his children again, but fully accepted God's way of solving his problems. On this occasion, there was palm wine and bamboo wine in abundance as two gourds had been delivered. He knew that his mother would be delighted to see the bamboo wine, which she preferred but which was not always available. When she drank bamboo wine she would say that she heard that the white man said it was good for the eyes, especially for people who were getting older.

"Hindowaa, how much progress are you making with the wedding plans? You are not keeping me informed," she said after taking a good gulp of the bamboo wine. "Please don't tell me that you have not started yet. You know the process very well because you have been married twice. We should not allow the chief to bear the entire burden alone. We have to provide goats, rice, palm oil, and plenty of palm wine and bamboo wine. That should be our own contribution. And this time we shall need beer; even our local gin should be available - in abundance. You know that this is a al marriage with the ruling house and that this is the first time the Hindowaa family is giving the chief a wife. You also know that we are the first family to give our chief a woman who knows the white man's book and is also a fine doctor."

Hindowaa had not yet finished his first serving of palm wine, but he saw that his mother was ready for a second one. It had been a long time since she had had bamboo wine and she was obviously determined to do justice to it. He poured her another cupfuland took a swallow of his own drink to fortify himself. Knowing that she was in good health and unlikely to have a heart attack, he said in a casual tone,

"Mother, I am surprised that you don't seem to be aware that Kunaafoh and the twins left for Ghana two days ago. The mission has transferred her. That is their rule; every few years they move the nuns to another country. If you want to check for yourself, you can go to the mission and ask the people there for Kunaafoh. She left two days ago."

He watched his mother closely in the ensuing silence and noticed that she had begun to sweat. All at once, she jumped to her feet with her hands over her head and ran into her bedroom shouting as if she had just been told that a close relative had died.

"Koooh, koooh, koooooh...Gbeeeh, ndupui, gbeeh ndupui, gbeeeh?... Gbeeh,ndupui,gbeeh,Ndupui,gbeeh?.. .Gbeeh,Ndupui,gbeeh, gbeeh?(Why child, why?...Why child, why?...Why child, why?")

She repeated the words like a funeral dirge, crying out loud while ripping her clothes apart. Then she started calling on her departed relatives to come because she was dying. Hindowaa did not know how to console her, so he left the room to give her time to grieve. She might even be able to come up with another creative solution to the new problem of telling the chief that Kunaafoh was now out of his reach. Hindowaa did not care what happened. He had said repeatedly that a marriage between Kunaafoh, a nun , and the chief would only happen over his dead body. Well, Kunaafoh had gone; she and her siblings were safe in Ghana. He thanked God and his ancestors for answering his prayers.

"Hindo, Hindo," Kigba called out from her room after a while.

Hindowaa found her sitting on the floor with her legs stretched right out as if she was bereaved. She had taken off some of her clothes, exposing her breasts which, he noticed, were sagging. They were the breasts which had suckled him, a fact which his mother had used to subject him to emotional blackmail whenever they were having an argument.

"Hindo, we are not going to argue now," she said as soon as he entered the room. She sounded breathless and desparate. "Time is against us. We have to leave tonight and go east. It is a long journey. We shall go to my oldest uncle who I know is still alive. We have to travel for very long time, but we have to get out of the reach of the chief because he will take severe measures against us when he finds out that Kunaafoh has left the country. He will never believe that we had no hand in the arrangement. How can I go and tell him this story? We leave tonight. We shall inform Boi-Kimbo when we arrive at my uncle's place and she and the children can join us there later. Hindo, before you pack few of your belongings, go quickly and tell your sisters and their husbands about the latest development. Swear them to secrecy, ask them to pray for us and say we shall stay in touch with them. I have not contacted my uncle for a long time, but I shall explain the circumstances to him and hope he will understand. We have to get out of here fast. I shall go ahead and wait for you by the river. The tide is full but soon it will start to recede. When you come we shall row across... I hope the canoe is on this side of the river. Let us hurry. It is dark outside, but no lamps, you hear; otherwise people will see us."

Hindowaa accepted his mother's assessment of their situation at once, as well as her proposed solution to the problem. There was no reason to argue with him. They had to escape. It was now a matter of survival. They had to be miles away from Talia by morning, so after seeing his sisters and their husbands, he joined his mother at the river. It was chilly and very dark when they ventured out. All nature was at rest, but there was no reason to believe that they were the only ones traveling at that time. Other people undertook such journeys when they had family emergencies; so united by the instinct of survival, they kept absolutely quiet as they waited to cross the long, meandering river, clutching their few belongings. A rush of fetid air assaulted their nostrils as if some rotting fish nearby was oozing maggots. For Kigba, that was an inauspicious sign, but she was certain that their ancestors would guarantee their safety.

Hindowaa thought it was their lucky night when they found the big canoe on their side of the river, for had it been on the other bank, he would have had to swim across to fetch it. At the height of the rains, the river had overflowed its banks, but since the wet season was coming to an end, the water level had begun to drop, signaling the start of the dry season when farmers could plant their crops. However, they had to wait for the river tide to recede sufficiently for them to make the crossing safely. Eventually, they were able to climb on board. Kigba sat facing Hindowaa, almost in a squatting position, and held on firmly to the edge of the canoe as her son plied the big paddle. It was not the first time Hindowaa had rowed across the big river in the rainy season, so he knew how to work the paddles to suit the present conditions. He stretched his shoulder muscles to their limit and in a short time began to experience a burning pain. Mother and son held their breath, intent on crossing the river and starting their journey to freedom.

It was when they were about half way across the river, according to Kigba's calculation, that Hindowaa began to say in a terrified voice, "Mother, they are coming! Mother, they are coming! Mother, mother, they are coming, I can see them; they are coming."

"Hindo, who are coming?" Kigba asked, panicking. "Come let me help you row. Who are coming?"

She got up and tried to grab the paddle from her son who was shouting by this time, "Ghosts are chasing after us. They are coming closer."

Hindowaa's panic stricken cries reached a crescendo as his mother tried to change places with him so as to row them to safety. Kigba was now convinced that her son was really mad, because she could not see what he was shouting about. In trying to sit down, she compromised the canoe's balance and it capsized.

Kigba's last sight of her son was of his arms clinging precariously to the canoe as it drifted toward the turbulent end of the river. Through her own resourcefulness and knowledge of the river, she landed safely on the other side. Hindowaa was still clinging to the canoe, but it had drifted out of sight and she could no longer see or hear him.

"Hindo, Hindo, Hindo, Hindoooo, Hindooo, Hindooo, please come back," she cried desperately. "Don't leave me. Please come back, my only son, please come back."

There was no reply, for Hindowaa had drowned at the turbulent end of the river in the darkness of the night. As Kigba lay on the other side of the bank, she thought about what she was going back to - an empty house and, without Hindowaa, an empty life. Whenever she told the story of that fateful last journey with her only son she always wept, painfully regretting that they had not shared the experience of dying together.

THE END

SIERRA LEONEAN WRITERS SERIES

Focusing on academic, fictional, and scientific writing that will complement other relevant materials used in schools, colleges, universities and other tertiary institutions, the Sierra Leonean Writers Series (SLWS) aims to promote good quality books by Sierra Leoneans, writers of Sierra Leonean descent from around the world, and writers writing on or about Sierra Leone. Even if the initial readership is made up of people outside Sierra Leone, it is the publisher's hope that students and other readers in Sierra Leone will eventually be at least some of the primary beneficiaries of these new works. Not only will people in Sierra Leone be able to read materials that relate to their own lives and experiences, budding writers will also be able to draw inspiration from the efforts of their compatriots and other established writers. Submitted work undergoes a rigorous peer review process before being accepted for publication, with an international editorial board providing guidance to writers.

For further information, please visit our website:

www.sl-writers-series.org

or contact the publisher, Dr. Osman A. Sankoh (Mallam O.)
publisher@sl-writers-series.org

Published Books

A. History and Political Science

SLWS H&PS-1

Joe A. D. Alie, 2007

ISBN: 3-9808084-5-9

Sierra Leone Since Independence – History of a Postcolonial State

A stimulating and informative account of Sierra Leone's political history from the last years of British colonial rule to the present. The book discusses some of the forces that have tended to unite and disintegrate the nation, paying particular attention to the deeds and misdeeds of the political elite. It concludes with an analysis of the major challenges facing Sierra Leone in the post-conflict period, as well as the prospects for building a progressive, democratic, peaceful and viable nation-state.

B. Creative Writing Series

SLWS CR-1

Osman A. Sankoh, 2001

ISBN: 3-00-003978-3

Hybrid Eyes – An African in Europe

This semi-autobiography critically examines the experiences of Africans and other minority communities in Germany as well as key values and stereotypes that many people in Africa hold about Europe. The author acknowledges the flaws of African culture and advances proposals for the way ahead.

SLWS CR-2

Sheikh Umarr Kamarah, 2002

ISBN: 3-9808084-0-8

Singing in Exile and The Child of War

This collection of poems examines the causes of the African (Sierra Leonean) condition, evaluates the African immigrant's situation in the West, hints at the role and culpability of corporate West in African wars and woes, and concludes that African must ultimately assume the responsibility of rebuilding their continent.

SLWS CR-3
Abdul B. Kamara, 2003
Unknown Destination
ISBN: 3-9808084-1-6
The book examines a wide spectrum of challenges that confronted African students in the aftermath of the economic reforms or structural adjustments of the 1980s, and the concomitant hardship that swept across Africa. The author uses his own real life-experiences to compare student life in the East as experienced in China, with that in the West (Germany), and adroitly analyses what these unforeseen cultural divergences implied for young Africans in search of higher education.

SLWS CR-4
Samuel Hinton, 2003
The Road to Kenema
ISBN: 3-9808084-3-2
In The Road To Kenema Samuel Hinton presents a poignant, sometimes searing portrait of a man who stands with one foot planted firmly in the ageless soil of Africa, the other on the promise-filled shores of America. Balancing memories of his homeland with dreams of his adopted country, Hinton takes his reader on a journey that is often upsetting, but always engaging. Each poem beckons, almost forces, the reader to experience the situation at hand...

SLWS CR-5
Karamoh Kabba, 2005
Morquee - The Political Drama of Wish over Wisdom
ISBN: 3-9808084-4-0
Morquee traces Sierra Leone's turbulent recent history through the eyes of one of the individuals caught up in it. With its patient description of how an innocent young man

can become tangled in a web of corruption, deceit and war, Morquee is a microcosm of the post-colonial experience in much of West Africa. Morquee is part of a renaissance in Sierra Leonean story-telling. The Sierra Leonean Writers Series is at the forefront of this movement. With this publication, Karamoh Kabba cements his status as a bright young hope for the Sierra Leonean novel. Home-grown creativity in Sierra Leone is on the rise again.

SLWS CR-6
Yema Lucilda Hunter, 2007
Redemption Song
ISBN: 3-980-8084-6-7
Told partly through the diaries of Emmanuel Martin, a boy on the threshold of adulthood, Redemption Song is the story of how war came to a peaceful, if impoverished, country and tore it apart. However, as Emmanuel grows up and his life unfolds, all is not doom and gloom...

SLWS CR-7
Mohamed Combo Kamanda, 2007
The Visa
ISBN: 3-980-8084-7-5
The Visa is a lucid, informative, educative and humorous play; it is truly a "travel ticket" into the two cultures: the Western Culture which shocks and transforms many Africans upon their arrival in Europe, and the African culture with its own uniqueness – you may call it a clash of cultures, races and value systems. The play touches on these issues in a light-hearted manner. ...

SLWS CR-8
J Sorie Conteh, 2007
In Search of Sons
ISBN: 3-980-8084-8-3
In this book, J. Sorie Conteh tells the universal story of the preference many societies/cultures in Africa have for more

sons in the family than girls. The story is set in the author's country, Sierra Leone, and tells the harrowing experience of a mother who tries to fulfil her husband's desire for more sons. She becomes pregnant but eventually dies in labour in search of sons...

SLWS CR-9
Michael Fayia Kallon, 2010
The Ghosts of Ngaingah
ISBN: 978-9988-1-3983-4
This is a story full of superstition, yet so credible. When a people neglect that which constitutes their collective consciousness and that which helps them to grow and prosper as a community, the negative effects are bound to hit them hard.

SLWS CR-10
J. Sorie Conteh, 2010
Family Affairs
ISBN: 978-9988-1-3984-1
In Family Affairs J. Sorie Conteh returns to the fictitious town of Talia which featured in his previous novel, In Search of Sons. Once again he has dealt with the stresses, strains and even tragedies that can arise within families when time-honoured beliefs and expectations are challenged. These are common themes in fiction. What makes Family Affairs particularly interesting is the obvious affection the author has for the people among whom this family drama unfolds. Except for one or two individuals, they are illiterate Mende people living in a small rural town in Sierra Leone. Without ever sounding patronizing, he has woven their concerns, customs and beliefs into a gripping story.